Def Jam

the men behind
the radical rise of **Def Jam**
Russell Simmons and Rick Rubin

by Alex Ogg

OMNIBUS PRESS

London/New York/Paris/Sydney/Copenhagen/Madrid/Tokyo

Cover designed by Fresh Lemon
Picture research by Nikki Lloyd

ISBN: 0.7119.8873.0
Order No: OP 48477

Exclusive Distributors:
Music Sales Limited,
8/9 Frith Street,
London W1D 3JB, UK.

Music Sales Corporation,
257 Park Avenue South,
New York, NY 10010, USA.

Macmillan Distribution Services,
53 Park West Drive,
Derrimut, Vic 3030,
Australia.

To the Music Trade only:
Music Sales Limited,
8/9 Frith Street,
London W1D 3JB, UK.

Printed in Great Britain by Creative Print & Design Wales (Ebbw Vale), Wales.
Typeset by Galleon Typesetting, Ipswich

A catalogue record for this book is available from the British Library.

www.omnibuspress.com

Contents

For Dawn

Acknowledgements

The author would like to thank Dawn and Hughie Wrench,
and Ellie Oggy or Laurence McGinty Jnr to be,
for the peace of mind and space of thought required.

Thanks to Chris Charlesworth for all his help throughout the project,
as well as James Sleigh and Nikki Lloyd at Omnibus.
Thanks as ever to Bill and Marion Ogg, and Sue and Michael.
Cheers to David Upshal and all those who agreed to interviews.
And as they say down the Roger Street 'hood,
Death to all quaslings and No to 5.30s, 24/7, 365.

Introduction

Hip hop's current stature as the most commercially potent and artistically resilient genre of popular music has much to do with the towering achievements of a label started in a New York student dorm by a punk rocker with a drum machine and an ambitious black businessman, who couldn't believe his new partner turned out to be a white guy just out of his teens.

Russell Simmons and Rick Rubin's unlikely alliance provided the launch-pad for the four most important architects of Eighties hip hop; Run-DMC, LL Cool J, The Beastie Boys and Public Enemy. Run-DMC imported hip hop from the Bronx to New York's suburbs but transmuted it irrevocably in the process, establishing an aesthetic of strutting local and personal pride and reducing hip hop's component elements to a straight dialogue between brutal, minimalist production and the youthful belligerence of two inimitable brothers in rhyme. LL Cool J, dripping in gold, testosterone, and an indomitable belief in the boundlessness of his own talent, became Def Jam's debut act and rap's first B-boy poster boy. The Beastie Boys outraged those to whom such a disposition came naturally, but more enduringly forged an accommodation of punk and hip hop protocols that, at least temporarily, sounded like the clashing of tectonic plates. And Public Enemy were simply the most influential artists of the decade, in any genre.

When Def Jam's founding partnership dissolved, Simmons went on to become one of the most successful black businessmen in America, his burgeoning empire incorporating interests in every conceivable medium, from clothing lines to publishing to television and the internet. Rubin, feeling he'd achieved all he could within hip hop, plotted his own maverick course, helping to promote a new musical extreme in thrash rock, reviving the American roots rock tradition, and generally working with whom the hell he felt like.

For all its achievements, by the early Nineties it was widely assumed that Def Jam's moment had passed. The label's profile certainly suffered from the commercial backdraft engendered by west coast gangsta rap. But Def Jam not only bounced back, it outpaced and out-classed those interlopers via the multi-platinum success of Jay-Z and DMX. In the process, it once again redefined the message and the medium. By the turn of the millennium, Def Jam had reasserted its claim as the blue chip hip hop marque.

This book explores the partnership between Simmons and Rubin, self-styled black hustler and style-shelved Jewish punk respectively, which lies at the heart of Def Jam's success. It also documents the roles played by the label's major artists and collaborators, and celebrates a combined legacy built on some of the finest music produced in the last quarter of the 20th century.

1

King Of Queens

"Disco music was black music made simple for everyone to dance to, that was always the best description of what it was. It was watered down, it was made by the industry for the people and not made by the people for the people. Our response to disco was hip hop."

— Russell Simmons

Hip hop's evolution from block party soundtrack to global pulse has been celebrated to the point where fact and mythology have intertwined and overlapped many times. And like claim-jumpers staking out their patch in the new gold rush, corporate sponsorship ensuring that for Klondike, read Nike, there is competition for the status of founding father. The faces of such titans as Kool DJ Herc, Afrika Bambaataa and Grandmaster Flash loom large, the 'holy trinity' claiming three places on hip hop's Mount Rushmore. Russell Wendell Simmons has the credentials to demand the fourth berth – would that he ever stayed still long enough for a sculptor to petrify his image.

A composite of Road Runner's kinetic legwork and nemesis Wile E. Coyote's bad posture, Simmons stalks the hip hop earth with ACME cell-phone welded to his ear, hatching plans, cutting deals and sniffing the wind for the latest idea. He may not be an artistic innovator to match those giants of the old school, but in 'taking care of business' he made rap music what it is today. And the debate still continues as to whether he legitimised or cheapened its parent hip hop culture in the process. As his friend Nelson George writes, "You can't understand the journey of this culture until you take the measure of this man."

Back in the day, hip hop's driving forces were fun, invention and competition. At this juncture, chasing the 'dead presidents' – a typically inventive linguistic reference to the portraits on dollar bill denominations rather than the static elders of Mount Rushmore – was entirely subservient to

1

chasing the opposite sex. Bambaataa and Herc both saw hip hop as an alternative to gang violence, a way of producing a sense of community and aspiration in disaffected black teenagers. These were puritans dressed as hedonists. Nobody was thinking that anyone would ever make any money out of all this. Russell Simmons had other ideas.

Hip hop began when Jamaican ex-pat Clive Campbell, aka DJ Kool Herc, hosted his first parties in the recreation room of his family's housing block, 1520 Sedgewick Towers, in the early Seventies. Based on his knowledge of dub reggae and the approach of reggae 'toasters' such as U-Roy, Herc started to accentuate the 'break', or climatic instrumental section, of records from disparate musical traditions. His 'merry-go-round' trilogy of James Brown's 'Give It Up Or Turnit A Loose', Michael Viner's Incredible Bongo Band's 'Bongo Rock' and Babe Ruth's 'The Mexican' was his signature sequence. Matching these innovations, his growing band of devotees improvised dance steps which incorporated gymnastic rolls, struts and spins. The fame of Herc and his 'breakdancers' or 'B-boys' spread beyond the Bronx as his party attendances swelled.

In his wake came Bambaataa, who formed the Zulu Nation after attending a Herc party in 1973, forsaking a youth spent running with gangs like the Black Spades. Bambaataa assembled a playlist of ultra-rare soul, funk and rock cuts, which fought for space on the twin turntables his mother bought him after graduation. Another acolyte was Grandmaster Flash, a sharp-featured, dextrous DJ who shared Herc's Jamaican roots and used his training at Samuel Gompers Vocational High School in the Bronx to construct the first cue monitor. Being able to pinpoint an entrance note on a record's groove allowed him to upstage Herc's breakdowns with his 'quick-mix theory'. At this juncture hip hop DJs developed a new arsenal of techniques in what amounted to creative hot-housing. Flash's apprentice, Grandwizard Theodore, developed the art of scratching – pushing the vinyl underneath the needle back and forward rapidly to create a high-pitched, rhythmic squeal.

Spurred by Herc's diverse musical tastes, which drew on the prevalent funk and disco staples but added obscure selections from rock, pop and jazz traditions, this new breed of DJ fought to outwit competitors by incorporating unique sounds in highly combative block party duels. Afrika Bambaataa, his eclecticism celebrated in his honorary title Master Of Records, segued selections from Filipino group Please, would-be synth lizard king Gary Numan alongside Hare Krishna consciousness records. Anything that offered an exciting or unusual instrumental twist was added to the repertoire, a jackdaw mentality that continues, via sampling and the vinyl one-upmanship of 'turntablists', to inform present day hip hop culture.

In the winter the more successful DJs would rent small clubs and community centres. Any proceeds generated from door receipts would be reinvested in improved sound systems in preparation for the outdoor summer gatherings – usually powered by electricity diverted from street lights. This party-based culture developed in tandem with urban graffiti; spray-can murals which had sprouted along the subway lines of New York boroughs since the early Seventies. Effectively guerrilla art, graffiti was embraced by its far-sighted custodians as a means of reclaiming uninviting, abandoned urban space as a legitimate canvas. Like other strands of the host culture hip hop, it gloried in individualism, often employing an elaborate, tenement-sized panoply of intricate art to express a simple signature, or 'tag'.

By the late Seventies Herc, Bambaataa and Flash were the linchpin DJs in this new culture, while breakdancers and graffiti artists fought to establish 'reps' in their chosen disciplines. In its crudest form, the first hip hop MC (master of ceremonies or microphone controller) was Kool Herc himself. He customised an echo box and microphone to exhort his party-goers to ever more gravity-defying feats of athleticism. However, this was hardly his forté and the role was soon delegated to friend Coke Le Rock, who would string a series of evocative rhymes together. His rhythmic epithets provided the foundation on which later MC teams such as Bambaataa's Soul Sonic Force and Flash's Furious Five would extemporise. Rapping, in a form recognisable to contemporary hip hop fans, began to develop among partygoers-turned-MCs such as the Treacherous Three, Cold Crush Brothers and Funky Four.

Though MCing/rapping subsequently became the dominant strain in hip hop culture, it only truly developed as an afterthought. The DJs were the original stars; they ran the parties and, with the exception of the 'mix tapes' which eventually circulated, it was only at parties you'd get to hear them. The thought of appearing *on* vinyl was light years away, even though vinyl itself, and the obscurity and elitism that surrounded the acquisition of the latest beats, was the new currency of exchange.

When hip hop did finally reach vinyl in October 1979, it was through the auspices of the Sugarhill Gang – a trio thrown together for the purpose by Sylvia Robinson of Sugar Hill Records. This cynical attempt to exploit the new phenomenon displayed little regard for the music's authenticity. Most controversially, some of MC Big Bank Hank's lines were lifted straight from a well-known routine used by rapper/DJ and Cold Crush Brothers' member Grandmaster Caz. Unlike Hank and his Sugarhill Gang brethren, who were considered remiss in dues-paying terms, Caz was a veteran of the cause. Despite this, the single sold millions of copies and announced hip hop as a viable commercial format. Everyone started to wonder if this ghetto craze had a future, a thought that had already occurred to Russell Simmons. In common with the old school Bronx originators, he was outraged by the Sugarhill Gang's opportunism. But while their grievances concerned the New Jersey's group's lack of integrity and skill, Simmons was more concerned by the fact that they'd got there first.

Born on 4 October 1957, which made him slightly older than the emerging hip hop generation, Simmons lived with his family in Jamaica, Queens, until 1965, later moving to the more affluent Hollis suburb, a small but populous area located between Jamaica and Queens Village. Largely facilitated by the national immigration act of 1965, Queens is the most multi-ethnic of New York's boroughs, with large populations of Greeks, Italians, Japanese, Chinese, Koreans, Puerto Ricans, Jews and Maltese. The borough boasts two million citizens who share 118 square miles of land mass.

Russell's father Daniel Simmons Snr was a poetry-writing teacher and public school attendance supervisor who subsequently became a professor of black history at Pace University in Manhattan, and who later contributed lines to Run-DMC's 'Thirty Days' and 'You're Blind'. Russell is similar in appearance, sharing his father's basset hound eyes and balding pate. His mother, the late Evelyn Simmons, was a pre-school teacher in Jamaica, Queens, who also dabbled in art and painting. They'd met at Howard University where Daniel Snr had earned a bachelor's degree in history and his wife-to-be degrees in sociology and psychology.

Russell was the middle of three brothers, sandwiched between Daniel Jnr and Joseph, sharing a bedroom with the latter while his elder brother occupied an attic room in their two-storey Hollis apartment. The area was generally regarded as middle class and aspirational, a fact attested to by little brother Joseph, who confirms that growing up in Hollis was "special". "Nice homes, manicured yards, and everything." The family also prayed daily and went to church every Sunday. Indeed, Joseph's memories of his youth are of being "surrounded by love" and having "everything a child could want". He recalls a time when every morning before school he received a small, inexpensive present, such as a balloon. Which contrasts with his elder brother's implication that his youthful environment was tough or arduous.

The children were strictly corralled by their firebrand mother, who nevertheless displayed a liberal streak when it came to her offspring's choice of professional vocations. Her lassitude was not endorsed by her husband, as Russell would find to his cost. Conversely, Daniel Snr, who mainly lectured during the evenings, also talked at great length about civil rights and black empowerment and encouraged his offspring to take part in demonstrations. He was delighted when his eldest son joined the Black Panthers.

Despite this, at his parents' insistence Russell attended integrated schools, largely because academic standards at neighbouring community institutions were inferior. But his friends remained the black youths he'd meet around the basketball courts of Hollis. As well as socialising with them he briefly ran with the Queens chapter of the Seven Immortals, an entity linked to one of the dominant Bronx gangs but which never matched its parent organisation in territorial ferocity or violence. He attained 'warlord' status during his 10th grade year, but the truth was that Simmons was never a street-fighter and his title was wholly symbolic.

Though a son of Queens to his marrow, Simmons was also regularly drawn to Harlem. Long considered the hub of black creativity in New York, the area above Central Park was famously described by author Ralph Ellison as "an alabaster vessel that holds the Black American heart". Harlem was also the birthplace of black nationalism and nurtured the idealism of Malcolm X and Marcus Garvey, while musicians such as Duke Ellington, Billie Holliday and Fats Waller routinely summoned their congregations there. Queens had no such identity, history or 'ebony chic'. But it did have great cultural diversity and a surfeit of bored suburban teenagers.

By the time he was a teenager, Simmons had developed what would become a lifelong devotion to looking 'fly'. Though he never went short of a meal, the household budget would not stretch to accommodate his tastes in A.J. Lester threads and his preferred three-stripe Pro-Keds sneakers. The easiest way to make up the financial shortfall turned out to be selling nickel bags of grass on 205th Street in Queens, a practice which was already rife. He'd been made aware of drugs through his elder brother's flourishing heroin addiction, though witnessing his problems first-hand ensured that Russell would avoid narcotics at all costs. But anything else, especially grass and angel dust, was considered fair game. He was strictly a small time operator, but at one point Simmons was involved in shooting a rival dealer who'd robbed him. Simmons missed. Later he gravitated to sucker-selling coca leaf incense to unwary punters who thought they were buying cocaine. This ruse developed while he was working the only day job he ever had, forced on him by his increasingly concerned father, at a juice store in Greenwich Village.

Unlike his brother, Russell never found himself in serious trouble with authority, apart from a night in the cells and a probation sentence after being caught smoking weed outside the public library on Jamaica Ave. The manner in which he later advertised this conviction testifies to the status value of a criminal past in the modern hip hop world. But however fashionable it may now be, Russell Simmons knew instinctively there were better, safer ways to turn a coin.

At his father's insistence, Simmons enrolled on a sociology course at City College of New York in the autumn of 1975, though this merely served as a smokescreen to his continuing pursuit of girls, acid and angel dust. But while there he met college peer Rudy Toppin, a similarly recalcitrant student who needed help promoting shows, which effectively amounted to distributing flyers, at Harlem's Charles' Gallery. It was Toppin who gave Simmons his nickname, 'Rush', reflecting his natural restlessness and energy (it later served as a testament to the speed at which his empire expanded on his way to becoming the first B-boy millionaire).

Though he didn't know it, promoting shows at Charles' Gallery would lead Simmons to hip hop. Most of the venue's regulars were there for the jazz, blues and disco nights, but increasingly the venue was also booking acts from the emergent hip hop culture. One night headliner DJ Easy G was accompanied by Eddie Cheeba, a crowd-pleasing MC whose slick routines encouraged audiences to chant slogans back and forth by way of repartee. Cheeba was adding his vocal embellishments to Parliament's 'Flashlight' when Simmons felt he'd just "witnessed the invention of the wheel".

As a youth Simmons' musical tastes had been informed by New York's WWRL station, which featured several of the jive-talking DJs who, depending on your view of history, either inspired hip hop or jumped on the bandwagon as it began to pick up velocity. Simmons' tastes, he claims, were geared towards the hard-bitten street soul of The Dells and Moments rather than Motown's more ornate, pop-orientated fare. He was hardly a true disciple of music, however, and his first love was always clothes. It was never "all about the music" for Russell Simmons, to use the vernacular. That alone is a stark contrast to the Bronx elders of hip hop, for whom the consumption of music was always a devotional activity, steeped in symbolism.

But Simmons was knocked out by Cheeba. One of the most successful DJs at the birth of hip hop alongside Pete Jones and the even more popular DJ Hollywood, Cheeba was tethered to the previous disco generation, but had started to employ short raps in the style of jive-talkers like Douglas 'Jocko' Henderson. Other name DJs included Johnny Thunderbird, who performed late night sets in his local Burger King, Reggie Wells and Junebug. These proto-hip hop DJs played regularly at the 371 club off Webster Avenue in the Bronx. As Kool DJ Red Alert, New York rap mainstay and cousin of Jazzy Jay, noted in *Ego Trip's Book Of Rap Lists*, "People such as Russell Simmons, who was a promoter at that point while going to City College, acknowledge what these people in the 371 crew were doing. After hearing about all these people, he started bringing them downtown, playing clubs like the Hotel Diplomat and other big spots."

Simmons leapt head first into the new music and its attendant culture. The vast potential audience that had not been tapped, at least in a monetary sense, began to dawn on him. So he started his research – checking out each of the clubs and DJs, noting the clientele, even taking in new wave venues such as the Mudd Club and the Peppermint Lounge. As Nelson George recalled, "There was a rebellious, nonconformist attitude in rap that Russell saw as analogous to the rock attitude he experienced hanging out at punk clubs."

The first party he threw was held at the Renaissance in Queens in 1977. The rental of the premises cost him $500, with $300 spent on flyers, but he managed to attract an audience of 800 (the club's capacity was 600). Kurtis Blow headlined. Blow, aka Curtis Walker, was programme director of City College's radio station and was nominally pursuing a degree in communications. Simmons first saw him on stage at Charles' Gallery, where he combined the roles of DJ and MC (he also played sets at Disco Fever and at Small's Paradise every Friday and Saturday night).

The initial adverts ran 'Rush Productions in Association With Rudy Toppin and Kurtis Blow'. A second event, advertised to his collegiate peers with flyers reading 'Rush – The Force in College Parties, Presents . . .' came a month later at the Hotel Diplomat in Times Square, where Blow was joined by Eddie Cheeba. Never backward at coming forward, Simmons earned considerable kudos by persuading Cheeba, then a huge star in his local community, to appear. Though promoter and DJ never actually got on, Simmons never considered a personality clash a hurdle to a commercially advantageous collaboration. *Business Never Personal* was an album title employed by future Def Jam signings EPMD, but it might equally have served as a rationale for Russell Simmons' business practices. Another promoter, the improbably titled Saint Saint James, ripped him off for nearly $2,000 on a show he was putting together featuring DJ Hollywood and Evelyn 'Champagne' King. But that didn't stop him employing James once Rush had become established.

Opening doors by dint of his legendary tenacity and a superhuman insulation to taking no for an answer, Simmons was beginning to carve out his niche. As a result his academic studies began to suffer even further; by the time he left college he was several credits short of his degree. This didn't sit well with his father, especially after one disastrous show in Harlem with zero attendance left him broke and meant he had to hit his mother for a loan. She handed over $2,000 in $100 bills. "It was that money that kept me afloat until Kurtis Blow's first record broke, and I entered the record business full force," he later told the *Final Call*.

Her errant progeny was maturing as a businessman and hype-merchant, which ensured the loan would be a one-off, as he had promised. Simmons concentrated on organised concerts rather than ad hoc gatherings, a more formalised vision of hip hop than the Bronx originals who set up block party jams, or hired school gymnasiums. That's one reason why DJs such as Cheeba and Hollywood were regarded as part of a separate culture by trailblazers like Flash and Bambaataa. Simmons, too, was viewed as something of an upstart outsider, but when he proved he could get his clients paid, Flash in particular started to warm to him. "The idea was to get artists who really moved you, who gave you goose bumps," Simmons later told *CNN*. "There wasn't any formula for these early artists, and today there still is not. It's just really what was relevant and what felt good. That was the criteria."

Soon he was booking shows for other hip hop luminaries such as Lovebug Starski, DJ Hollywood and Grandwizard Theodore throughout the five boroughs of New York. He even helped Flash crack the previously hip hop-resistant Manhattan by cross-promoting him to R&B audiences. He also cheekily re-branded Harlem native Blow 'Queen's number 1 rapper'. It was Simmons who brought Blow and Flash together. When the DJ couldn't afford to bring all his MCs out to Queens, he would use Blow as an adjunct member of the Furious Five. Soon a minor itinerary developed, a circuit including venues such as Small's Paradise, the Renaissance Ballroom, Club 371 and Broadway International. Of course, there was competition; other promoters included actor Ving Rhames' brother Junior and Black Expo alumnus Jerry Roebuck. But soon Simmons had established a reputation as hip hop's number one party promoter.

Artist management was the next key building block in a strategy to attain first-mover status within the rapidly evolving hip hop firmament. He took the step up from merely promoting acts by signing Kurtis Blow to his Rush Artistic Management company. It was Simmons who suggested he change his name to Kurtis Blow instead of his previous billing as Kool DJ Kurt (a tribute to Kool Herc). Blow signified "hard-hitting, like a death blow", he maintained, but it was also a reference by Simmons to Walker's refusal to give up the fake cocaine or coca leaf incense scam.

Billboard writer Robert 'Rocky' Ford Jr was researching a piece on breakbeat culture and the new DJs when he saw one of Simmons' promotional stickers on the B.M.T. subway in New York in 1979. Later, spotting Russell's younger brother Joseph sticking up a poster for one of Russell's parties, he decided to write a story about the young entrepreneur. Simmons agreed, in turn soaking up Ford's inside track on the machinations of the music industry. Ford briefed him on the principles of artist management, advancing two immutable tenets; find a distinctive trait to make artists marketable and hire an entertainment attorney to review the contracts over any live bookings. "He taught me that I should have a full understanding of any business before I pursue it," Simmons reflected to *Black Enterprise*. "Every time I go into a new venture, I find a rabbi who has the business acumen to help me understand the mechanics of that industry, the costs involved in developing a product, and what you need to do in order to make a profit."

Ford and colleague J.B. Moore, who worked as an advertising executive at *Billboard*, were invited to attend an August 1979 show at the Hotel Diplomat, featuring Kurtis Blow, Eddie Cheeba, Lovebug Starski and Grandmaster Flash. By this time they'd come up with the idea of producing a rap record "about Santa Claus coming to Harlem" based on the poem 'The Night Before Christmas'. Their idea – that the novelty factor might make audiences more amenable to a rap record – may seem patronising in retrospect, but it demonstrates how far away from the music industry's mainstream hip hop existed. In the event Ford also helped convince Blow that Russell Simmons was not just a party promoter, but the man to take over his management – despite the fact that Blow's initial inclination was to sign with Ford because of his contacts and clout within the industry.

Ford's original choice of MC had been Cheeba, having become an ardent fan during his research. But he and Moore were dissuaded when Blow put in a performance that, according to Simmons' memory, demonstrated "more charisma than the others". Had Ford stuck to their original suggestion, the course of hip hop might have changed substantively. For a start, Cheeba might have retained his pre-eminence, and thus his status as a pioneer after successive rap histories have denigrated his role to that of footnote.

Simmons grasped the organic nature of hip hop immediately as an inclusive, community-bred phenomenon, with a potential reach beyond the chart fixations of Motown and the largely faceless disco years that followed. "Our response to disco was hip hop. The rap DJ's response to music, the reason it grew up, is because he turned on black radio and you'd hear 'YMCA' by The Village People or 'I Love America' by Patrick Gilbert or all these records that were foreign to us." Simmons never intended to restrict his audience to his local neighbourhood, but it was important to him that the music and artists reflected their origins honestly. As he told *HHC* magazine in 1995, it was important that black people reaped the rewards of their creativity, unlike the preceding rock'n'roll generation. "They had the king of rock'n'roll, the king of blues, the king of jazz – they was always white. But they couldn't do another Elvis this time. This time niggas wasn't having it. This time black people really have some stake in some shit that they invented." Simmons, in collaboration with Rocky Ford and Kurtis Blow, was all set to release the first hip hop record. The only problem was finding a backer to help finance the recording. Then someone else got there first.

The arrival of the Sugarhill Gang's début single may have confirmed Simmons' belief that hip hop had the potential to attract a mass audience, but that was small consolation. Many aficionados, including Afrika Bambaataa, cite the Fatback Band's 'King Tim III (Personality Jock)', the B-side to their 1979 single 'Candy Sweet', as the first hip hop record. But 'Rapper's Delight', released on 13 October 1979, boasted the small matter of 14 million sales worldwide to hallmark its status as the first rap record proper. Many, such as Grandmixer D.ST and Simmons' friend Jazzy Jay, believe its release killed the hip hop culture stone dead. There is some merit in that argument. Musically, hip hop had mutated songs and beats from myriad traditions and styles, and it was that process, rather than any kind of finished product, which defined hip hop. As soon as it carved its initials on vinyl, hip hop became a different entity altogether, formalised and self-referential. But Simmons now had a proven market to operate in.

Simmons was at a show at the Armory in Queens when he first heard 'Rapper's Delight'. In *Life And Def*, he qualifies his disposition as "wrecked". Though concerned that the token rap hit had eluded them, the ad hoc quartet of Simmons, Ford, Moore and Blow persevered, completing 'Christmas Rappin''. The finished version was co-credited to Ford, Moore and Simmons, though Russell insists that his younger brother Joseph wrote "the entire second half of that record and didn't get any credit", including the famous "throw your hands in the air" section.

The single was cut at Greene Street Studios with engineer Rodney Hiu (who later worked with Pete Rock and CL Smooth as well as a succession of R&B and rock acts), and featured Queens jazz musicians Eddie Martinez (guitar), Denzel Miller (keyboards), Trevor Gale (drums) and Larry Smith (bass), collectively suggested for the task by Ford. Smith later became part of Rush's inner circle, becoming Simmons' original partner, and went on to play key roles in the future of Simmons' businesses, particularly with respect to little brother Joey's Run-DMC.

No one in the industry thought that the success of 'Rapper's Delight' was about to be repeated any time soon. But Simmons had a plan up his sleeve. Having identified PolyGram's R&B roster as the best possible outlet for his acts, he produced a series of test pressings of 'Christmas Rappin'' and distributed them to influential DJs. Then 'fake' orders were placed identifying the record as PolyGram product, ensuring interest would be generated within the R&B department at the 'mystery' orders. It worked. Ultimately it was a white English A&R executive who signed the distribution deal, which underlines the scepticism with which hip hop continued to be viewed even by the black music establishment. 'Christmas Rappin'' made its official début on Mercury Records in the autumn of 1979. It also made Blow the first rap artist to gain a major label contract and the attendant promotion and celebrity. Aided by radio support from DJ Mr Magic, it was this record that introduced hip hop to *Yo! MTV Raps* producer Ted Demme, among many others. After a few plays on mainstream black radio by WBLS' prime time DJ Frankie Crocker, the song took off. Overjoyed, Russell vaulted the stairs to tell his parents, then "just stared at the speakers", so awed was he by the recognition. The royalty cheque that eventually came through enabled Simmons to move out to Brooklyn with girlfriend Paulette Mims.

Blow, an able showman on his own merits, cemented his status as 'first rap star' with the release of 'The Breaks (Part One)'. It anticipated Grandmaster Flash's 'The Message' as a record that surveyed the inequities of life in black urban society, albeit obliquely ('dem's da breaks' was a popular expression referring to fate's fickle hand). One of the soundtrack records of New York in the summer of 1980, it went on to sell more than half a million copies and was awarded gold certification – the first time a rap record had passed that milestone.

Simmons was convinced he was marketing the new 'king of rap', and started to advertise Blow's shows as such. Indeed, Blow was earning good money on the road, partly because hip hop's one MC and one DJ blue-print meant not having to split the gate with other musicians. Simmons even secured Blow a support tour to the Commodores, but also put him forward for concerts at 'white' venues like the Mudd Club, where DJ Anita Sarko occasionally mixed in hip hop with the latest new wave releases. An eponymous début album followed, one of the first in what was previously considered a singles genre. Blow, whose on-stage personality ironically recalled a rap Lionel Richie, was unquestionably the leader of the pack for a brief moment.

As his fame grew, he employed a who's who of DJs so he could concentrate on MCing. The first of these was Russell's own little brother, Joseph 'Run' Simmons, who was billed 'son of Kurtis Blow' in tribute to DJ Hollywood's deck maestro and 'disco son' DJ Small. Joseph would also trade raps with Blow on stage. As he recalled in his autobiography, "Since Russell and Kurtis were tight, Kurtis came over a lot. Sometimes he would sleep at my house . . . When Kurtis came around the house I would come out and rap. I had a little bit of skill at the time, and Kurtis was always down with giving me pointers and stuff." When Run broke his arm Davy D (later a successful solo artist and producer) took over, before Kool DJ AJ, who wrote Blow's other big hit, 'If I Ruled The World', stepped behind the decks.

Simmons used the connections he'd made selling Kurtis Blow to Poly-Gram to secure a regular sideline income by running club promotions for the label. As Darryl 'DMC' McDaniels, a regular visitor to Simmons' house in Hollis recalled, "He was a renaissance man of the streets. I mean, he was into hip hop. He was into partying and had his own company, Rush Productions . . . He was into selling fake cocaine. He was into everything that a young B-boy growing up in Hollis would be into, but he was also in college and highly ambitious."

Blow's career faded following the cool reception that greeted his subsequent *Deuce* and *Tough* albums. He actually recorded an astonishing six full-length albums for Mercury when his real strength was in the singles market. Afterwards he concentrated on production work (enjoying success with Sweet G, the Fearless Four, Dr Jeckyll & Mr Hyde, Lovebug Starski and Angela Wimbush, as well as much of the Fat Boys' early output). He made a clutch of TV appearances before orchestrating rap nostalgia compilations and even a hip hop musical, *Echo Park*. If Blow failed to make the most of his early breakthrough, it was through no fault of Simmons, who invested a great deal of effort in his grooming. But by the time it became apparent Blow was never going to make the transition to the mainstream audience that had once seemed assured, Simmons had already hedged his bets with a series of other artists.

Following 'Rapper's Delight', others began to explore the possibilities of moving from live to recorded performance. Lovebug Starski's 'Gigolette' was issued on Disco Fever's in-house label, while another party promoter, Paul Winley, released Afrika Bambaataa's live Zulu Nation Throwdown tape. Enjoy Records, like Sugar Hill, was run by an R&B veteran (Bobby Robinson, whose son was a member of the Treacherous Three). He was fleet of foot enough to document the emerging music via Grandmaster Flash's 'Superrappin' ' and the Funky Four's 'Rappin' and Rockin' '. But Sugar Hill dominated recorded rap music between 1979 and 1982, releasing sparkling efforts by the Crash Crew, West Street Mob and Positive Force.

It was Grandmaster Flash, who'd defected from Enjoy Records along with the Funky Four and Treacherous Three, who truly upped the ante with the DJ odyssey 'Adventures Of Grandmaster Flash On The Wheels Of Steel' and especially 'The Message'. The latter took everyone by surprise, not least the group itself who initially refused to have anything to do with it, by tackling issues way outside hip hop's traditional party remit. Other successful Sugar Hill hits included the Funky Four Plus One's 'That's The Joint', Sequence's 'Funk You Up' and Spoonie Gee's 'Monster Jam'. However, hip hop's first record label never truly evolved beyond its initial, highly opportunistic stature. Its reflexes were sharp enough to document what was happening on the street, but Sugar Hill's view of hip hop was as one-dimensional as some of the major label executives who believed it had no future. Its business practices were also highly questionable. CBS crucially passed on a distribution deal due to the involvement in its affairs of Roulette Records' legendary Morris Levy – the man, backed by Genovese Mafia connections, who said on his deathbed, while waiting to start a prison term, "Artists . . . are just imbeciles."

When Sugar Hill did sign with MCA in 1983, the distribution deal was rumoured to have been brokered by Sal Pisello, another feared mobster.

The two parties quickly ended up in court, just when Sugar Hill should have been benefiting from their pioneering status as hip hop went global. For the record, Simmons always enjoyed 'cordial' relations with both Sylvia and Joe Robinson, but it was significant that he never managed a Sugar Hill act – principally because the label's executives went out of their way to discourage outside involvement with their artists. This prefigured Simmons' own problems with combining the roles of manager and label executive. But ultimately it was Sugar Hill's complacency, and refusal to sign a new generation of artists (turning down LL Cool J, for example, and missing out on Run-DMC) that left the door open for a more resourceful and receptive label to outflank them. "Russell Simmons had taken [Sugar Hill's] blueprint, said, 'Thank you,' and applied a little college education to the marketing and doing the shit right, rather than keeping it in the ghetto," reckons Sugar Hill house band member Doug Wimbish. Or, as Joey Robinson Jr, Sugar Hill's head of A&R remembers, "Rap music started changing. Run-DMC came out, LL Cool J, Public Enemy, and it went to another dimension. And while hip hop was changing, we were in the midst of litigation."

The idea of becoming a record mogul was deferred during the early Eighties as Simmons built his roster of management clients. Among them were the Fearless Four, who released two distinctive records for Bobby Robinson's Enjoy label in 1982, 'It's Magic' and 'Rockin' It', before Simmons brokered a major label contract with Elektra – the first for a rap group rather than solo artist. But their career faltered after initially making a strong impact with their Kurtis Blow collaboration 'Problems Of The World Today', an over-obvious attempt to rewrite 'The Message'. But soon they'd been dropped by Elektra, who never really understood what they'd taken on. It was the second major stumble in Simmons' career. He'd now secured two major label contracts for his clients, only to be bitterly disappointed at their inability to market and develop those artists.

A couple of projects during this period required Simmons' creative input. In 1982 he served as producer for Larry Smith's band, Orange Krush, which also featured Rush client Alyson Williams on vocals. Their rap-disco hybrid 'Action' provides an important footnote in Def Jam's history, as it later provided the musical blueprint for Run-DMC's début single. Smith, who was also producing funk stalwarts Con Funk Shun, also worked with Simmons on Jimmy Spicer's single 'The Bubble Bunch'. Simmons, inevitably, managed the veteran rapper, whose 'Super Rhymes'

14

incorporated a dictum that could have come straight from Simmons: "And whenever you say disco, I say the beat".

The Orange Krush sessions fomented the idea of releasing a record representing the new generation of MCs. It was originally slated to feature Simmons' younger brother Joseph 'Run' Simmons, champing at the bit to take his turn behind the microphone, as well as producer/DJ Davy D and Cool Lady Blue, the English ex-pat punk and promoter at roller-skating rink turned exotic hip hop nightclub, the Roxy. The group was tentatively called the Okay Crew. Joseph had been pestering his brother for years to let him make a record, having served his apprenticeship with Kurtis Blow from the age of 11. Russell kept telling him he needed to get his high school diploma first, standing firm on academic standards in a manner that would have pleased his father.

Joseph was keen to bring his best pal on board, Darryl McDaniels, whom he'd known since kindergarten, instead of the suggested cast of accomplices. By the time he and McDaniels had graduated together from St Pascal's Catholic School and the basketball courts of the Police Athletic League (PAL), they'd had hip hop drip-fed to them for nearly five years. McDaniels, a straight-A student with an elder brother who worshipped Earth Wind & Fire, had grown up a 15-minute walk away, and been brought up by similarly strict, middle-class parents.

McDaniels was also a would-be DJ, having given Joseph Simmons a crash course in operating the turntables prior to his alliance with Blow. Before taking the acronym DMC, which he stumbled over in typing class, he called himself Grandmaster Get High – inspired by hearing Grandmaster Flash perform 'Superrappin' ' on a mix tape, though the alias was also conceived in tribute to his favoured leisure activity of smoking weed. Though his first love was horror movies, he became immersed in hip hop culture as it spread through New York's boroughs. McDaniels and Simmons would gather alongside friends Butter Love, Terrible T and Runny Ray, aka the Hollis Crew, in DMC's basement. "The basement was important because it was the only place where a turntable and mixer were available," remembers Joseph Simmons. McDaniels had the luxury of two twin $12 turntables and a $40 mixer, courtesy of his elder brother Alford. Their other chief stomping grounds were Jamaica Park and the local high school yard on Hollis Avenue, which hosted impromptu DJ parties.

After Joseph had played out a few times under his appellation 'the Son of Kurtis Blow', he started to invite DMC along, starting with a show supporting Sweet G at Le Chateau in Queens in 1981. Scared witless at the prospect, DMC got himself silly drunk. But his more experienced partner offered him some latitude, and the pairing became permanent. Joseph was already cocksure after his stint with Kurtis Blow, who remembers: "Before we made our first records, we were rapping five or six years in the clubs, and the block parties, on the streets. Run [Simmons] used to go around to every block party in Queens and rock on the microphone, so he had the experience to handle an audience."

Russell, writing the introduction to his little brother's memoir, *It's Like That*, noted how quickly his upstart brother conquered the drum machine and turntable he acquired as a pre-teen. "He was the fastest DJ I had ever seen. He was so fast that he could literally cut the air." Russell Simmons claims to have given Joseph the nickname Run due to this speed of hand-eye co-ordination. But both Run and McDaniels insist it was down to his innate verbosity, an ability to run off at the mouth on any subject, and that it was Simmons' friend Rudy Sply who first coined it.

Even though they went on to attend different high schools in Manhattan and Queens, Run and DMC became inseparable. Their inspirations were Afrika Bambaataa's Zulu Nation, Flash, the Funky Four and the Cold Crush Brothers, acts who were beginning to veer away from the simplistic party rhymes that characterised early hip hop. Both DJs-turned-rappers were enthralled by the mix tapes that were beginning to circulate in Queens, which lured them further into the culture. "You got to the jam, say Russell Simmons, he'll throw a party," remembers DMC. "You'll go there, Grandmaster Flash and The Furious Five performing, or DJ Hollywood. Somebody will sneak a tape in, or somebody will get a tape up in the DJ booth. You'll make a tape. You tape the show, bring it out on the streets, sell it for $6 to $10, a lot of tapes were sold like that. My first tape I bought was the Cold Crush Brothers tape, $6 I paid for it. It was like an album to me."

At that stage, they reasoned, the polite, mannered records emerging from Sugar Hill, Enjoy and other pioneering imprints failed to document the raw, urgent vibe of the original practitioners. It was their calling, they believed, to provide that missing link. "We took that street thing," says DMC. "That's one thing Run-DMC did, we took that original street thing before Sugar Hill Records got their hands on 'Rappers Delight', and we kept that alive, and that's why we're here today."

First they also had to overcome Russell Simmons' disparaging remarks that DMC didn't have a 'good voice' for rapping – a bemusing verdict given his later stature in the industry. "Russell didn't like my style," remembers DMC. Not for the last time, it was pressure from inside his own camp that won Simmons over. "They had record ideas and stuff and I was like – finish school . . . I thought, I ain't gonna fuck with 'em," recalls Simmons. "Then people around me started telling me, 'Fuck with your brother, he's right with his shit, and fuck with DMC cos he's right with his shit.' " After abandoning the Okay Crew project, Simmons tried to record his younger brother solo on a prototype rap entitled 'Street Kid' – an upstart 'My Generation' rhyme co-written by Orange Krush drummer Trevor Gale. Which rather contradicts Run's assertion in his auto-biography that he told his brother, "If I can't be down with Dee (DMC), I really don't want to make records." However, it's equally true that DMC would never have had his stab at the microphone had he not been taken under his friend's wing. "He [Run] wanted to dominate in this new craft," recalls DMC. "And, fortunately, he wanted me to come along for the ride." It also helped Run to have DMC in his corner, to prevent Russell moving him away from the sort of music he wanted to make. Simmons finally relented after failing to shop the 'Street Kid' demo to several major labels.

In 1983, while Run was studying mortuary science at La Guardia Com-munity College and DMC had enrolled at St John's on a business manage-ment degree, Run called his friend to say he was going into the studio to cut a record. He needed some help to finish the lyrics for a track he'd been working on called 'It's Like That'. When DMC came through, he added the track's emphatic counter-punch, "And that's the way it is". They showed the lyrics to Russell, who immediately packed them off to the studio. But even at this stage, his younger brother had to hold firm and insist that DMC was part of the proceedings.

'It's Like That' had the duo formalising rhymes they'd been messing about with for years, while the rhythm track served as a musical tribute to the two definitive hip hop records of the era, 'Planet Rock' and 'The Message'. Purpose-built to appeal to radio, its percussive crunch was nev-ertheless both innovative and alarming, indicative of a powerful new sonic aesthetic which Run-DMC would patent. Even better was the B-side cut 'Sucker MC's (Krush-Groove 1)', their tribute to pioneering MC teams like the Cold Crush Brothers. The call and response rhymes established Run-DMC's dynamic, with each partner finishing the other's sentences intuitively, giving heightened rhythmic emphasis to the lyrics pay-off lines, which arrived at dizzying pace.

Larry Smith, the duo's producer through to their second album, *King Of Rock*, was invited to recreate the backing track from Orange Krush's 'Action' for 'Sucker MC's'. It employed a beat authored by Russell Simmons – something he later claimed was "the single most creative thing I've ever done". The finished 'Sucker MC's' yielded nothing so conventional as a bass line. "Larry's asking us what music to put on it," recalls DMC. "We don't want no music, we want this to be a park jam, we want this to be a party in the basement. Put the beat on, we're gonna put vocals on the record." Ironically, despite their reverence for the Bronx party jams which spawned the original hip hop movement, 'It's Like That' and 'Sucker MC's' would effectively kill off hip hop's first wave, as breakbeat culture was subsumed by the possibilities of the drum machine.

It was during the 'It's Like That' sessions at Larry Smith's attic in Queens that Russell rang to tell the duo they would be called Run-DMC. DMC was mortified, as he recalled in *The Show*. "Russell called and said, 'The name of your group is going to be Run-DMC.' Right now, when I say that, it sounds def, cos Run-DMC is a household word. But imagine that name never existed on the earth. You're standing there. Your manager calls and says, 'The name of your group is going to be Run-DMC.' I just saw Joe's face cringe. He said, 'Here, take the phone.' He gave me the phone. Russell said, 'D, the name of the group is Run-DMC.' I still remember that day in Larry's attic. I was standing there. He said Run-DMC. It was the worst, stupidest thing I ever heard." They entertained notions of being called something more fittingly hip hop, like the Sure Shot Two. Russell waved away their protests. Though mystified at his reasoning, in employing a name that distanced the group from their forebears, Simmons played no small part in establishing the 'new school' aesthetic in which Run-DMC's music would prosper.

A demo of 'It's Like That' and 'Sucker MC's' was despatched to Corey Robbins and Steve Plotnicki at Profile Records. Their second release had been a single by Alonzo 'Lonnie Love' Brown of Rush clients Dr Jeckyll & Mr Hyde, which cemented the connection with Russell Simmons. Though Plotnicki later spent more time establishing the franchise for the *Robot Wars* TV series, Profile was the only rap label to retain its independence until it was finally bought out by Arista in the Nineties. Despite registering several gold records at Mercury with Kurtis Blow, Simmons believed the independent label offered the best bet for the project. The deal was cut on a 10-point contract with a $25,000 advance for the first album. 'It's Like That' sold 20,000 copies on 12-inch. The B-side took on a life of its own, however, its insistent beats fatally upstaging more venerable rappers who were still trying to find new ways of recycling old Chic rhythms. "It was just a beat and rappers," recalls DMC, "unheard of. *Ridiculous*." As Sasha Frere-Jones wrote for *Vibe's History of Hip Hop*, " . . . rap was no longer folk music; it was now a portable, formal conceit and whoever could do it best would win."

Of all the stylistic innovations to shape modern rap, the most indelible contribution came from Run-DMC. After their intervention, hip hop incrementally gravitated from the periphery of popular music to its heart, while the unmistakable sonic gear change immediately rendered the acoustics of the old school quaint and its adherents museum curios. Run-DMC were bright, well-adjusted suburban kids in reality. But their brooding and confrontational records spoke of an alternative reality that fellow suburbanites were happy to take as the gospel of the street. As Rick Rubin once stated: "With Run-DMC and the suburban rap school we looked at that [ghetto] life as a cowboy movie. To us, it was like Clint Eastwood. We could talk about those things because they weren't that close to home."

Jason Mizell, a wild youth and another friend from the basketball courts of Queens, came on board as the duo's DJ. He'd made his name playing in local parks as part of Two-Fifth Down, and had a reputation for taking nonsense from no one. His reputation would ensure that no locals 'messed' with the group, in addition to his skills as a DJ. DMC gave him the stage name Jam Master Jay, thus completing Run-DMC's line-up. But the transition from old to new school was not entirely smooth. Russell Simmons booked them for their first appearance before a 'proper' hip hop crowd at the Disco Fever in the Bronx in the spring of 1983. Things got off on the wrong footing when Jay missed the gig because his ride never turned up. The MCing duo were then greeted with gales of laughter as they took the stage. It was bad enough that these hip hop pretenders hailed from the Queens (considered 'soft' by Bronx residents), but their chequered sports jackets did not impress anyone – DMC had actually borrowed his suit from his father's wardrobe. He was so humiliated by the experience that he almost gave up the idea of being a rapper on the spot. It was only later that they began to wear their 'street' clothes on stage, reinforcing their distance from the old school rappers, some of whom would have looked overdressed had they been appearing in *Cabaret*.

It is Russell Simmons who is usually regarded as the pivotal force in moulding Run-DMC's presentation, though Run gives Jam Master Jay credit for establishing the trio's dress code. After they started to earn decent money from live shows, all three invested large proportions of their salaries in the finest boutiques Jamaica Avenue had to offer, from whence came the leather suits and gold chains. Their feet, meanwhile, embarked on a mutually rewarding and monogamous relationship with Adidas sneakers, worn bereft of laces. With their sideburns, outsized Cazal glasses and black velour fedoras, Run-DMC looked more like an obscure Jesuit sect than hip hop outlaws. But somehow it worked. Somehow it was cool.

For Russell Simmons, who 'refined' the look to give it visual cohesion, the clothes merely reflected the group's individuality. "Joey as a kid always had a disdain for people who went the most obvious way. The reason that he, DMC and Jam Master Jay dressed the way they did was because they wanted to make a statement about the community. They believed that the route they were following was really the guts of rap itself. It was not about being successful or about any commercial gains. It was about the new phrase, 'keeping it real'." Of course, 'keeping it real' has since become a hollow cliché mouthed by a succession of MCs who couldn't plot an original course if their next bottle of Cristal depended on it, but back in 1983 the expression actually meant something. Run-DMC looked, sounded, felt – authentic. "If you take a look at the pop cultural landscape or the black political landscape now, there aren't a lot of heroes," Russell Simmons said at the time. "If you're a 15-year-old black male in high school and look around, you wonder what you can do with your life. How do you better yourself? Run-DMC has opened up a whole new avenue of ambition. You can grow up to be like Run-DMC. It's possible."

A glut of 12-inch singles followed, including 'Rock Box', the first of a trilogy of attempts to cross-pollinate rap with rock dynamics. It included an overbearing guitar solo from session musician and occasional Orange Krush member Eddie Martinez, who'd previously graced such AOR staples as Robert Palmer's 'Addicted To Love'. It didn't quite work. It sounded like a square peg being knocked into a round hole. Yet it served as a useful trial run. As Simmons recalled on *The Show*: "Our whole thing was, let's try to be real. And the realest thing you could do, was just put a drumbeat with nothing but a drumbeat. And loud. So we wanted guitars. We had always scratched guitars, but not guitar riffs, just the noise. You cut the beat and you give it dynamics." The two MCs only knew about the Martinez overdub well after the fact, and were initially outraged that their freestyle now had loud rock guitar stamped all over it. The video, too, was aimed squarely at marketing the group to a rock audience. 'Rock Box' was "a very calculated and successful attempt to merge the hip hop and rock aesthetic," reckons Nelson George. "That's why Russell Simmons shot the video at Danceteria. There's a little white kid who runs through the crowd – very calculated. The Danceteria was where uptown and downtown met. Madonna would be at that club. Joe Jackson would be at that club. So would Kurtis Blow. The actual setting was very important in terms of what they were trying to accomplish with the video."

2

The Odd Couple

"Both Rick and Russell were adventurous, innovative, and creative. The difference was that while Rick was that way for the hell of it, Russell was focused on how they could get paid for being that way."

– DMC

Run-DMC, Kurtis Blow and Rush's other clients had made Russell Simmons the main man in the nascent hip hop market, with his connections seemingly extending to every major participant. Rick Rubin, meanwhile, was a long-haired lover of punk rock from Lido Beach, Long Island. Born Frederick Jay Rubin in 1963, the only child of a well-to-do Jewish family, he was tutored in his adolescent tastes by the likes of Black Flag, the Dead Kennedys and X, although he never gave up on his teenage favourites, AC/DC and Aerosmith. Inspired by punk rock's DIY ethos, he briefly played guitar in the charmingly titled Pricks, who never made it out of Long Island.

By the time he'd enrolled at NYU to study film and video, Rubin had formed a new group, Hose, inspired by San Francisco's deranged art-punk terrorists Flipper. Their début single, 1982's 'Mobo', featured a discernably Flipper-like demolition of 'We're All Going To The Zoo Tomorrow' on its flipside. Other staples of their live set included a cover version of Black Sabbath's 'Sweet Leaf', played at approximately half speed. Despite a press release insisting "the world can't get enough of their tightly arranged mood/concept pieces", Hose were not embraced with anything approaching enthusiasm, even in an era where audiences' indulgence of independent record-making was at its zenith. "Truly awful", was acquaintance Jim Finnigan's verdict. Both Hose's records were released with the assistance of Ed Bahlman of 99 Records, though the label carried the legend Def Jam. 'Mobo' was given the catalogue number DEF-SP–1. The follow-up EP *Hose*, whose lead track was 'Only

The Astronaut Knows The Truth', additionally featured covers of Rick James's 'Superfreak' and Hot Chocolate's 'You Sexy Thang'.

Bahlman and 99 Records also released material by the Bush Tetras, ESG and Liquid Liquid, whose 'Cavern' was illegally appropriated on Grandmaster Flash's 'White Lines', leading to a protracted law suit with Sugar Hill. Bahlman was crucial in Def Jam's development in that, during the time they spent together, he taught Rubin the basics of record production and record mastering. Rubin, meanwhile, tried his hand at promoting – disastrously attempting to fuse his disparate influences by pairing Heart Attack, a highly political New York hardcore band, with Liquid Liquid and the Treacherous Three at the Hotel Diplomat.

Rubin first encountered hip hop via Mr Magic's WBLS radio show. At that time, he was the only source by which a young white kid could access the music. "I didn't have an older brother or sister listening to Led Zeppelin or who got to see The Doors," Rubin recalls. "That was all very old news to me, it didn't exist. They weren't coming around every six months to tour. It wasn't a real thing. And then, all the black kids [at school] liked rap records, and one week their favourite would be one group, and then a new single would come out and they would have a new favourite group. It was that immediate. It was a very immediate, progressive audience. It was very exciting, and you could be part of it. You could go and hear it and see it and feel it and touch it."

His infatuation with what he heard sparked into a full-scale love affair with hip hop after 'It's Like That' dropped. Run-DMC immediately became his favourite band. It's not hard to see the parallels between their sound and the music he'd consumed as an adolescent. As he admitted to *Rolling Stone*, "I liked punk rock music and for me, hip hop was black punk, and I like white punk and black punk equally. I like fringe music. It just seemed like, at the moment in time while I was at NYU, the punk scene was kind of waning and the hip hop scene was thriving. If it had been five years before, I probably would have produced punk rock first." And, after being the only punk rock fan in high school, he wasn't too perturbed by the fact that his peers didn't share his tastes, though by 1983 he'd found a soulmate (and roommate) in Adam Horovitz of The Beastie Boys.

Rubin wasn't alone in finding parity in the spirit of hip hop and punk. Indeed, there had already been some cross-fertilisation between the two camps, especially at the 'art-rock' end of the punk spectrum. As Afrika Bambaataa later confirmed, "It was the punk rockers and new wavers that were the first of all white people to accept this music. They were bringing me down to the punk rock clubs to mix. You used to see punk rockers come up to jam at the hardcore black and Hispanic neighbourhoods." Blondie's 1981 chart-topper 'The Rapture' played tribute to hip hop grandees such as Grandmaster Flash and Fab Five Freddy, while the Manhattan epicentre of the music, the Roxy, was run by ex-punk Cool Lady Blue, who'd previously served with Malcolm McLaren. Another McLaren client, John Lydon, cemented the punk-hip hop alliance by dovetailing brilliantly with Afrika Bambaataa on their 1983 collaboration 'World Destruction'. A year later the Cold Crush Brothers acknowledged the common ground with 'Punk Rock Rap'. As Jon Savage wrote in *England's Dreaming*, rap was: "The black punk: aggression, politics and empowerment translated into black music after 1982." But not all attempts to marry the two cultures proved so fertile. When the Clash played for 17 nights at Times Square's Bond's International Casino, their specially selected support acts (Grandmaster Flash and the Treacherous Three) were bottled off stage. Russell Simmons hung out with the Clash at famed after-hours drinking hole Save the Robots. But generally he was dismissive of the punk-rap axis. "Punk, new wave, alternative – most of it came and went."

As a willing acolyte of hip hop, Rubin spent several weeks checking out the Negril, soaking up the atmosphere. At that time it was the only place in Manhattan that would touch hip hop, also doubling as a reggae venue. He had to travel to the Bronx to find the records Mr Magic played, which weren't readily available outside of the borough. At the Negril he eventually befriended Jazzy Jay of Afrika Bambaataa's Soul Sonic Force. As well as pointing out what the really hot breakbeat records were, Jazzy Jay, who had a sideline building speaker cabinets at college, taught Rubin how to programme drum beats. They started to discuss making records together, too. "I'd go to clubs and hear this music and love it," remembers Rubin. "Then I would, always as a fan, go out and buy the records. But the records didn't really reflect what I would hear at the clubs. So, just really as a hobby and for fun, I started making records that sounded like what I heard at the clubs – almost like a documentarian, really." He and Jazzy originally intended to remix a song by the Sex Pistols. Eventually those ideas were jettisoned and they started to work on what would become 'It's Yours'. But they needed someone to rap over it.

The first choice was Kool Moe Dee, but neither he nor fellow Treacherous Three member Special K could get a release from their Sugar Hill contract. So Rubin and Jazzy enlisted the services of Special K's brother

T-La Rock instead. "It took us two years to get the record placed," remembers Jazzy. That was partly because Rubin was so obsessive about the quality of the finished product. 'It's Yours' was made "just from a fan's point of view," Rubin asserts, but it's apparent that he took being a fan seriously. Rubin told David Toop that his approach was just "being in tune with everything. You can't do it by listening to music. Pro-wrestling is real important. Movies. You know, everything. You have to make records the way you live your life."

The record's rallying cry: "Musical myth-making people of the universe, this is yours!" jump-started the single and provided an unequivocal introduction to Def Jam's legacy. Though it featured the label's now famous "stylus" logo, an overhead view of the tone arm of a Technics 1200 turntable designed by Rubin, it actually released via Arthur Baker's Party Time label, after Rubin rejected early interest from Profile. Party Time's previous forays into the hip hop idiom had included Dimples D's 'Sucker DJs', an answer record to Run-DMC's 'Sucker MC's' – the record that inspired Rick Rubin to get involved in hip hop (it also featured the début vinyl appearance of producer Marley Marl).

'It's Yours', which featured Adam Horovitz on 'background vocals', also announced Rubin's obsession with bass; the deeper, the better. Jazzy Jay, who nicknamed Rubin the 'bass-master', has a quality anecdote about Rubin trying to squeeze the biggest sound system possible into his tiny MGB sportster (at this stage the preferred method of road-testing a record was to play it at extreme volume in your car). When Rubin turned the system up full, he immediately blew his tail lights and licence plates clean away.

When 'It's Yours' finally reached Russell Simmons' ears, he was astounded to learn that a hip hop record could breach the airwaves without recourse to his management or promotional skills. Jazzy Jay hollered out to Simmons one night at a club, asking if he'd like to meet the man behind the record. After overcoming his surprise at Rubin's colour, they began to talk and discovered a shared interest in making 'hard' hip hop records. Though they'd never previously spoken, Simmons and Rubin had certainly attended many of the same venues, particularly new wave nightclub Danceteria.

Simmons was subsequently invited to Rubin's dorm, a bombsite littered with record crates and adorned by tacky wrestling and heavy metal posters. Rubin set up his drum machine and played Simmons a selection of beats he'd programmed, which Simmons described as "hit records in the making". Simmons then talked about his experiences in the industry, and how he felt he'd been ripped off by a series of record companies, including independents like Profile with whom he'd been wrangling over Run-DMC, and Mercury, who had offered Kurtis Blow little support since his breakthrough. Rubin, for his part, appreciated the fact that Simmons had kept going because it was a "love" rather than "a business thing". For his part, Rubin had never received a penny for 'It's Yours'. Rubin could therefore sympathise with Simmons, who'd made "about 20 hit records that sold a lot, and he was broke. He never got paid either. So I said, 'this is dumb. They're not really doing much for us, and they're not paying us, so let's do it ourselves. At least we can make sure we get paid and our artists get paid.'"

Rubin persuaded Simmons that they should think about forging Def Jam as a unique entity and remain independent. The label name, which he'd already invoked, reflected current hip hop vernacular, the term def being a popular superlative indicating 'definitive' status. Or so Rubin thought. In his autobiography, Simmons contends that it was Rubin misspelling the black slang term 'death', usually pronounced 'def', that inspired the name. That explanation seems unlikely, however, given that Rubin had already used it on punk releases several months previously.

The initial investment was $4,000 each. Russell immediately got to work, using his network of contacts to gain the ear of *Billboard* magazine, where he boldly claimed: "The purpose of this company is to educate people as to the value of real street music by putting out records that nobody in the business would distribute but us." Def Jam 'proper' was founded in the summer of 1984, long after the first flowering of hip hop, but nicely on cue to benefit from the commercial harvest.

By dint of walking before he could crawl, and then running before he could walk, Simmons had established himself as hip hop's pre-eminent promoter. And an early and characteristic decision to diversify as soon as he'd made a success of his preceding venture brought further success. In the wake of Kurtis Blow's breakthrough with 'Christmas Rappin' ', his client roster mushroomed. This was principally because he was one of the few to believe the hip hop phenomenon had the longevity to justify proper artist representation – a leap of faith in a culture still dominated by the singular, one-off event. Among his clients were Spyder D, who contributed to hip hop's brief fascination with the Smurfs ('Smerphie's Dance'), Spyder's wife Sparky D, one of the first female MCs to reach vinyl, and R&B singer Alyson Williams, the daughter of bandleader

Bobby Booker. The most interesting of the Rush management crop, however, were Whodini, Stetsasonic and Jeckyll And Hyde, a trio of acts who left their stamp on hip hop for a variety of reasons.

Whodini, comprising Jalil Hutchins, John 'Ecstacy' Fletcher and Drew 'Grandmaster Dee' Carter, were among the most versatile and gifted of the formative hip hop acts. While their material blended the new school electro aesthetic with funk and R&B, their stage show, incorporating complex dance routines from U.T.F.O.'s Dr Ice and Kongol Kid, readily differentiated them from competing entities. Chuck D remembers Whodini as "probably the most tightly performing yet underrated outfit in the rap game," and recalls, with gratitude, Fletcher helping him out with stage tips. Their origins lay in 1982's 'Magic's Wand', commissioned by Barry Weiss at Jive, a white executive who, next to Simmons, has had the most longstanding association with hip hop in the record industry. It was intended as a collaboration with WHBI's Mr Magic but when the DJ passed, his assistant and his friend (respectively Hutchins and Fletcher) were invited to remould a keyboard track that Thomas Dolby had submitted to Weiss. Later Whodini collaborated with Larry Smith on a succession of fine singles including 'Five Minutes Of Funk' and 'Freaks Come Out At Night'. Both were included on their gold-certificated 1984 album *Escape*, one of the first fully realised hip hop albums, and their R&B leanings are frequently advanced as a precursor to swingbeat.

Whodini were soon outflanked by new school rappers though, most of them, ironically, from Simmons' own Def Jam stable. Simmons himself considered Whodini "hip hop for adult black people who hated rap", which suggests his heart was in it. It's a quote that's also illustrative of Simmons' position in the great hip hop versus rap debate, placing him in direct opposition to his Bronx forerunners Flash, Bambaataa and Herc, for whom rap was a term covering hip hop's *nouveaux riches* and Johnnycome-latelys. After setbacks with Jive, Whodini never recovered their equilibrium and their career petered out towards the end of the Eighties, despite an attempted comeback for MCA. Chuck D of Public Enemy brought them back together in 1994 to appear on Terminator X's *Godfathers Of Threatt* album, a reunion with producer Larry Smith. They contributed one notable new track, 'It All Comes Down To Money', though the line "the type of businessman who doesn't really have a plan" did not refer to Simmons, as some imagined. Indeed, the Terminator X collaboration arose out of his urging the group to cut a new album. Later they tried a third comeback for So So Def in 1996, signed by Jermaine Dupri, who as a teenager had breakdanced on their *Fresh Fest* tours. The album bombed and the two parties parted in acrimony.

Fellow Brooklynites Stetsasonic were billed by Simmons as the 'first hip hop band' in recognition of their accommodation of live instrumentation alongside drum machines, turntables and a human beatbox, and a musical doctrine that anticipated rap's later dalliances with jazz and reggae. They were among the first to pursue Afrocentric themes before the discourse became fashionable in the late Eighties, spurring the Jungle Brothers and A Tribe Called Quest to pursue similar themes as part of the Native Tongue collective. Stetsasonic's love of the continent was reciprocated when they toured Africa, and they were joined by Winnie Mandela and Reverend Jesse Jackson on stage at a memorable Brixton Academy show. Their albums *On Fire* (1986) and *In Full Gear* (1988) boasted some of the most articulate lyrics in the hip hop pantheon, notably on 'Talkin' All That Jazz', a landmark single which eloquently defended the integrity of those involved in sampling, after they'd heard producer-songwriter Mtume claim that the practice constituted artistic theft, or 'Memorex music'.

Linchpin members Prince Paul (Houston) and Daddy-O (Glenn Bolton) eventually parted after the former produced 1989's epochal De La Soul album *3 Feet High And Rising*. Its runaway success led to ructions in the Stetsasonic camp, which intensified after they recorded a third album that neither of the main protagonists felt entirely satisfied with. "After I listened to it," recalls Daddy-O, "I thought, well, for what it's worth, I think it's a good album. But the effort was so divided, it was crazy. All the Daddy-O tracks sound like Daddy-O, and all the Prince Paul tracks sound like Prince Paul, nothing like we were when we started." Prince Paul later set up his own boutique label within the Def Jam empire, but came a cropper, before reuniting with fellow Stetsasonic member Fruitkwan and RZA of the Wu-Tang Clan to form the Gravediggaz. For his part, Daddy-O collaborated with Mary J. Blige, the Red Hot Chili Peppers and Queen Latifah whilst pursuing a solo career. The achievements of both, in a number of fields, substantiated their emphatic repudiation of Mtume's view of the musicality of hip hop.

Dr Jeckyll & Mr Hyde comprised Andre Harrell (Jeckyll) and Alonzo 'Lonnie Love' Brown (Mr Hyde). 1981's 'Genius Rap', one of several hip hop jams based on the Tom Tom Club's 'Genius Of Love', had saved record label Profile from bankruptcy (which was just as well for Run-DMC) by shifting 150,000 copies. It provided the duo with their five minutes of fame, though audiences were nonplussed when confronted by performers dressed in strait-laced suits and ties, and their début album bombed. Both Harrell and Brown were transparent about their plans to succeed in the music industry behind the scenes if they didn't make it as artists. An early promotional picture had one of the pair holding a copy of *Billboard*, the other *The Wall Street Journal*. Harrell soon landed himself a staff job with Rush *en route* to becoming a leading black music executive.

Managing such a large stable of artists stretched Simmons, but an effective means of marshalling his energies presented itself in timely fashion. In the summer of 1984 he was approached by Ricky Walker with the idea of promoting a tour featuring rappers and breakdancers. The event was not without precedent. In November 1982, Fab Five Freddy and Bernard Zekri set up 'the European B-Boy Roadshow', later dubbed the 'New York City Rap Tour'. Playing to audiences in Paris and London, it featured Afrika Bambaataa, Ramellzee and Grandmixer D.ST, alongside breakdancers and graffiti artists. Walker, an established concert promoter, thought there was scope for a similar concept that would take in major American cities. The Swatch Watch New York City *Fresh Fest* featured Run-DMC, Whodini, Kurtis Blow and the Fat Boys. The latter, the only group not overseen by Simmons, were managed by Charles Stettler, who negotiated the sponsorship deal with Swatch. The show grossed $3.5 million over its 27 performances, and featured 10-year-old Jermaine Dupri, later head of the So So Def empire, making his stage bow as a breakdancer. Its financial success astounded industry experts. While the short-term dividend was a coast to coast drugs binge for the artists involved, its lasting impact was to spread the word about hip hop to previously insulated metropolises across America.

Operating out of a tiny two-roof office at 1133 Broadway, south of 26th Street, Rush, later renamed Rush Artist Management in 1986, was adorned by a huge mural painted by graffiti artist and design associate Cey Adams, (one-time room-mate of Adam Horovitz of The Beastie Boys), who later formed the Drawing Board agency with artist and later film director Steve Carr. Simmons had begun to build up an intimate staff circle, many of whom graduated to secure board-level industry posts. Employing Theodore Roosevelt's measure of a good businessman, "the best executive has the sense enough to pick good men, and the self-restraint enough to keep from meddling," time would judge Simmons an unqualified success. His first recruit was secretary Heidi Smith, whom Simmons met when she was assistant to Robert 'Rocky' Ford, before Ford's business went bankrupt. Andre Harrell was drafted in as A&R

executive in 1985, and eventually became vice-president at Rush, while also entertaining Simmons as a long-stay house-guest in Queens.

Harrell subsequently established Uptown Enterprises, which enjoyed major crossover R&B success by harnessing the genius of Harlem producer Teddy Riley to the swingbeat generation of Jodeci, Mary J. Blige and Riley's own band, Guy, as well as overweight rapper Heavy D. The latter's success was a personal vindication. Harrell tried on numerous occasions to get Simmons to sign his friend, but Simmons resisted, considering "the overweight lover of rap from money-earnin' Mount Vernon" "too R&B" for the rest of Def Jam's roster. Later, Harrell encouraged the early career of Sean 'Puff Daddy' Combs, who went from work experience to CEO at Uptown, before a temporary falling out led to him setting up Bad Boy. Simmons became fast friends with Combs after they met in 1988, despite his aborted move to lure LL Cool J from Def Jam in the Nineties. In fact, such sharp practice probably only increased their mutual respect. With Simmons' help, Harrell finished up as the president of Motown on a package worth $30 million, before he was fired in 1997 after 18 months of poor sales. Simmons remains furious about his treatment. "The scumbags in this business, who recycle white executives like returnable bottles, wouldn't give him a shot," he railed in his autobiography. Still fondly nicknamed Dr Jeckyll by his old sparring partner, Harrell has remained a close confidant of Simmons ever since.

However, Simmons' most important appointment was future business partner Lyor Cohen, another employee on whose floor he would sleep for a protracted period. Cohen, an imposing presence at over six foot five inches, was proud to boast he oversaw the 'detail' work at Rush Management. Others attest to the fact he kept the operation shipshape by yelling at anyone foolish enough to show an ounce less commitment than he and Simmons did to Rush, and later Def Jam. DMC gave him the nickname 'Mr Handle-It-Make-It-Happen' in tribute to his results-orientated approach.

Cohen was raised in Israel and Los Angeles having been born in New York to an affluent Jewish family. He gained a degree in international finance and marketing from the University of Miami in the early Eighties. In his year out from his studies, he travelled to Ecuador and made an unsuccessful bid to launch a shrimp-farming business. After graduation he returned to Los Angeles to take up a banking post, which bored him rigid. While there he stumbled across his first rap performance by Egyptian Lover and the World Class Wrecking Cru (who featured a pre-NWA Dr Dre). Impressed by the 16,000-plus audience the event attracted, despite a total absence of media coverage, he made a characteristically rational decision. Hip hop was going to be his "way in". In the sleevenotes to Def Jam's 10th Year Anniversary box set, he recalls: "I was desperate to make an impact. It wasn't like I heard the cash registers ringing. I just wanted to find out where I belonged. I said to myself, 'I'm sure I can get some white boys interested in this. It's too black, it's too counter-cultural, it's too loud, it's too aggressive, it's too your-parents-are-going-to-hate-it.' It was everything that teenagers wanted, the logical extension of rock'n'roll with an extra scary element of race."

Cohen began promoting shows at the Mix Club in Los Angeles, hosting hardcore shows by So-Cal punk bands Social Distortion and the Circle Jerks. But when he booked Run-DMC for a show at the Hollywood Palladium, it led to a meeting with Simmons and an invitation to join him back in New York. He made the move in January 1985. At first he worked as assistant to Andre Harrell, before taking over as road manager for Run-DMC and overseeing the *Fresh Fest* tour packages. Nobody paid any heed to the fact that he was often the only white face in the clubs, a towering, gum-chewing presence directing operations on the front line. "Lyor's name was Little Israel back then," DMC recalls, "all the homies knew him as that."

Eventually he was handed the reins of Rush on a day-to-day basis, leaving Simmons' hands free to devote more time to Def Jam when the label took off. He would introduce a welter of new talent to Rush, including Jazzy Jeff and the Fresh Prince, featuring future mega-star Will Smith, Eric B and Rakim and EPMD. He helped sign 3rd Bass and Slick Rick to Def Jam and pioneered Rush's street marketing, inaugurating the now common practice of giving away free cassettes to influential club DJs. His reputation was also built on the fierce support he gave artists he brought under the Def Jam or Rush umbrellas. "Not to get into the sociology too much," surmised Bill Stephney to *Newsweek*, "but one can argue that a white hip hop executive who shows he respects the music will get more respect than a black hip hop executive who shows respect for the music."

Simmons also hired Bill Adler, a freelance journalist whom he'd first met in 1980 after he'd written a feature on Kurtis Blow for the *New York Daily News* and a subsequent piece for *People* about the rap venue Disco Fever. Simmons made him his director of publicity in 1984. Tony Rome became Rush's road manager, also handling Whodini and later LL Cool J. Yale graduate Lisa Cortes became Lyor Cohen's assistant, and later founded Rush Producers Management. It's worth noting the loyalty afforded Simmons by those he employed – many of these original employ-ees remained key staff throughout Rush's existence, many later graduating to Def Jam. By the autumn of 1985 Rush had relocated to 40 East 19th Street, a former dance studio that still boasted panelled mirrors and wooden floorboards.

Despite a growing array of interests, the priority act for Rush was Run–DMC, whose momentum was building impressively. Yet their affairs were still sufficiently hand-to-mouth to necessitate hastily convened recording sessions for their second album, *King Of Rock*. They succumbed to Profile's timetable in order to secure the second part of their advance, though Simmons held enough cards to effect a re-negotiation of their con-tract had he not been so desperate for ready cash. Despite the success of the title-track, take two in the group's attempt to reconcile rock with rap, the results were patchy. The album was blighted by clashes of ego and musical conflicts. Simmons has subsequently claimed he was infuriated by the R&B leanings of Larry Smith. Smith, the group's producer and some-time road manager, added a bass line on 'You Talk Too Much' without his knowledge. Smith thought he was adding musicality. Simmons thought he was softening the sound.

Also heavily involved in producing *King Of Rock* was Rick Rubin. He was beginning to wield his influence on the trio, encouraging them to push the rock dynamics to the forefront and adding his own guitar work to a few tracks. In an attempt to satisfy the divergent influences being brought to bear on the record, hundreds of edits were completed before the album was finalised, despite the punishing schedule. But it was Rubin who emerged with the clearest vision of what Run–DMC needed. Schooled on old AC/DC records, he was suspicious of anything that diluted the trio's sonic fundamentalism. "The less going on in a record, and the clearer and more in-your-face it is, the better," he later told *Mojo* magazine. But someone really should have told Run that there were four Beatles, not three ("Every jam we play, we break two needles/There's three of us, but we're not the Beatles") – a lyrical oversight on the title-track that puts their relationship with the wider world of pop in context.

Despite its uneven sound, the album achieved platinum sales. But real confirmation of Run–DMC's stature came equally from peer approval. They were thrilled to appear alongside long-time heroes the Cold Crush Brothers at a performance at Columbia University in April 1985. Indeed, being tied to an independent label with restricted finances meant that they had to make their money on the road. At their peak they could secure

$150,000 a night. Small wonder, then, that Simmons organised annual cross-country treks like the *Fresh Fest* tour.

In the meantime, Def Jam was about to launch itself as a record company proper. Simmons, emboldened by Rubin, started to talk up the idea of a label. Following the success of *King Of Rock*, they were sounded out by a number of interested parties about distributing the mooted imprint. They attended several conferences, and at one stage were flown to Los Angeles to speak with Warner Brothers' president Mo Austin. But with the cards stacked in their favour, they could afford to wait for the right deal to come to them. And despite Simmons' characteristic myopia when it came to A&R, they'd struck on the right act to launch the label.

3

Some Guy Named Rick Called . . .

"Around '84 we were in a bar and Russ was telling me, 'I'm sick of making other people rich. I want to own my own shit, my own record label, my own movie company.' What I really thought was that he was drunk. There weren't a lot of blacks thinking that way back then. There weren't a lot of examples to follow."
— Gary Harris, former Def Jam executive

LL Cool J, or James Todd Smith, was a precocious 16-year-old from St Albans in Queens, who had been mailing demo tapes to anyone who'd listen. Finally, he sent one to an address he'd found on the back of a 12-inch record he'd bought at Record Explosion on Jamaica Avenue, T-La Rock and Jazzy Jay's 'It's Yours'.

Despite his later image as rap's grandest showman, Smith was an introverted youth who managed to find expression through hip hop culture. He had grown up with the nascent movement, embracing its energy as a youth, before becoming its crossover every-man poster boy, bowing to stylistic peer pressure and promoting a persona that was inoffensive and amiable rather than bland — a balance that his Nineties challenger and namesake Will Smith never quite mastered. Catholic-educated, he was nine years old when he started rapping, by which time he'd been unfortunate enough to witness the shooting of his mother and his jazz saxophonist grandfather by his own 'buck wild' father. Afterwards he was mercilessly beaten by the man his mother took up with while recovering from her injuries. It wasn't the best start in life. The result was a reputation as a 'problem child' who was regularly expelled from school, and briefly joined the Muslim sect Five Percent Nation.

At the age of 11 he saw the Sugarhill Gang, Crash Crew and Funky Four Plus One perform at the Harlem Armory, and he grasped a means to transcend his circumstances. Here were people saying things in a dialect he understood, expressing themselves in unequivocal terms that had the punch and emphasis of a street-corner slanging match. The cars and women they rapped about were less relevant. "I got into rap for the power," he confirmed in his autobiography. "I wanted to be heard. I wanted to make a record and hear it on the radio. It was just that simple." So he sought refuge from his abusive stepfather by writing page upon page of rhymes.

By the time he'd turned 13, the 'name' DJs in Queens were the Albino Twins, the Disco Twins and Jay Philpot. The latter, the state heavyweight wrestling champion and later a student at City College, gave Smith his shot. He proved his mettle on the microphone, though it was only after performing over a rival's beats that he won Philpot's respect, and chastisement. After obtaining his grandparents' permission, Philpot gave Smith rides to his shows, adopting him as his front-line MC. Like just about everyone else in the game at this stage, Smith, who took the name LL Cool J (or Ladies Love Cool James) wasn't paid for his efforts. And like most everyone else, he didn't care. But he did have plans. He started mailing out tapes to addresses jotted down from record sleeves. He tried all the big hip hop imprints, Sugar Hill, Enjoy, Next Plateau, Tommy Boy, Profile, as well as the majors. Nobody expressed any interest whatsoever, though he did build up enough rejection slips "to start a fire". At least eight tapes were sent to Sugar Hill alone. His mother encouraged his interest by investing $600 in a drum machine, just as his enthusiasm was starting to wane. Finally, together with a friend called Finesse who provided some elementary scratching, he came up with a new tape, and mailed it to Def Jam.

Rubin had put his phone number on the back of 'It's Yours', which was a positive incitement to the ambitious young rapper. LL kept reaching his answering machine, but finally spoke to Rubin in person. All Rubin would offer was a half-hearted promise that he'd get back to him. Smith kept ringing to check if he'd received his tape. Rubin would pretend he hadn't – in truth it was sitting with a big box of cassettes in his dorm room, waiting to be discovered.

Eventually, on returning home one night, LL's grandmother informed him that "some guy named Rick called". He arranged to travel to Rubin's dorm in University Place, where his future label boss greeted him in the lobby. As he recalled in his autobiography, he was entirely wrong-footed by the shuffling, podgy vision which greeted him. "As I stood there, I thought of all these great things to say, like, 'Yo, man, I'm ready to be a star,' and, 'There's plenty more where that came from.' Then maybe I would hit him off with the rap I'd written the night before. But when he was finally standing there in front of me, all that came out of my mouth was, 'Yo! I thought you were black!' " LL later found out that his meeting with Rubin was due to Beastie Boy Adam Horovitz's discovery of the tape in the gulag that was Rubin's dorm. The two immediately started working together, LL improvising lines over Rubin's scuttling, hop-scotch drum patterns. They taped the results, which Rubin suggested they take over to Russell Simmons, "the money man", at his offices on Broadway.

Having passed through a minuscule reception area presided over by Heidi Smith, they were confronted by a desk-bound Russell Simmons, who never shied away from embossing his image as the great playmaker, especially in eyeball-to-eyeball meetings. According to LL, his tape was brushed aside. "Nah! It's the same old thing. That's just like the Treacherous Three and everybody else!" was how LL recalled his verdict. Still, Rubin believed in his talent, and organised a proper recording session to cut 'I Need A Beat'. It changed Simmons' mind instantly. "He really liked that record," LL remembers. With a potential tie-up with a major in the offing, Simmons was still considering his options. But eventually he got frustrated by lack of corporate faith in hip hop, which he'd experienced first-hand at Rush. "Every time we would bring an artist to a major label, they would always say that the marketplace is saturated," he complained. "You know the funny thing is, when LL Cool J came out, there were already 'too many rap artists for radio.' " "So what happened was," concludes LL, "instead of them taking that record and going to a distributor and trying to get it distributed, and having problems with the money, they decided to form an independent company called Def Jam and put that record out."

'I Need A Beat' is a production that Rubin is still proud of. "That's a really sparse record, pretty much all one drum machine, vocals, and a couple of little musical nuances here and there, a little bit of scratching." It was exactly what he was looking for to launch Def Jam. "They came up with some deal that would benefit them more than me," recalls LL. "But, of course, I signed anyway. I didn't care at all. I really would have done it for free."

The 12-inch took off immediately thanks to the patronage of DJs like Red Alert and stations like KISS-FM. It also scored on the west coast, thanks to KDAY's Greg Mack, and Russell's diligence. "A guy named Russell Simmons came up to me and said, 'Greg, I'm Run's brother and I'm starting this record company,' " remembers Mack. " 'I got this lil' artist named LL Cool J. He's about 16. I wish you would give his single a shot and play it.' The next thing you know, LL just blew up. And with every group that Russell brought me, it was the same thing."

LL's fanbase exploded after some stunning live shows, appearing along-side Jay Philpot, renamed Cut Creator (although the original Cut Creator on 'I Need A Beat', was a friend from Corona in Queens). He became so popular so quickly that Rubin and Simmons were forced to enlist Cornell Clark, who'd worked with the Fearless Four and Kurtis Blow, as his personal manager. Clark, a diffident man who was nevertheless a former professional dancer and karate expert, made an unlikely but fruitful alliance with the brash young star.

Clark convinced him to hang out on the set of Simmons' new movie *Krush Groove*, in the hope of talking himself into a bit part. Producer George Jackson was persuaded to offer him a cameo, in which he 'spontaneously' rapped 'I Can't Live Without My Radio'. When Simmons booked him to record a video for the song later that week, LL overslept and missed the date. He was chewed out by Simmons over the $50,000 that his no-show allegedly cost, though that figure is likely to have been exaggerated. 'Radio' was a big hit, regardless. But the success quickly inflated LL's already gargantuan ego. As he later reflected, "I was 16 years old and thought I was grown, but I was a very troubled young man." His grandmother was utterly unconvinced about his new career, especially as the late shows on weekends left him too exhausted to go to school. Eventually she issued him with an ultimatum; he left home rather than give up on the music industry. Despite his success and celebrity, he suddenly had no one to turn to. He claims to have spent two weeks sleeping on subway trains. Then his manager learned of the situation and offered him his basement in Ozone Park, Queens.

It was in that basement that he wrote most of the material for his début album, *Radio*. Simmons and Rubin remedied his immediate financial plight by presenting him with a cheque for $50,000. Dazzled, he made straight for Revel Knox Hats on Jamaica Avenue and blew a chunk of it on a new supply of his trademark Kangol headgear. He then bought his mother a Mercury Cougar, though that was far from the end of his high-rolling. The first cheque was soon followed by a second instalment to the same value, for royalties from 'I Need A Beat'. Simmons was just as excited. "It was great. I made my first $300,000. I was actually more excited about that milestone than when I made my first million years later."

Radio, which cost just $7,000 to record in New York's tiny Chung

King, was a fantastic example of raw, flashy adolescent pop noise. 'Rock The Bells', his biggest single so far, went on to sell 900,000 copies with LL on beatbox cruise control. He started spending and partying like tomorrow was a foreign country. His particular obsession was gold chains – to the point where he had to attend muscle-building classes in order to get his neck and shoulders in good enough shape to bear all the gilt. He also purchased over a dozen vehicles, including three sports cars in the course of one American tour. You can blame Rush and Def Jam for not advising him better, but it doesn't sound like LL would have listened if Donald Trump and Warren Buffet had been sitting on his chest.

Unsurprisingly, LL's breakthrough brought tensions. Simmons kept putting Run-DMC on the same bill as LL, and Run in particular didn't take kindly to a younger pretender stepping on his turf. "LL Cool J was always one step behind us," remembers Run. "His whole career was like one year we'd love him, the next year we'd hate him. LL was always giving us a strong run for our money." The two parties shared more than joint management. Aged 16, LL penned 'Can You Rock It Like This?' for Run-DMC's *King Of Rock*. He also wrote 'Rock The Bells' as a homage to *Raising Hell*'s 'Peter Piper', which he'd heard them working on in the studio. He thought he might just use the same Bob James break, 'Take Me To The Mardia Gras'. When Run found out he was livid, so LL changed the song's musical foundation to incorporate Trouble Funk samples and AC/DC's 'Let's Get It Up' instead.

DMC admits the relationship on tour could be fractious. "Run and LL would fight every night," he recalls. In particular, LL liked to trump the headliners by proclaiming the auditorium was *his* house. "Run would run into the dressing room and get in his [LL's] face. 'Don't say you're from Hollis! You ain't from motherfucking Hollis! And stop saying your house! This is my tour!'" Stetsasonic's Daddy-O reckons the pecking order within the Rush family was always a prickly issue. In 1987, when two separate Def Jam itineraries crossed in Atlanta (Run-DMC having toured with The Beastie Boys, Stetsasonic with Public Enemy, Eric B and Rakim and LL), he witnessed LL being told he couldn't use his stage props, essentially an oversized radio, because Run-DMC were headlining. "He didn't like performing on Run's set, so he hurt 'em! And it was the first night I seen him rip his shirt off."

If Def Jam had struck first time out with LL Cool J, a few of their pitches in its early release schedule flew wide of the coconut shy. Indeed, a couple took out the goldfish on the next stall. The most fascinating was a release by Jazzy Jay, 'Def Jam', a tribute to the new label's aesthetic, backed by 'Cold Chillin' In The Spot'. The B-side is a collector's item for more than monetary reasons. It features Russell Simmons' own lamentable attempts at freestyling, verses which mainly consist of telling 'Doctor' Andre Harrell, in situ at the studio the night the record was cut, that he can't appear because his label might sue Def Jam. The record bombed so completely its anonymity alone would have kept the lawyers at bay in any case. To give credit to Simmons, he's a man who has always recognised his own limitations – unlike, say, Puff Daddy – even if it takes a little rubbing against them before those limitations are acknowledged.

'I Need A Beat' and 'Def Jam' were two of seven singles the label issued in its first year, by which time Simmons and Rubin were ready to sign a $600,000 distribution and promotion contract with CBS. The major had passed on a similar deal with Sugar Hill in 1983 due to the Englewood imprint's unwholesome reputation, but was still interested in exploiting this new youth phenomenon. When negotiations were completed, Rubin was so excited he made a photocopy of the cheque to show his parents. The backing meant Def Jam could relocate to a new 'complex', in reality a cramped three-storey building at 298 Elizabeth Street in Greenwich Village, which overlooked a daily gathering of crackheads on the street outside. Indeed, it was that assembly line of users and their empty crack vials that inspired Chuck D to write Public Enemy's 'Night Of The Living Baseheads'. Rubin moved into the third floor, while Def Jam occupied the second floor and Rush Management the first. The basement housed a recording studio.

LL's breakthrough confirmed Simmons' presence in the hip hop market as both a label head and artist manager. While some point to the limited role he has had in unearthing artist talent, usually having to be persuaded by those around him with better instincts, his greatest contribution has been his ability to recruit to his cause those with the vision he lacked. To this end, he started to beef up Def Jam's staff. As well as the aforementioned Rush personnel, a who's who of modern rap executives and industry movers embarked on careers with Def Jam; Dante Ross, Bill Stephney, Lisa Cortes, Sean Casarov, Faith Newman, Dave Klein, Hank Shocklee and Lindsay Williams among them. As one-time Def Jam associate Nelson George points out, "Within five years all would be vice presidents at major labels, owners of their own boutique labels, or both." Dante Ross is a good example. He graduated from messenger boy at Def Jam to an A&R post, signing white rap act 3rd Bass. He then moved to Tommy Boy, discovering Queen Latifah, then Elektra, where he signed Brand Nubian among others.

It is almost impossible to name an artist, label, fashion or trend in hip hop that hasn't been touched profoundly either by Rush or Def Jam. In March 2000 *HHC* produced a poll of the greatest albums in the genre. Whilst Public Enemy were predictably at number one, most of the other critical records of the last 15 years boasted some link back to Def Jam. In second place were the Wu-Tang Clan, whose Method Man signed a solo contract with Def Jam. Nas, the Queens prodigy at number three, had been signed to Sony by Faith Newman and discovered by MC Serch of 3rd Bass. At number four were Rush clients Eric B & Rakim. At six was De La Soul's *3 Feet High And Rising*, produced by Rush client Prince Paul. The list goes on.

Simmons' empire-building has been likened to that of Motown's Berry Gordy, previously the outstanding figure in the black music business, or the business of black music. Indeed, that opinion was shared by some in the Def Jam organisation, like Cey Adams. "At that time, Def Jam was closer to the way Motown was – it was a family. It had a lot to do with the fact that Russell and Rick were spearheading every project, but it also had a lot to do with the fact that it was before people were making a lot of money." The Motown analogy is something that Simmons himself implicitly acknowledged in the exaggerated biopic of his life, *Krush Groove*. In one of the opening scenes, he follows Run-DMC into a church to confront his father (played by Simmons Snr in person) to request money to help fund his record label. He is mocked thus: "You [Run] Lionel Richie, You [DMC] Prince, here comes Berry Gordy!" As co-producer and story consultant on the film, it's impossible that Russell Simmons would have allowed this allusion to Gordy in the final script if he didn't want to encourage the comparison.

But unlike Gordy, Simmons' approach did not revolve around trying to market his artists to a mainstream white audience. As David Morse wrote in his 1971 book on Motown, "Its [first] attempts to reach white audiences – and so, indirectly, to break down barriers between black and white – put it in the mainstream of black American opinion, which, under the leadership of Martin Luther King, was still very much concerned with integration and racial harmony. Since then the idea of Black Power, however interpreted, and the new role of pop music as an outlet for white American dissent have made Motown and its tuxedo-clad artists seem both square and Uncle Tom." Maura Sheehy also observed the simple but hugely significant dichotomy at work. "Like Gordy, Simmons is building a large, diverse organisation into a black entertainment company, only Simmons' motivating impulse is to make his characters as 'black' as possible."

Simmons never wanted to sanitise or mould his artists. As he wrote in *Life And Def:* "Unlike Motown, I don't believe in catering to the so-called mainstream by altering your look or slang or music. I see hip hop culture as the new American mainstream. We don't change for you; you adapt to us." There was an intuitive understanding that these MCs and DJs, initially friends and acquaintances rather than business clients, came fully-formed with their own intrinsic identities and agendas. Just as punk had killed off the effete prog rock bands, hip hop made some established black artists look like out of touch dinosaurs. As Simmons admitted to Stephen Holden of *The New York Times*: "In black America, your neighbour is much more likely to be someone like LL Cool J or Oran 'Juice' Jones than Bill Cosby . . . A lot of the black stars being developed by record companies have images that are so untouchable that kids just don't relate to them. Our acts are people with strong, colourful images that urban kids already know, because they live next door to them."

Nelson George noted the comparison with Gordy in *Hip Hop Nation*, but prefers to liken Simmons to Sammy Davis Jnr for his ability to network and integrate with the white establishment, in music, film or anything else he feels like tackling, without compromising his own agenda. But there were definite similarities between Gordy and Simmons, the two men for whom 'music mogul' has become an almost inevitable suffix. Both benefited from parental loans, an indication of backgrounds where aspiration was matched by *relative* affluence. They also employed hugely important, hardcore businessmen as first lieutenants – in Simmons' case Cohen, in Gordy's Jay Lasker. Lasker later recounted to the *Sunday Times*: "I'll tell you the truth, I never learned to love music. I stayed in the record business not because I love records but because I love business. And it paid well." That mirrors Cohen's outlook perfectly. Gordy also staked everything on a film enterprise with the purpose of launching Diana Ross. Simmons was about to do something very similar, only with his own 'persona' getting the star billing.

Krush Groove is considered by many puritans to be the best hip hop movie around. It told Simmons' story in a simplistic but appealing rags to riches vernacular and was directed by Michael Schultz, one of the pioneers of African-American film. Run-DMC, The Beastie Boys and Dr Jeckyll

41

and Mr Hyde all got screen time. Alongside *Wild Style*, the low-budget document of breakdancing and graffing filmed by Charlie Ahearn, it is a time-capsule of a revolution in progress.

Simmons had been toying with the idea of making a movie for some time, encouraged by Kurtis Blow, who was keen to develop a parallel acting career. But Simmons knew little about the industry, and fretted over who he should take the project to. *Breakin'*, a hip hop exploitation movie made in Los Angeles, had been directed by Joel Silberg, and produced by Menachem Golan and cousin Yoram Globus. An energetic if clichéd cash-in on the west coast breakdancing phenomenon, featuring Lucinda Dickey in the lead and introducing west coast rapper Ice-T to movie-goers, it spawned a less impressive sequel, *Breakin' 2: Electric Boogaloo*, within a year of release, but also a soundtrack album that went platinum. Golan, a protégé of exploitation king Roger Corman, wanted to pull the same trick on the east coast, focusing on MCs rather than breakdancers. But after initial negotiations Simmons chose to run with George Jackson, who headed Richard Pryor's film company and later took over as Motown CEO. Jackson had been planning a hip hop movie since he caught the Long Beach Arena leg of the 1984 *Fresh Fest* tour. "We saw the birth of a cultural phenomenon," Jackson reflected. "We knew this hip hop shit was going to be big, and we decided instantly to make a film." Golan and Globus did get their hip hop movie in the end – the appalling *Rappin'*. But once Jackson had wined and dined Simmons, persuading the members of Run-DMC to commit to the project was straightforward.

Simmons suggested Schultz as the man to direct, having been impressed by his coming-of-age classic *Cooley High*. Via his connections with Mo Austin, which he'd established while shopping Def Jam to potential backers, Simmons convinced Warner Brothers to distribute the finished film. It was Jackson's suggestion that the basis be Simmons' own life and times. That tactic was bound to appeal to his ego, but it also gave the film a workable narrative structure. Simmons' part was taken by Blair Underwood, later Jonathan Rollins in *L.A. Law*, while Rick Rubin played himself – neither the most demanding role or performance. Simmons also had a walk-on part as the promoter Crockett, presumably so that acting could be added to his ever lengthening résumé. Rubin and Simmons each received $15,000 for their input.

The opening scenes featured Run-DMC in the studio, before the film cut to Rubin's dorm from where Def Jam was first run (real-life Rush assistant Heidi Smith plays 'Carmen', the indignant receptionist). There's a presumably intentional interlude where Underwood's character under-scores the hierarchy of the relationship with Rubin, who is unable to cope with the orders created by the interest in Run-DMC. "A hit record is the worst thing that could have happened to us," Rubin protests, unconvinc-ingly. Simmons is less bashful, grabbing the phone and insisting that the label will deliver. Given that we know it was Rubin's idea to set up Def Jam in the first place, this suggests further revisionism on the scriptwriter's, and presumably Simmons', behalf.

Later, in the scene in which he begs for money from his father to tide the business over, the Simmons/Underwood composite character is told that it's "God's will" he be tested. Again, the cynical might suggest this was an attempt by Simmons to mythologise his struggle. There are further scenes, similarly contrived, in which he and Rubin attempt to convince a caricature bank manager that they're good for a $5,000 loan to give the business some collateral. That's the same figure that Simmons admitted in an on-line interview for ABC News that he'd put by from his work with Kurtis Blow and others in order to start Def Jam.

Later in the film, as Run-DMC takes off, the plot centres on the ten-sions success engenders between the two brothers. Run is portrayed as the ungrateful bad guy and Russell the 'angel' who'd done everything for him. The fact that Run-DMC were never a Def Jam act is readily glossed over in Ralph Farquhar's screenplay. Finally, Russell's character gets the girl, in this case Prince protégé Sheila 'E' Escovedo. Thus inspired by his alter-ego's romantic triumph, Russell himself started dating actor Shari Headley on the set, the first of his tedious 'famous people' conquests recalled in unwarranted detail in his autobiography. Yet for all that it's a fun film, despite marrying fact and fiction in a slightly unconvincing manner. "Every scene [that he was in] had me either rapping or sitting there writing rhymes," confirms DMC, "which was pretty accurate for what I did in real life. And they made Run the raunchy, energetic kid eager for fame by any means, which he was in real life."

In a belated quest for authenticity, several scenes, including the finale, were set in the legendary South Bronx venue Disco Fever, with real-life owner Sal Abottiello appearing in cameo. As the *Vibe History Of Hip Hop* noted, "The granddaddy sequence of them all was Run [DMC]'s climac-tic taking of the stage near the end of the film to demand exactly whose house – and by extension, movie and genre and art form – this really is." The film grossed over $3 million in its first weekend of release, demon-strating America's growing appetite for hip hop and Run-DMC's box office appeal. However, Simmons and Rubin had no claim on royalties. Simmons himself admits to naivety about the whole process, especially in failing to secure any intellectual rights to *Krush Groove*. From a $2 million budget, the film eventually achieved a domestic gross of $11 million.

Though it is generally lauded as a pivotal cinematic moment, several things annoyed Simmons about the final version. He wasn't aware that Jackson had cut a deal with Charles Stettler to give the Fat Boys a movie deal, which eventually resulted in the deplorable *Disorderlies*. Which explains their prominence in the film, where they variously beat-box on a college stairwell and munch their way through an all-you-can-eat menu in grandiose style without moving the plot along an inch. He also regretted the lack of 'edge' in the final print. Nevertheless, *Krush Groove* is still an enjoyable, though mercilessly stylised, document of the hip hop world. Indeed, it was not until the Nineties and John Singleton's *Boyz N The Hood*, a film which Simmons almost produced, and the Hughes Brothers' *Menace II Society*, that hip hop and cinema began to enjoy each other's company again.

Run-DMC, who came out of *Krush Groove* with their reputations intact if not necessarily enhanced, finished on the set and immediately jumped on a plane to start their *Raising Hell* tour. By the time it was completed they'd become the first rap act to play on *Dick Clark's American Bandstand*. Just as significantly, they were the only rap group to perform at Live Aid – though they were only added to the Philadelphia bill, at the personal request of Bill Graham, when it was realised that only three out of the 70 acts booked were black. It wasn't an auspicious arrangement, as they appeared early on the bill in blazing sunlight in front of an audience bemused by their presence. But taking part was important from a historical standpoint. They were then contacted by Little Steven Van Zandt of Bruce Springsteen's E Street Band about performing on an anti-apartheid record. With typical American insularity, none of the group knew of the artistic boycott of Sun City, though they were happy to contribute to the record once they'd swatted up.

Run-DMC played a more substantive role in dismantling *musical* apartheid. 1986 was the year in which they finally smashed the barriers between hip hop and rock, and to an extent, black and white. *Raising Hell*, Run-DMC's third album, sold more than a million copies in its first five weeks of release. This time the quality and breadth of the material was outstanding, particularly the defence of rap linguistics that was 'You Be Illin' ', its lyric inspired by Prince's 'Raspberry Beret', and 'My Adidas', a tribute to their trademark footwear that also referenced their *Live Aid* appearance. But it was their collaboration with Aerosmith, the lapsed kings of arena rock whose career looked as dried up as singer Steven Tyler's skin, that gave the album real impetus. When Rubin broached the idea of including a version of 'Walk This Way', which he thought might be "a nice little kicker to the album", he received short shrift from the group. Aerosmith had nothing to lose, whereas Run-DMC's growing credibility was on the line.

But the collaboration was not as revolutionary as might first have appeared. The opening beats of 'Walk This Way' were a popular breakbeat staple that Jam Master Jay and myriad other hip hop DJs had been using for years. However, they knew the track only by its LP title – *Toys In The Attic* – and they'd never left the needle on the record beyond the intro. "We were gonna cut the beat back and forth, that's how we gonna make this record," recalls Simmons. "It's not gonna be any singing or none of that crap. Rick Rubin was like, 'No, let's call up Aerosmith.' I said, 'Who?' 'Aerosmith.' 'Who are they?' 'That's the people from *Toys In The Attic*; that's the band.' Run and DMC were not for the idea. I was a little bit in the middle about, 'Are you gonna rap those lyrics?' But we had a lot of fun making it."

The band's initial protestations that the song's lyrics were "hillbilly shit" were waved away, and the sessions convened. Rubin's first contact with the band was to establish the exact nature of said hillbilly shit, which DMC had sat down with a pen and paper to transcribe but couldn't fathom. While Jam Master Jay was in favour, the two MCs remained deeply sceptical about the entire enterprise, but were eventually persuaded by Rubin. In the meantime, he'd invited Aerosmith over for the weekend to re-record the track.

Rubin, as a star-struck 20-something producer, was able to savour being in the studio with one of the two bands, alongside AC/DC, that he'd loved beyond any others as a teenager. Indeed, he even got to coach Joe Perry on his guitar performance when he felt his idol wasn't ripping into it as well as he'd seen him play live. Despite Aerosmith's legendary drug intake, by this time both Tyler and Perry were 'clean' and didn't party with their collaborators, who were newer in the game with a developing taste for drugs. The two parties got on fine, though Aerosmith have done little to acknowledge the part Run-DMC played in restoring their fortunes. Steven Tyler did acknowledge to Robert Sandall of Q that: "A lot of black guys have always come to our shows. But it was a gas to hear these dudes from New York City funk the shit out of that tune." And funk the shit out of their nose-diving careers, too.

Much of 'Walk This Way's success can be attributed to the video that accompanied the single. Its no-brainer symbolism was ready-made for MTV; rock and rap band sharing adjoining studios end up breaking down the barriers together. Its suitability for the medium arose specifically out of design rather than accident. Central to Russell Simmons' strategy to increase Run-DMC's visibility to suburban audiences was access to MTV. As he later told Ifé Oshun: "You know when Run-DMC got on MTV, the only person that was black on MTV was Michael Jackson . . . So there was a dramatic difference between Michael Jackson and normal kids who spoke to young black America's heart, and now all young America's heart . . . Now MTV is integrated, and kids understand each other better . . . from the trailers to the projects to Beverly Hills . . . they all have a dialogue, they're sharing an understanding." Or, as he later told Fayette Hickox in *Interview* magazine, "Michael Jackson is great for what he is – but you don't know anybody like that. The closest Run-DMC comes to a costume is a black leather outfit . . . It's important to look like your audience. If it's real, don't change it."

MTV was the medium that legitimised music video. Though it lost millions in the year of its launch, 1981, it became a uniquely potent showcase for record companies attempting to market their wares. But, by 1983, *The New York Times* was able to point out that "The program can be watched for hours at a time without detecting the presence of a single black performer." A growing consensus railed against the musical policy, insensitively brick-batted by MTV president Bob Pittman as, "The mostly white rock audience was more excited about its music than the mostly black audience was about its music – rhythm and blues, or disco, or whatever you want to call it."

R&B singer Rick James led the upsurge in protest, disgusted that his hugely successful singles 'Super Freak' and 'Give It To Me Baby', from his multi-million selling *Street Songs*, were being ignored. In interviews he repeatedly condemned MTV as a racist network. Simmons was part of a Rush delegation who picketed the station, though it's hard to imagine him pounding the streets outside their Manhattan offices for very long when there were phones at Def Jam's offices to pound. If pushed, he'll admit, "We didn't *really* picket. We let Rick James do the picketing." The conflict intensified when Michael Jackson – who later requested that all mentions of his name on the show should be prefixed 'King Of Pop' in return for exclusive previews of his videos – became a mainstream pop star. When his handlers discovered that MTV were not disposed to playing his 'Billie Jean' promo, CBS president Walter Yetnikoff legendarily threatened to refuse MTV access to any of the label's artists (though years later Pittman would rubbish this story). Soon Jackson was joined by the likes of Lionel Richie and Prince in steady rotation. But MTV distanced itself from rap, the music which had all but consumed black listening tastes by the late-Eighties. With rare exceptions, such as Grandmixer D.ST, hip hop was an unwelcome guest. Run-DMC's 'Rock Box' was played, but it needed the concession of an Eddie Martinez guitar solo to get it that far. Not until Run-DMC were accompanied on video by some family friendly, time-honoured rawk stars was this situation reversed.

After 'Walk This Way' the colour barrier at MTV collapsed, as legions of rappers, from Salt-N-Pepa to Tone Loc, crashed through the ideological hole between rock and rap flagged up in the video. They came to realise, as Bill Stephney notes, that MTV, "had changed rap. It's not music any more, it's visual art. The best rap doesn't mean anything if the kids aren't into the video." Other rappers filmed promos, but Simmons and Rubin deliberately and doggedly targeted MTV with acts such as LL Cool J, and later, Public Enemy. Rubin was good friends with the supportive Peter Doherty, who held a senior post at MTV and encouraged young intern the late Ted Demme to push rap. It was their joint efforts that led to the founding of *Yo! MTV Raps* in 1988, hosted by Fab Five Freddy, before Ed Lover and Dr Dre, formerly of Def Jam quartet Original Concept, took over its week-night slot. It soon became MTV's most popular show. Later, with the rise of gangsta rap, station execs grew fearful of the music's violent cadences. MTV never came to terms with NWA, after having spoon-fed the world both Vanilla Ice and MC Hammer. But as Ted Demme confirms, "[Run-DMC's] videos were fantastic, and they were the leaders. They took hip hop into the video millennium, if you will."

'Walk This Way' peaked at number four in the American survey in the autumn of 1986 and stayed on the charts for 16 weeks. Run-DMC were depicted on a landmark front cover for *Rolling Stone* magazine, while *Raising Hell* became the first rap album to reach number one on the R&B charts. The album had an effect as profound as 'Sucker MC's' in broadening hip hop's reach and appeal, evangelising contemporary MCs, a generation for whom Run-DMC's influence is both readily apparent and universally acknowledged.

The *Raising Hell* dates of 1986 saw Run-DMC tour in triumph

alongside a clutch of Simmons-managed acts, while Lyor Cohen negotiated a sponsorship deal with Adidas estimated to be worth $1.5 million.
Business executives were, if not running a slide rule over hip hop, awak-
ening to its importance as a marketing tool. The future synthesis of music,
fashion and business that made hip hop the dominant cultural trend of the
Nineties was prefigured by the deal. Russell Simmons had long noted the
financial benefits such sponsorship afforded sports stars like Michael
Jordan, who'd far outstripped his basketball salary by hooking up with
Nike. And, despite Run-DMC's oft-quoted mantra, "Don't want nobody's name on my behind" (a reference to Calvin Klein on 'Rock Box'),
sneakers were evidently a different proposition. Indeed, the sports shoe has
proved an artefact of almost mythical importance to hip hop consumers.
There's an amusing extract in DMC's autobiography in which he con-
fesses to feeling pity for a group of shabbily dressed fans who confront him
for autographs while at a car wash. "It was pretty apparent that some of
them were just making it from payday to payday. I looked at some of their
sneakers, which were off-brand and really worn, and I just started feeling
guilty."

Simmons and Cohen set up the deal with the precision of a bank heist.
Adidas big-hitters were flown over from Germany to attend Run-DMC's
triumphant Madison Square Garden performance, headed by deal-broker
Angelo Anastasio. It was some show they caught. Run varied his usual
opening mantra, "This is Run's muthafuckin' house", to "I beg your
pardon, this is Run's muthafuckin' Garden!" With the group at the apex
of its powers, Run orchestrated one of rap's truly iconic set-pieces. "At
the spur of the moment – things were at an all-time high – I had everyone
in the whole Garden lift their sneakers in the air," he recalled in his autobiography. "The spotlight was racing across the crowd, and twenty thousand pairs of Adidas were raised." As he later reasoned in *The Show*,
"Everybody had no shoestrings in 'em, so it was easy to take 'em off."
DMC, too, was taken aback with their new sponsorship. "They even had
the box black, something they never did." Anastasio was sold on the idea,
though you can't help feeling that Russell Simmons or Cohen might have
suggested the sneakers-in-the-air gesture as a sweetener.

The release of 'My Adidas' as a single could only have pleased the band's
new paymasters. Run, meanwhile, was overjoyed at the prospect not only
of banking the footwear giant's giant cheque, but also having his own
brand of sneaker. For a B-boy, it doesn't get much sweeter than that. The
presence of Carlton Ridenhour, later to become famous as Chuck D of

Public Enemy, who had been invited to the show as part of Rush and Def Jam's efforts to get him to sign, was just as significant for rap's history.

However, two incidents took some of the shine away from Run-DMC's tenure as ringmasters. Nominated in five categories for an American Music Award in 1986, they came home empty-handed. It seemed to them an open rebuttal of rap music, as lesser acts such as New Edition collected trophies they thought rightfully theirs (New Edition's leader Mike Bivens acknowledged that fact in his acceptance speech). For some, this was evidence of the intrinsic resistance, or veiled racism, behind the music industry's response to rap.

As if to confirm these cultural gatekeepers' worst suspicions, there was violence at some venues on Run-DMC's tour of that year. None of it was the fault of any of the acts, but it did bring hip hop an undeserved reputation for confrontation. The worst problems arose in August at a Long Beach, Los Angeles performance where a local turf war between rival Crips and Bloods gangs was relocated to the venue. Run-DMC were bemused by the politics at ground zero, though they had been briefed to avoid wearing prominent red or blue in light of the gang affiliations. They were left cowering in their dressing room as the dancefloor erupted into a war-zone before they'd even taken the stage. Support act Whodini came rushing backstage and described seeing a man thrown from the balcony onto the floor of the auditorium. According to DJ Greg Mack, who was in the audience, the security guards were being actively targeted by gang members, and were so scared they started taking their uniforms off. Soon the group, and rap music in general, was in the dock about lyrics that incited violence – a signpost to the bloody times that lay ahead for rap music as it emerged from an altogether more innocent era.

4

Skills That Pay The Bills

"It's really a New York thing. When we were growing up, clubs wouldn't only play rap or punk or funk – you'd go to hear a hardcore band and they'd play James Brown on the PA between the sets."

– Adam Yauch, June 1994

A few years before pixelated pariahs Beavis and Butthead became the targets of moral indignation, three obnoxious, whiny adolescents drew them a route map. The Beastie Boys were, and are, a quintessential, yet atypical hip hop act. Their presence came at a tangent to its conventions on both a musical and personal level. The trio are from affluent back-grounds, for a start, despite their street–smart, wisecracking ways. And they were white. As in, not black. All of these factors had reverberations, but none of them overshadows or dilutes their central contribution to the commercial and artistic rise of hip hop.

Their presence underscores rap's links to a previous rebellious counter-culture, that of punk rock – or more strictly its 'hardcore' derivative, in which idiom they initially operated. The son of an art dealer, Michael Diamond attended St Ann's, an exclusive private school in Brooklyn, before becoming vocalist for The Young Aborigines, alongside guitarist John Berry and drummer Kate Schellenbach. They played exactly two shows – on the same day – before breaking up. By 1981 they were recon-stituted as The Beastie Boys, at which time architect's son Adam Yauch was drafted into the line-up on bass. Yauch and Diamond originally met at a show headlined by Bad Brains, the wild but breathlessly inventive Rasta-punks who spearheaded the New York hardcore scene of the early Eighties after relocating from Washington. Bad Brains patented a frenetic, life-affirming stage show, incorporating singer H.R's improbable back-flips, with occasional and wholly contrasting diversions into sweet-textured reggae. Though it took time to appreciate the musicality beneath

50

Bad Brains' sonic blur, many of those who looked deeper became converts (The Beastie Boys attempted to sign the band to Grand Royal in the mid-Nineties before another old fan and mutual acquaintance, Madonna, gave them a contract with Maverick).

There had been no precedent for a black band playing punk music, just as The Beastie Boys would become the first recognisable white hip hop act. Both Diamond and Yauch embraced the Manhattan punk scene wholeheartedly. Diamond described his first meeting with Yauch to the *NME* in 1988. "I was going to a lot of punk rock shows on my own because I didn't have any friends who were into that. And because I was young and he was young, a lot younger than most people at the gigs, we became part of this group of kids who went to clubs and to see bands together." However, being imbued with a natural New York reticent cool, they did not become fast friends immediately. "We scowled at each other for some time first."

Their intuitive sarcasm and preference for clowning about above any kind of work ethic placed them at odds with the puritanical wing of straight edge hardcore, patented by Bad Brains' long time Washington DC friends Minor Threat (of whom Rick Rubin was also a big fan), but at this stage hardcore was still an inclusive movement. Indeed, the putative Beastie Boys were all fans of Minor Threat's Dischord label and its DIY ethos, and played regular gigs at venues like the A7, and eventually supported Bad Brains at Max's Kansas City at the invitation of HR. Their first release, the *Pollywog Stew* EP, was housed on friend and record shop owner Dave Parson's Rat Cage label. Recorded in 1981 and released early the next year, its roughshod production and simpleton musical values did little to set the band apart from a peer group that now included Kraut and the Nihilistics (with whom they were unfavourably compared). But early songs such as 'Egg Raid On Mojo' (revisited as 'Egg Man' on *Paul's Boutique*) and 'Michelle's Farm' highlighted an engaging propensity for, respectively, ragging on neighbourhood fashion victims and self-parody.

The final permanent member of The Beastie Boys was Adam Horovitz, son of playwright Israel Horovitz, who replaced Berry. He too was enmeshed in the burgeoning New York hardcore community, to whom his band The Young And The Useless were component parts. Their sets were littered with Dickies-inspired cover versions of hokum pop tunes such as 'Grease' and 'Billy, Don't Be A Hero' rather than original material. Horovitz met his new bandmates at a show by the Funky Four Plus One, signed to groundbreaking hip hop imprint Sugar Hill. Despite later accusations that the trio were merely cultural tourists, or worse, pirates, their attendance proves all three were keen to investigate New York's emergent new black music strain. But they retained their punk attitude, proudly extolling the virtues of being "loud, obnoxious and ugly", according to Kate Schellenbach, who played drums for the group in the early days. The new line-up increasingly left hardcore behind as they began to incorporate hip hop cadences, adapting readily to its precepts of creative freedom and imagination. With hardcore, an attempt to reinvent punk as a suburban American phenomenon, hip hop shared the advantage of refusing to acknowledge musical ineptitude as a barrier to entry.

The Beastie Boys' learning curve took in all of hip hop's non-linear trajectory, from street battle tapes popular in the Bronx to its first vinyl releases via the Sugarhill Gang, Grandmaster Flash and Afrika Bambaataa. The wildly eclectic DJing of the latter, in particular, proved a singular inspiration. These influences were distilled into their second release, 'Cookie Puss', which mixed rudimentary hip hop beats with the group's trademark sniggering, shouty vocal duels and an abusive telephone sketch based on a real conversation with a receptionist of the Carvel ice cream company (which made Cookie Puss ice cream cake). Though the musical register changed, the group's juvenile, class clown behaviour only intensified. This could be indulged more fully after they left the bosom of their families to move into new, rat-infested quarters in Chinatown, living below a sweatshop and above a whorehouse. The move was funded, they suggested, by a $40,000 payment from British Airways over their illegal use of the band's 'Beastie Revolution' (though biographer Angus Batey suggests this was an early example of Beastie Boys' myth-making).

Rick Rubin saw in The Beastie Boys a bunch of kids that shared both his background and aspirations. "I was chairman of the social committee [at NYU] and a DJ," he told *The Source*, "and The Beastie Boys started coming to these parties at my dorm. They asked me to DJ for them since I was a friend of theirs and I had a bubble machine." Diamond confirms the mutual attraction. "We hooked up with Rick Rubin because we wanted to MC in our live shows and needed a DJ to do so, and he had turntables. He definitely swayed us in that he told us to forget the other stuff we were doing and just concentrate on the rap stuff. He had this PA in the room and we'd listen to all the new 12-inch singles in there and Horovitz would make beats on his drum machine." While hanging out together in Rubin's dorm, Diamond helped scan through the demo tapes that were pouring in. In the process he helped 'discover' "people like LL Cool J and Public

Enemy, who had their shit together but -couldn't get a deal." While it's true that Rubin ostensibly got the jobs as Beastie Boys' DJ because he had the equipment to provide some kind of legitimate musical context, he also had useful connections. He introduced Russell Simmons to them at new wave club Danceteria. "They were wearing red sweatsuits and stripes, red pumas and do-rags," Simmons remembers. "They were assholes."

Their metamorphosis from snide punks to bratty rappers was a gradual one. "When we'd play a show, the first 15 minutes would be hardcore, and then Rick Rubin would come up and we'd start to rap," Horovitz told reporters. "Eventually, we switched over to doing only rap. But it was a mellow transition for us. Half our act was rap, anyway." As Diamond concluded in an interview with *Newsday* in 1992, "Attitude-wise, hardcore and rap are remarkably similar. The energy is the same. And you can express yourself without having had to study music for 15 years. I used to say that the only difference was that with punk rock you have funny haircuts, whereas with rap you have funny hats." He added further context to the Beasties' assimilation of contrasting musical interests in 1998. "New York [in the Eighties] was a different city to how it is now. For a start, you had a totally integrated club scene, which has never been the case anywhere in America and isn't the case in New York now. And it was wide open musically. Hardcore punk and rap was happening pretty much concurrently in the city, the punk clubs were the first to play rap records for a white audience and so as hardcore petered out, what was left? There were still incredible, groundbreaking rap records coming out. I remember at the Danceteria they'd play Kurtis Blow, then Spoonie G, then the Cure's 'Boys Don't Cry'. It was all, in this weird way, considered dance music." While others depicted their musical redefinition as a quantum leap, the group considered it to be a natural evolution. "When you think about it, hardcore and hip hop aren't really that different," reckoned Horovitz. "In hardcore, you've got your verse and your chorus. In a rap song, it's kind of the same thing. And the attitude is the same – it's a city attitude."

The transition saw Schellenbach exit, later to found Luscious Jackson, though she ascribed her departure to Rubin encouraging the band to incorporate 'sexist' japes and sketches. Others were suspicious of Rubin's objectives, hardcore author Steven Blush remarking that Rubin was "quick to throw dad's money around". Rubin, meanwhile, used the term precocious to describe The Beastie Boys, which offers a variation on the usual trilogy of snotty, bratty and obnoxious. As Simmons recalled in *Life And Def*, however, reservations within the hip hop community about The

Beastie Boys were predicated on their colour rather than their deport-ment. "A lot of people were mad at me for managing them, at least at first. I remember there were discussions that the Beasties were a rip-off of black artists. To me the Beasties were honest. They were doing their version of black music." Nelson George, in defence of charges that The Beastie Boys were appropriating black territory, makes the following point: "It is one of the rare moments in pop history that a successful white group practised a black music style with a black person so intimately involved in guiding their careers."

To be fair to him, Simmons has always been more interested in the colour of money than skin pigment, and he also sponsored the career of another white hip hop group, 3rd Bass. At this stage he'd tried and failed to export Run-DMC to suburban audiences, where the bulk-buying power resides in America. This was a golden opportunity to rectify that failure. The trick was not to alienate indigenous hip hop fans in the process. All parties, conscious of their credibility for different reasons, trod carefully until they'd successfully circumnavigated the debate. As Ted Demme, co-founder of *Yo! MTV Raps* notes, "The fact that they were white did not hurt them, but they didn't exploit it like Vanilla Ice did. They were true artists who did things their own way and were so original that you just couldn't help but love them." Or as Yauch modestly informed Joanne Carnegie for *Creem*: "We got called a few names, but once people hear us, they automatically realize how great we really are."

Now a fully-fledged hip hop group, they adopted suitable nomen-clature. Diamond, rejecting a given name that many rappers would have killed for, became Mike D, Yauch took the acronym MCA and Horovitz was now Ad-Rock. They largely abandoned musical instruments to con-centrate on three-way tag-team rapping, backed by Rubin on turntables, himself re-christened DJ Double R. Simmons started finding them spots on hip hop bills. "Rick started getting tight with Russell," remembers Yauch. "We really formed into a hip hop group as Russell was starting to manage us. We started playing real shows, opening for Kurtis Blow or the Fat Boys. It was scary at first. One time Russell put us in a limousine and sent us out to the Encore club in Queens. We were definitely the only white people for miles, and we were getting out of, like, a stretch limou-sine. How much more obnoxious and conspicuous could we have possibly been?" But few who knew them doubted that their snotty attitudes were an image rather than a conviction. "There was a very sweet period in '84, '85, when Russ would throw these parties and the entire Rush/Def

Jam posse would be in the house – Run-DMC, Whodini and Kurtis Blow, Beastie Boys, LL would all show up," remembers Bill Adler. "It was just fun, loose, and when they could relax and didn't have to be the Beasties, they could be charming, they could be warm."

It's important to point out that, while it was Rubin who was the principal musical collaborator in the band's development, Simmons ". . . took us all under his wing," as Diamond told Scott Mehno in 1987. It was Simmons who dissuaded them from their initial inclination to dress in tracksuits and ape Run-DMC's style, insisting they would be seen as fake. As Adler remembers, "Russell looked at the Beasties in these extravagant matching red Chinese gym suits and said, 'No. N-O! You've gotta be who you are and who you've been.' "

As Def Jam grew, Simmons became convinced of The Beastie Boys' potential to sell hip hop records to a mainstream audience, as publicist Leyla Turkkan recalls. "Russell was obsessed with them. This was back in those Danceteria days when everybody was really high on coke. All he could talk about was The Beastie Boys, and I just didn't believe it was going to work. We had a bet going on whether they would ever fill Madison Square Garden, because I didn't think it was going to go over. I lost." Others, like Jazzy Jay, just looked on them as part of the furniture. "The Beastie Boys were just hang-out partners. The founders and the saviours of rap they never were, but I don't think they ever portrayed themselves to be." At this stage, the fact that Simmons was both the group's manager and label head didn't seem too problematic to either party, though it later became the kernel of the argument on which their relationship would rupture.

LL Cool J's 'I Need A Beat' became the first Def Jam release under the aegis of Simmons and Rubin. The man who claimed to have discovered him, Mike Diamond, was ready to record with his own group. 'Rock Hard'/'Beastie Groove', released in November 1984, was built over a sample of AC/DC's 'Back In Black' (later also used by KRS-One's Boogie Down Productions). While Run-DMC had dabbled with a rap-rock hybrid on 'Rock Box', released a few months previously, The Beastie Boys' effort was less gimmicky and harder-hitting. 'Beastie Groove' more accurately anticipated the contents of the band's début album, and included Horovitz's first eulogy to penis envy: "I'm a man who needs no introduction/Got a big tool of reproduction". In the mid-Eighties, discussion of the enormity of one's male appendage was routine. The Beastie Boys discussed it more than most.

But if they were to connect with mainstream America, which was Simmons' big idea, they needed exposure beyond the hip hop circuit. A classic Simmons hustle provided the answer. He'd been contacted by Madonna's management in an attempt to secure behemoth B-boys The Fat Boys as tour support. At that time, Simmons had a stake in just about every hip hop act extant, and was considered the go-to-guy for those outsiders looking in on the scene. Simmons, carefully neglecting to mention that The Fat Boys were actually nothing to do with him, suggested Run-DMC instead. As Yauch recalled to *The Source*, Run-DMC were "too expensive so Russell offered a good deal on us." Even now, the image of Simmons the cultural shopkeeper, offering discounts on his non-branded goods, is hard to resist.

Madonna had been exposed to hip hop culture as a regular at Cool Lady Blue's Roxy club and Danceteria, and later became a fan of both The Beastie Boys and Public Enemy. Even so, Horovitz was bemused by the connection. "It's not like any of us knew Madonna [though they worked at one point with her original producer Mark Kamins], but we all used to hang out at Danceteria so we knew about each other. I don't know why she thought it would be a good idea, though. It was a terrible idea!"

While it gave The Beastie Boys a deal of notoriety, it's easy to overestimate the importance of the Madonna tour in winning converts. But then, as Simmons reasoned, "Every night they'd make 95 per cent of the people in the audience hate them. But they built that other five per cent into a fan base." The tour also established their reputation for mayhem, which was more than tacitly encouraged by Simmons. Band friend Jarvis was appointed tour manager, by dint of having a valid driving licence. "I remember Russell saying, 'Either it works, or let's get thrown off the tour in as big a style as we can.'" Their on-stage antics made the latter a distinct possibility, as Simmons remembers. "They used to go out in front of Madonna's fans and run around on stage and lip-sync. They'd be joking and falling over while the lip-syncing was supposed to be going on." Horovitz reckons it was Simmons' 'greatest coup'. "At the time she [Madonna] was just becoming massive and wanted to retain some cool . . . and it's true she took a shine to Yauch."

When deafening boos greeted their appearance at Madison Square Garden, Yauch responded with a stream of expletives. "They were very bad boys," Madonna later recalled. "They said 'fuck' all the time on stage. The audience always booed them and they always told everyone to fuck off. I just loved them for that. I couldn't understand why everyone hated them. I thought they were so adorable." Nevertheless, wiser counsels prevailed upon her to boot the band off the tour. She chose not to, after Simmons sent Yauch to her dressing room to plead their case.

While touring with Madonna The Beastie Boys hooked up with photographer Glen Friedman, who'd been a fan since their bawling hardcore days. The prints of their ad hoc photo session were passed to Def Jam. "After Russell Simmons saw the shoot I did with The Beastie Boys," Friedman recalls, "he decided that Def Jam and Rush would never have a group come to California without seeing me. I ended up helping them with promotion and always doing photo sessions with the groups that I liked, until the point came when they asked me to make it back to New York in '86." Friedman would have a big impact on Def Jam's visual profile, subsequently photographing a number of Def Jam record sleeves, including Slick Rick's début, before becoming, in Simmons' words, his "social and political conscience".

With Rubin bowing to other commitments, The Beastie Boys employed Dr Dre (Andre Brown) of Original Concept as their new DJ. Also signed to Def Jam, Original Concept's 'Total Confusion' had been a further attempt to meld a rock-rap fusion, this time using a sample of Led Zeppelin's 'Kashmir', though their one *bona fide* hit was 'Pump That Bass'. "After Rick finished the Madonna tour," remembers Dre, "he said, 'Hey, you DJ pretty good, why don't you get down with these guys?'" There were also protracted discussions, quite openly raised, as to whether Yauch and Horovitz should dispense with the services of Diamond. The two Adams had roomed together and considered Diamond the junior partner and the butt of their practical jokes. "I was shocked that there was a discussion about that," Simmons later protested. "He was the only original member, right? That's fucked up."

The Beasties toured as opening act on the 1986 Def Jam *Raising Hell* package tour featuring Run-DMC, LL Cool J and Whodini. It was a deliberate effort not only to bolster their credibility with hip hop audiences, but also to promote the Def Jam brand. But as Dre remembers, the excess just carried over from the Madonna tour. "On the *Raising Hell* tour with Run-DMC, our breakfast was Scotch, Jack Daniels and Budweiser beer, and my mouthwash was gin and tonic. Everyone always wanted to ride on our bus because of the stories. We had Nintendo, the radio, the best stuff in the bar. But everyone was scared for us to ride on their bus." But unlike the Madonna trek, people were now paying attention, as DMC remembers: "From day one they were killing. Even when nobody knew them. It could be a completely black, negro, southern crowd there to see Run-DMC and Whodini, but when the Beasties came on it wasn't like people were walking around getting hot dogs – they really paid attention to them white boys."

But their appearance at the Apollo Theater saw them push the envelope a little too far, much to Dre's embarrassment. "Everybody was like, 'Look, whatever you do, don't say "nigger" ' – because it was part of what we did, before a lot of people were doing that in hip hop. They didn't mean it in a negative way, they meant it as something warm and generous to their audience. But Russell grabs me and says, 'Don't let 'em do it.' And I'm like, 'What am I gonna do? I'm in the back, DJing.' So they're out there doing 'She's On It' and Ad-Rock says, 'All you niggers, wave your hands in the air!' I've never seen so many blank stares! Mike looks back like he doesn't know what to do, but Yauch was like, I'm out of here! And Ad-Rock's going, 'Come on y'all, come on y'all,' and nobody's waving back. They finished the song, dropped the mics, and ran off the stage. I'm still out there, and everybody's kind of looking at me. I run upstairs to the dressing rooms, and everything's gone. They weren't even on the tour bus. They all jumped in a cab and went home."

Crucial to the group's subsequent success was Simmons' decision to sign Def Jam to Columbia Records. The major, then the largest record company in the world, had been looking for an alliance with a 'street' label, and had already attempted to cosy up to Tommy Boy, Def Jam's chief competitor as an independent hip hop label. Simmons, who was keen to expand his operation, used the credibility he'd built up with the success of LL Cool J to close the deal (for an undisclosed figure thought to be in the region of $1 million). Columbia brought improved distribution, promotion and a proper studio budget. It also provided far greater fiscal resources, though Simmons' insistence that financial decisions went through him (at least as far as royalty payments went) is instructive in any assessment of the man. It later allowed him to test the old adage that he who pays the piper calls the tune, or more accurately, chooses not to pay the piper until he comes up with a new album. Columbia felt they were getting an established star with excellent career prospects in LL Cool J, and in Simmons a label spokesman who could sell ice cubes to Inuits, or more accurately, deliver a white rock audience to hip hop artists. They were also getting a great talent scout in Rubin, as anyone with a passing knowledge of the hip hop scene knew. The Beastie Boys were very much a side-dish.

Sessions for The Beastie Boys' début album began in the summer of

1986. Simmons, his finger rigidly on the financial pulse, encouraged their habit of recording late at night, thereby keeping down studio bills. That the nocturnal Beastie Boys came back with the fastest selling début of all time surprised everyone, not least the band itself. *Licensed To Ill* is hardly rocket science, or even rock science, though its extensive use of tape loops did presage sampling, later rap's lingua franca. 'Rhymin' & Stealin' ' introduced the album and thematic, pugilistic John Bonham drum samples drawn from Led Zeppelin's 'When The Levee Breaks' providing the initial rhythmic wallop, augmented by SP–12-pogrammed beats and the grunted, truculent vocals that became the group's trademark. There was also a snatch of the Clash's 'I Fought The Law' thrown in for good measure. It was a sound that was immediately intoxicating as well as inordinately, unapologetically youthful.

In addition to a musical debt, the Beasties also acknowledged Zeppelin in the artwork, by Steve Byram and David Gamboli (credited as World B Omes to avoid paying his agent). An airliner with Beastie Boys insignia is depicted, before the gatefold sleeve is opened to reveal its ruptured nose concertina'd into a mountainside. "It was inspired by stories about Led Zeppelin's private jet," reveals Rubin. "The grandiosity of rock decadence, in the form of a private plane being smashed. That, and extreme excess turning into extreme violence."

The album's centrepiece was '(You Gotta) Fight For Your Right (To Party)', embracing sentiments which recalcitrant know-everything 'life's not fair' teenagers worldwide could wholeheartedly endorse. Columbia heard '(You Gotta) Fight For Your Right (To Party)' for the first time and "flipped", according to Beastie Boys' press representative and writer, Bill Adler. It took off as soon as it hit radio, though the Beasties insist to this day that initial quantities were purchased by an indigenous hip hop audience. It was also not the group nor their management's preferred selection – having already issued 'She's On It' and 'Hold It Now, Hit It', they wanted 'Slow Ride'. But Columbia were insistent. Rubin's fingerprints were all over '(You Gotta) Fight For Your Right (To Party)'. "That was really my rock and roll roots coming out," he recalls. "Much like 'Walk This Way' was kind of different than the rest of the Run-DMC album, I really wanted to do a straight-up rock song that incorporated rap, but something that really blurred the line and that's what it did." It was the final song recorded for the album. It reached the US Top 10 in March 1997, astounding all connected to the band. "None of us knew they would sell records," shrugs Simmons. "The only people that we made

Licensed for were the people who they hung out with, the people they thought were fashion-forward. Those guys didn't make records like '(You Gotta) Fight For Your Right (To Party)' because they thought they'd make any money. It was a fucking joke."

Licensed To Ill had important antecedents in LL Cool J's *Radio* and Run-DMC's *Raising Hell*, but was the more conventional rock album and therefore the most accessible to attitudinal white kids who gloried in its outsider/misunderstood rhetoric (though we should dignify at least a section of the audience with spotting, and relishing, the role-playing going on). The follow-up single, 'No Sleep Till Brooklyn', started out as the B-side to 'She's Crafty' and fomented a crass youth club chant out of a dumb 'da-da-da' chorus, an aesthetic approach that owed more to Motorhead than hip hop. The metal guitar riffs were provided by Kerry King of Slayer, though The Beastie Boys dismissed Rubin's idea for a video effect that would make King appear 60ft tall – one of their first creative clashes.

If 'No Sleep' was baloney, there was genuine wit and invention on other tracks, such as 'Brass Monkey', a homage to low-cost alcohol solutions. Both the deceptively complex 'Slow And Low' and 'Paul Revere', which included a particularly nasty line about 'doing' the sheriff's daughter with a baseball bat, were written with the help of Run-DMC. The latter track, an old school homage framed over back-spun funk, became the B-side to 'It's The New Style'. It was pushed to black radio prior to '(You Gotta) Fight For Your Right (To Party)' making a splash on rock stations. It was pretty obvious which approach was winning, however. As Robert Christgau wrote for the *Village Voice*, "The wisecracking arrogance of this record is the only rock and roll attitude that means diddley right now."

Licensed To Ill was indeed the perfect arranged marriage between rock'n'roll exhibitionism (Zeppelin, Kiss, Pistols) and hard rhyming, as the Beasties trawled the dustbins of American junk culture for whatever artefacts they deemed serviceable, the smell of week-old pizza and testosterone that accompanied that process being equally important to the finished record. An obsession with their own bodily functions, and those of women, seemed completely appropriate, almost unremarkable in the context, while their lowbrow philosophical scratchings provided the perfect riposte to being brought up the progeny of intellectuals. "They really made an album that was great and it represented the ideas and attitudes of a lot of kids who didn't have their own rap artists yet," Simmons surmises. "It really took all the alternative music and the rap music and put it into a little box and made it nicely packaged. And it was real." *Licensed To Ill* became the best selling début LP in Columbia's history and the first *Billboard* number one rap album. Columbia clearly hadn't wholly expected this turn of events. They initially shipped only 100,000 copies before demand outstripped supply. "Pretty soon, Columbia started saying, 'What's going on here?' Diamond recalls. "They didn't believe people wanted to hear The Beastie Boys."

But back to that credibility hurdle. The record was sprayed with hip hop jargon and reference points in an effort to reinforce the Beasties' grass roots authenticity. They were well aware that they were white kids operating in a black musical idiom, and while women and gays were randomly targeted, there was nothing derogatory to the black community. While this is hardly an apologetic record, that meant *Licensed to Ill* conveyed a contrary feeling of desperately wanting to belong. Importantly though, with the possible exception of 'Paul Revere', The Beastie Boys made no attempt to approximate black rapping styles, retaining their own vocal ticks and cadences. That prompted hip-hoppers like Q-Tip of A Tribe Called Quest to welcome them with open arms. "They don't try to be black. They're just themselves – not trying to be something they're not." But not everyone was convinced, among them MC Serch of fellow white rappers 3rd Bass. "To me, they were the Anti-Christ. They didn't go to Union Square. I was [a white MC] busting my ass in the streets going through what I considered the proper hip hop, urban channels and these guys go on tour with Run-DMC. To me, they were the worst possible thing to happen to hip hop culture."

Others wanted to question the group on a couple of small textural points. The Beastie Boys' reputation for juvenile sexism had been exacerbated by dubious press comments made by Horovitz on the subject of homosexuality (the original working title of the album, rejected by Columbia, was *Don't Be A Faggot*). Nobody was quite sure whether the preppy antics were those of clumsy character actors or these guys really were the jerk-offs depicted on *Licensed To Ill*. They eventually came to realise the responsibility that their success carried with it as a Buddha-embracing, conscience-led global wake-up act in the Nineties. In the meantime, however, there were front pages to dominate, and leader writers to outrage. Which made them naturals for MTV, then establishing itself as a powerful brand leader and marketing tool. "MTV loved them," notes Ted Demme, the programme's founder, "because they were knuckle-heads, they represented rock and roll – they went nuts, they got drunk, they crashed things. They did what every good rock band does except that they did hip hop."

By the time The Beastie Boys and Run–DMC reached Britain in May 1987, The Beastie Boys were already generating more column inches than their better established headliners. The uninitiated, and some of those with vested interests, hyped up the potential for chaos. Simmons even concocted a 'fight' story between the members of the Beasties and Run–DMC at a pre-tour party. "I told Yauch to go punch [Jam Master] Jay in the face. We got on the cover of every paper all round the world. The Beasties did it 'cos it was fun. I did it because it would make us money." Much of the pre-tour reportage focused on the Beasties' use of a go-go dancer, Eloise, who appeared caged on stage alongside a huge hydraulically operated phallus. They also appeared in front of a Budweiser banner before the brewery objected to their patronage, this being a long time before commerce co-opted hip hop as a powerful marketing tool which can buy them leverage in niche urban communities.

British tabloids mercilessly hyped the 'depravity' of The Beastie Boys, picking up on American stories including the judgement in Jacksonville overturned by the group's lawyers that all tickets and promotional material surrounding their performance had to feature explicit warnings of the group's 'sexism'. Conservative MP Peter Bruinvels demanded the band be denied entry to the country. The *News Of The World* gave succour to another right-wing rent-a-quote MP, Geoffrey Dickens. "I want these diabolical creatures banned from these shores," he fumed, on cue. Douglas Hurd at the Home Office was said to have "examined the matter carefully", but was not minded to refuse the group work permits. But the Beasties were initially complicit partners in the media-baiting. "We were in London and MCA jumped off the third-floor balcony into the pool," remembers Dre, who later opted out of the madness to be replaced by DJ Hurricane. "We were banned from Holiday Inns for the rest of our lives. I still can't get into a Holiday Inn! I tried the other day and they said, 'We have your picture with those other guys.'" They also pursued girls with messianic zeal, legendarily attempting to live up to Led Zeppelin's *Hammer Of The Gods* manifesto of sordid bacchanalia. "Ad-Rock would try to get the older, sophisticated girls," remembers Dre. "Yauch would fuck anybody – he'd fuck the fish if they were in the fishbowl. Then he'd act like he was the holiest man – that's what would kill me."

Tour manager John Reid later suggested to Q magazine that the band's management cut deals with the press in order to keep their profile newsworthy. That Faustian pact unravelled when the *Daily Mirror* accused them of mocking terminally ill children at a festival in Montreux, Switzerland, shortly before they reached Britain. The band have always maintained that the story by hack Gill Pringle, which echoes The Sex Pistols' Bill Grundy fracas, was entirely fictitious. The paper later printed a tiny retraction after the *Sun* ran a spoiler story in which Yauch was quoted as saying the Beasties "knew where to draw the line".

While glorying in behaviour that would have delighted tennis superbrat John McEnroe, The Beastie Boys were similarly treated to some unjust line calls. Pringle's piece engendered a sense of hostility toward the band from 'right-thinking' tabloid readers. Their show at the Brixton Academy was accompanied by massed ranks of horse-mounted police. There was no trouble, apart from an unsubstantiated Garry Bushell report about anti-white literature being distributed in the venue. However, in Liverpool, one of two dates added after the Beasties became tabloid sensations, the group were targeted by bottle-throwing punters chanting football songs, who'd swallowed the Pringle story uncritically. The projection of The Beastie Boys as a band who humiliated dying children was an act of tabloid insanity which mirrored the urban myth, which also originated in Liverpool, that local councils had banned the use of black bin liners for fear of causing racial offence.

After dodging the projectiles, the Beasties returned to the stage equipped with baseball bats and defiantly attempted to parry the flying glass. "Miraculously I don't think I got hit," complained Diamond, "and we were like ducks in a shooting gallery! After about three songs it was obvious that it wasn't going to let up, so we just had to down tools and get out of there. Once we were on the bus, we thought: Thank God it's over. All English people are assholes." Audience member Joanna Marie Clark complained one of the beer cans deflected by Horovitz struck her. Horovitz was thrown into the cells, while protesting his total innocence (he was cleared, largely on the evidence of an off-duty policeman, in November 1987). Photographer Ricky Powell was at the show, and reported that Ad-Rock's jail time "wasn't that bad. He was in with some old-timers who were telling him dope stories." Alongside the rap-loving cop, another unlikely advocate stepped up to defend the group during this difficult period. In an interview with the *Los Angeles Times*, Ad-Rock's father Israel Horovitz noted: "If people can't see the humor and satire in the record [*Licensed To Ill*], I don't know what to say to them. It's all so obvious. I think the thing that makes the record so good is that it shows a real understanding of people; maybe not an understanding of 49-year-olds, but certainly of 17-year-olds. I am delighted beyond description; it's like a kid taking over the family store."

In the tour's aftermath a new Beastie Boys-inspired craze began to sweep Britain. Diamond had begun wearing Volkswagen marques as a parody of Rakim's Mercedes-Benz pendants. Soon badges were being ripped from the radiators of Volkswagens nationwide – resulting in the car manufacturer offering to give them away free to provide some respite to their customers. Bizarrely the UK's hugely influential Mo Wax label began after James Lavelle purchased stolen Volkswagen insignia from his partner-to-be Tim Goldsworthy.

The Beastie Boys, on their return, slipped into indolence. Some observers thought they might never record again. Horovitz pursued an acting career, appearing in *Lost Angels* and TV's *The Equalizer*, while his relationship with Brat Pack actress Molly Ringwald, whom he'd met through the inclusion of 'She's Crafty' on the soundtrack to *The Pickup Artist*, kept the celebrity gossip columns buzzing. Diamond and Yauch concentrated on a variety of side projects.

Some of the internal tensions were ascribed to Rubin 'favouring' Horovitz. That may have had more to do with the fact that they spent a summer sharing the same dorm and enjoyed a personal friendship outside of the group. Rubin denied, and still denies, ever trying to create disharmony within the group. "When we became successful," he told James Brown of *NME*, "we'd still hang out but there'd be all these business managers and other people telling the other two I was trying to split the band. It's success: suddenly there's so much pressure being applied to every situation by so many people. Also, people change." But Yauch remains embittered. "I was really upset and pissed at Rick Rubin, feeling like Def Jam and Rush Management had gone on a really selfish tangent. We started getting sick of the band and what it represented, like we were ashamed to be a part of it. We decided to take some time apart from each other."

Musical differences were another factor, as Rubin later confirmed to *Mojo*. "I was more into the rock stuff; they were more interested in punk stuff, or Adam Horovitz was always into Bill Withers, Al Green, smooth, soul sounds, and the funk drum beats." There were also rumblings over a film script that came to nothing. Provisionally entitled *Scared Stupid*, the plot was set in a haunted house, but there were arguments over the royalty points. Universal offered the group money to finance the film, but Rubin pointed out that they couldn't record any music for it under their Def Jam contract. The project was spiked. Simmons regrets that outcome. "That was stupid. No record company should do that. What I should have done was tell Rick, 'Forget it. They think it's a better opportunity. It's a bigger budget. It's a different kind of film. It protects our music.' I was young and inexperienced and made the mistake of not protecting them. Rick made the mistake of not understanding that you can't control it all." Rumours also abounded that Simmons had earmarked Yauch for a solo career.

All of which meant Columbia's understandable ambitions for a follow-up album were frustrated. According to Rubin, they responded by refusing to pay the group's royalties until they fulfilled their part of their contract and furnished them with new material. However, others, notably Bill Adler, believe Simmons was at the heart of the dispute. Seeing the band party and spend without focusing on 'the business', he held back royalties for fear they'd smoke and drink themselves back to square one, and lose all the impetus they'd created. All three core members of The Beastie Boys were outraged, and it's possible their indignation gave them something to unite around just as their career was dissipating. So they went fishing for a new contract, believing they were entitled to do so because Simmons' decision to withhold royalties would render their existing agreements invalid. Or, as Yauch confessed to author Steve Blush, "Russell put pressure on us to go back in the studio with Rick. I didn't want to go in the fuckin' studio with Rick. I thought he ripped us off and I didn't get along with him that well."

Thereafter it got nasty as the group hung out at the Mondrian Hotel in Los Angeles. "That's where Russsell's guys tried to slap the subpoena on us," remembered Horovitz. "For two days they waited outside our rooms because you just have to be touched with the subpoena and you're caught, it's like a game. We got security to chuck them out. We called all our friends up in LA and got them to come over with disguises and we were all dressed up and Yauch had a big curly afro wig and I had long robes and they were trying to get at us but couldn't work out who was who." Lawyers wrote to Simmons in 1987 to terminate their association with both Rush Management and Def Jam. Simmons, backed by Columbia, insisted that it was the Beasties who were in breach of their contract by failing to provide a follow-up album. Beastie Boys' lawyer Robert Weiner publicly contested Def Jam's ability to pay the $2 million The Beastie Boys were due, asserting that was the real reason behind the dispute.

It's hard to say whether Simmons' decision to stall on payments did his record label long-term damage, but it certainly cost them their prize asset. It also blew the illusion of a Def Jam 'family', as the band muttered darkly about the abuse of their friendship. "How can you not dislike someone who stole from you?" Diamond told *Rolling Stone* magazine. Asked in a subsequent interview if they'd learned any lessons from their past, he offered this sporting analogy: "Of course. We were playing softball the other day, and I should have known that Russell can hit the ball really hard. I just figured I could just play shallow instead of deep." Diamond certainly saw Simmons as the villain. "The thing about all these manipulator guys like Russell and Malcolm McLaren is they take what essentially happened by accident and they take the credit for it." They were still angry by the advent of their 1994 album *Ill Communication*, where an aside on 'B-Boys Makin' With The Freak Freak' noted: "Got fat bass lines like Russell Simmons steals money."

Rubin was more sanguine about the group's departure, figuring they'd never get round to recording another record anyway. But he did rue the loss of their goodwill. "I think the success destroyed our relationship. We were not friends again for a very long time. I think a lot of that really stemmed from the media. Probably because they were white, The Beastie Boys didn't have the same credibility as Run-DMC or LL Cool J. A lot of the press looked at them like the Monkees, like this put-together thing. The perception was that it was my record, that they were a fabrication." Simmons, too, had regrets. "When the fights started between Rick and the group, I regret that I didn't get involved in a more meaningful way."

The Beastie Boys washed up on Capitol in a deal thought to be worth $3 million, signed by A&R executive Tim Carr, who convinced his boss David Berman they were a good investment. "They were, without doubt, the smartest bunch of really arrogant kids I had ever met," Berman reflected. "We just went to Capitol and said, 'We need a whole shit-load of money to do anything we feel like doing at any time,'" recalled Yauch. "And they said, 'That's cool,' and gave us a whole suitcase full of money." Putting together a new album was his way of forcing the situation and getting away from Def Jam, even though "we almost dreaded getting back together". Simmons couldn't stop them, but announced his intention to release an album of outtakes that he owned, with new backing tracks, entitled *Whitehouse*. His rationale? "They owe me," he told *Rolling Stone*. "That's eight gold records I've got to replace." Diamond dismissed the record in an interview with Ted Mico of *Melody Maker*. "It's up here in Russell's head. That's all it's ever been. The tragedy is that Russell is someone who really likes music, but he never got someone in to organise things so he didn't have to play by the rules of this bullshit industry. They still owe us a lot of money, but we don't know when or how much we're going to receive."

The Beastie Boys put geographical as well as philosophical distance between themselves and Def Jam by relocating to Los Angeles, where they regrouped for 1989's *Paul's Boutique*, an album considered by many to be hip hop's *Sgt. Pepper's Lonely Heart's Club Band*. Had success not soured their relationship, it would have ranked alongside anything on the Def Jam roster. As their former publicist Leyla Turkkan notes, "All the really hard-core hip hop heads wouldn't publicly admit it, but quietly, they'd all say to me, 'Oh, my God, the beats on this record are the most unbelievable thing on earth.' From Chuck D to LL Cool J to KRS-One, they were all in awe of *Paul's Boutique*."

Built on an artful patchwork of samples, ranging from Alice Cooper to Tito Puente, the album's dense, wraparound layers of sound and in-jokes were pieced together over a 16-month period by the Dust Brothers, previously successful with charismatic but erratic pop-rapper Tone Loc. Ironically Matt Dike, one third of the Dust Brothers and charitably likened by Yauch to Phil Spector because "he's a little weird", had first got involved in hip hop through his admiration of Rubin's work. But The Beastie Boys were keen to avoid a situation in which their producers would again steal the limelight. "They became very paranoid of people getting credit for things that they were doing," remembers Glen Friedman. "Everyone was treating them as though they were the puppets of Rick and Russell. Business-wise, they were never the greatest people to deal with. But after that period, it got ridiculous."

And they were determined not to do any more laps on the pop star treadmill. "If we were doing something too commercial with the music," recalls Dust Brother John King, "they would say, 'Nah, I don't like that.' They didn't want it to blow up. Yauch said, 'We won't promote this at all, it'll be a cool thing that people find out about.'" The band's love affair with Def Jam may have withered, but not to the extent where they couldn't obtain clearance for a sample of Public Enemy's 'Bring Tha Noise'.

With the media sensing a promotional face-off to dovetail the legal shenanigans, *Paul's Boutique* was lined up against Def Jam's 'core' project of the summer of 1989, LL Cool J's *Walking With A Panther*. It came up short, at least commercially. Sales of approximately 800,000 (a fifth as many as their début) must have horrified the accountants at Capitol. One of the problems was that, in the period since the release of *Licensed To Ill*, groundbreaking hip hop albums had emerged from Public Enemy and Eric B and Rakim. More importantly, the classy samples and skits of De La Soul's *3 Feet High And Rising* had anticipated, if not necessarily bettered, the Beasties' new eclecticism.

The band had also run up a huge recording tab, a situation you cannot imagine their previous label head allowing to pass. Capitol responded by severing the dollar drip-feed – effectively refusing to commit more money to promoting the record. Berman had been fired, allegedly as a direct result of signing the band. Instead, Capitol left The Beastie Boys to their own devices in their self-constructed G-Son studio complex. In a climate of low expectations they once again prospered, primarily as a result of exploring live instrumentation again. 1992's *Check Your Head* took their label by surprise by restoring their commercial standing, reaching the American Top Ten, as rumbling hip hop and funk rubbed shoulders with thrash-punk, in a schizophrenic programme that recalled the approach of old favourites Bad Brains. Elsewhere, street-smarts replaced the dumb splenetics of old. 'Pass The Mic' notably offered a weary lament on hip hop's lyrical descent into repetition and crass materialism.

Meanwhile Diamond was, if not truly retracing his footsteps, picking up a few markers from Russell Simmons by remoulding himself as a hip hop entrepreneur, albeit one whose primary motive was fun rather than profit. The result was Grand Royal, named after a phrase coined by friend and occasional collaborator Biz Markie. Part of its rationale was informed by the group's experiences with Def Jam. "When Rick Rubin and Russell Simmons began the label out of Rick's NYU dorm room we were really closely involved," Mike D told Simon Reynolds for *ID* magazine, "and were actually instrumental in discovering LL Cool J and Public Enemy. Then, as it started to sell a lot of records, Def Jam got less family-oriented. It became a big biz label, it just took us a while to get our shit together." After releasing the first records by Schellenbach's Luscious Jackson, the label has shipped material from Scottish indie pop-punkers Bis, Sean Lennon, Atari Teenage Riot, DJ Hurricane and others. The whole ethos of the label's A&R policy has remained "what we think is cool". Contracts were occasionally signed on napkins. There is a publishing concern, also called Grand Royal, edited by Bob Mack, and Diamond's own clothing line, X-Large (though Horovitz still prefers to promote Free Fashion, or "wear whatever you can get for free"). Unlike Simmons, Diamond cares little about the bottom line. His maxim: "The only thing between you and other people's money is the other people," is more of a cool phrase than a business agenda.

Yauch, meanwhile, embarked on a spiritual quest that eventually ended with him being the chief proponent of the Tibet Freedom Movement. Horovitz delved further into film work and spent much of his time tinkering with electronic instruments. Their records, *Ill Communication* (1994) and *Hello Nasty* (1998), continued to earn rave notices, revealing a band at ease with itself after past tribulations. The former's 'Sure Shot' closed the book on the band's previous sexism; their playfulness now tempered with concerned, but never pious, social commentary. Significantly *Hello Nasty*'s 'Intergalactic' paid homage to the group's twig on hip hop's family tree. Still a hip hop band? Definitely.

Later Horovitz apologised for what he called the "shitty, ignorant things we said on our first album". But the new puritans met with some resistance. There was a stand-off with The Prodigy at the Reading Festival in 1998, when The Beastie Boys asked the Essex techno mavens not to play their song 'Smack My Bitch Up'. "When we called, we asked them if they would consider not playing the song," Yauch told journalists. "We explained that although this may sound hypocritical, we recently have been trying to be more careful in choosing what songs we play, as well as changing some of the lyrics in songs we do play." Prodigy mainman Liam Howlett was not impressed. "During that whole Reading thing The Beastie Boys really let themselves down. They think they have the power to come over to England and tell a band not to play one of their songs – it's pathetic . . . I always used to like The Beastie Boys because they stood against all that American crap, but when I spoke to them they just seemed to be full of all that self-improvement, learning-to-be-a-better-person type of bullshit. I mean, you know, I think I'm intelligent enough to look at those early Beastie Boys records and see the tongue-in-cheek humour."

Rolling Stone's Greg Heller asked Rubin if he shared Horovitz's sense of regret over previous affronts. "I have no regrets at all," Rubin replied. "Listening back to it, you can be horrified by some of the things that were said, but in the spirit it was done in at the time, it was just fun. Nothing was done with any malice or negative intent. There was a certain amount of locker-room humor, guys trying to make each other laugh. Whatever got a rise, made it to the record. Obviously he felt the need to [apologise], and I could never judge him on that. If he felt a sense of freedom by doing that, all the power to him. People should do whatever they need to do to feel good. I hope that by doing that, it gave him some solace."

The Beastie Boys remain the epitome of New York cool, for all the right reasons. Would they have achieved what they have done had they stayed at Def Jam? Possibly. But the clash of egos was never going to be tidily resolved, and they've learnt to make an asset out of adversity, so it's probably the best outcome for all concerned that they got out when they did. And in *Licensed To Ill* they gave Def Jam what is still the biggest seller in its history. Indeed, there has been something of a reconciliation. *Grand Royal* magazine ran an interview a couple of years back under the less-than-tantalising headline, "An Impromptu Car Phone Conversation With Russell Simmons". "Russell Simmons and us go back a ways," the article, written by Diamond, begins. "As you probably know, though, when it came time to get paid, Russell dipped with the money. But we're not the type to hold a grudge, and plus, Russell's always been a snap."

The problems with Rubin were less easily resolved. While the rumour that they once drove up to his LA mansion in order to piss on his front gate may be apocryphal, you wouldn't bet against it.

5

Fight The Power

"Don't blame me for being preachy if the next man is not saying a Goddamn thing."

– Chuck D, 1994

Chuck D has always freely nominated Run-DMC as the greatest rap act of any generation. But the integrity of such a judgement, though held with conviction, is forfeited when that rarest of traits in the rap game, modesty, is brushed aside. Public Enemy have exerted an influence in the development of late 20th century music that only The Beatles and The Sex Pistols can truly rival. Like those groups, their impact is not confined merely to music but also myriad social spheres. "I wanted to make a rap group that was as big as Run-DMC," recalls Chuck. "I wanted to change how people looked at rap music. I wanted to change how black people thought of ourselves." Goals that the group have tangibly achieved.

Like other great insurrectionists, Public Enemy were never a wholly unambiguous proposition, and came yoked with idiosyncratic contradictions and complications. Even today, when their overwhelmingly constructive contribution is routinely acknowledged even by a conservative, rock-focused music press, there are many who cannot utter their name without reference to perceived racism. Yet as much as anti-Semitic and anti-white allegations sullied their reputation for a time, few of those same critics would take similar umbrage with John Lennon's remarks about Jewish Beatles' manager Brian Epstein, or The Sex Pistols' flirtation with Nazi imagery, a shameful discourse to which both David Bowie and Eric Clapton have succumbed. Few writers introduce a Clash retrospective by decrying them for shooting innocent pigeons or fibbing about their backgrounds, or dismiss The Rolling Stones for one member's predisposition to sex with underage girls. Critics' favourite Elvis Costello has to answer for his use of the word nigger in dubious circumstances, while *Pet Sounds*, considered America's defining piece of late 20th century art by so many, was recorded by a group who brought a psychotic killer into America's midst. You don't throw away the copybook for the sake of a single blot, however heinous. God may be in the details, but the big picture is what enthrals the congregation and fills the pews.

One of the other things often missed in discussions of Public Enemy is the work-rate and commitment levels that underpinned their career. As much as it is a story of terrific, irresistible records, their rise was also prompted by shoestring touring, allegiance to a multitude of causes and the belief that music was a way of opening up a dialogue rather than final-ising a position. Chuck D led his team – many of whom were not coinci-dentally drilled and attired in army fatigues – like a marine sergeant at boot camp. As he once elaborated, "Our attitude to music is a cross between a sports team and military corps: win, crush, destroy."

Alcohol and drugs were frowned upon, despite Flavor Flav's later well publicised problems. "You won't see Public Enemy with no 40s and no blunts and putting anything in our bodies that'll be detrimental to our existence," finger-wagged Chuck D in 1994. "It hasn't anything to do with religion. It's common sense. You got people who get pissed off if you put bullshit gas in their car, but they drink a 40." In contrast to today's celebrity-hugging (and worse) rap superstars, nobody was invited back-stage after a Public Enemy show. Even when such legends as Magic Johnson caught a performance, there was no cow-towing to the great and good. That discipline, by anyone's standards, runs contrary to the world inhabited by contemporary rappers, who rarely look beyond getting paid and getting laid. But Chuck instilled in his troops a steely sense of unity and rigid professionalism. He once confessed to spending days sitting in front of a blackboard, working out possible song titles before any studio work was convened. There's a wonderful inset in his *Fight The Power* auto-biography where he lists his favourite DJs, including his own, Terminator X. "Over a thousand shows; very few mistakes." Not so much damned by faint praise as praised by faint damnation.

Public Enemy underwrote hip hop's expansion by touring with rock bands ranging from the Sisters of Mercy to U2 and co-opting their audi-ences. In the process they built an elaborate cantilever construct out of the rope bridge between rock and rap that Run-DMC had erected with Aerosmith. They were quick to learn from the white rock world without compromising on their mission statement: to empower the community from whence they came. Public Enemy trekked around the world and embraced the cultures they found – unlike so many rappers who bitch constantly about European or Oriental temperatures and takeaway menus, while romanticising the cuisine of their local Burger King. In the process Public Enemy gave hip hop the global status it now wallows in, taking hip hop from the gangland slums of the Bronx to the hipper homes of every continent via their native borough of Long Island.

Unlike the Bronx, there were no gangs in Long Island, essentially because it was too lower-middle class. "What Long Island does have," wrote local music journalist Letta Tayler, "is proximity to New York City, one of the biggest pop music meccas. It also has an enormous number of kids who are just affluent enough to buy turntables and amps and electric guitars, and whose parents usually are lucky enough to have a garage or a basement where they can plug them in. Above all, it is suburbia, producing youths whose experiences, when they sing about them, strike a chord with similar youths in similar housing tracts across the nation."

The borough became the favoured suburban destination for aspirational African-Americans from other parts of New York City during the Fifties and Sixties. "So when rap was developing in the mid-Seventies in the projects of Harlem and the Bronx," recalls Bill Stephney, "basically those people were our cousins. Every weekend we'd go visit them and we'd be an extended part of the hip hop nation that was developing." Soon Long Island would boast its own hip hop venues – the Roosevelt Rollerskating Rink, the Hempstead Elks Club and the Hempstead Holiday Inn. Artists including Grandmaster Flash and Afrika Bambaataa would make the trip.

The origins of Public Enemy reside in that Long Island of the early Eighties, where Stephney hosted a rap show on Radio station WBAU. Hank 'Shocklee' Boxley was a local DJ operating under the guise of Spectrum City, the largest and most respected DJ operation in the locale. His near-neighbour Carlton Ridenhour, aka Chuck D, was an amateur cartoonist studying graphic design at Adelphi University.

Ridenhour was born in Flush, Queens, and grew up in Queensbridge before the family moved to Long Island, settling in Roosevelt. Curtis Mayfield, Otis Redding and James Brown records were constantly on the stereo, their pro-black sentiments endorsed by Chuck's parents. There was, similarly, an in-bred conviction about the struggle for racial equality, something he saw denied his peers. "My people were very informative, they told me who I was. I remember there was a tendency to call us 'negro' or 'coloured' and my Mom said, 'No, you're black!' My Pa said,

'You're black!'" As a kid his first love was sports, and the New York Knicks, Jets and Mets, while his musical favourites included Abba as well as the soul and R&B greats.

After graduating from high school he half-heartedly enrolled on his course at Adelphi University in 1979, just as hip hop was beginning to blow up in New York. He'd first encountered the culture a couple of years previously. "I first heard a hip hop tape in 1977. It was a tape from a neighbour who was a couple of years younger than me. I was about 17 at the time and it had this DJ named Hollywood and also a DJ named DJ Smalls. They were on the tape and they were playing a record by the Jacksons called 'Music's Takin' Over'. The thing that I couldn't understand is, how long they was extending this part that was the instrumental, that was a small lead into the song. I kept hearing it come back and come back and I was wondering how they was doing it. The DJ was doing it and the MC navigated it and my curiosity just turned me out. I was just confused on what was going on and fascinated at the same time."

By this time Bronx mix tapes had reached outlying New York districts. But the local stars were just as important as quasi-mythical Bronx figures like Grandmaster Flash and Bambaataa. "I was from Long Island," remembers Chuck, "so Hank Shocklee had an operation called Spectrum. Being from Roosevelt, to me they was the bomb, because they had the clean system and they played the records that everybody wanted to hear and check out. And tapes came from the city with DJ Hollywood and Eddie Cheeba, who I was just fascinated by, the way that they actually played the records."

He reappraised the art form again when he caught a show by Grandmaster Flash and the Furious Five at the Roosevelt roller-skating rink in 1979. "For the total B-boy style, when I first heard Grandmaster Flash and MC Melle Mel, I was saying: 'Those guys are doing it right.' Although it was two different types, because Eddie Cheeba and DJ Hollywood was more like club [orientated] and you had to be a certain age to get in the club. I actually was on that line to get in the clubs, I checked them out. On the other hand you had Flash and Melle Mel from the parks, and I also checked them out too. So it was two different styles, and from Long Island Spectrum was able to do both of them. So I was kind of a local supporter as well as hearing these sounds from the city."

One of the principal attractions of rap to an articulate young man like Chuck D was the scope it afforded practitioners to explore concepts. "[I liked] the large volume of words," he conceded. But he immediately observed the pitfalls facing hip hop. "I remember the early Eighties well. The first companies to release the music were black-run independents like Sugar Hill and Enjoy, which treated rap like a fad, preparing to bail out if it flopped, as disco had two or three years earlier. The contracts were dungeons on paper, and trend-setters like the Furious Five, Spoonie Gee, Fearless Four, Treacherous Three and Cold Crush Brothers took an exploitative hit like a pack of bluesmen in a concrete Delta."

He started performing his first MC spots at the Adelphi's Thursday Night Throwdown, where Hank Shocklee saw him perform. They already knew each other after Chuck had attended one of his parties the previous summer. When Chuck pointed out that the turnout might have been affected by the shoddy artwork on their flyers, which even misspelt Spectrum, he received short shrift. Shocklee had just blown the money he'd been given to buy a graduation yearbook and entrance to the prom, and was figuring out how to break the news to his parents. It was not the perfect time to reproach him about his promotional ineptness.

But after hearing Chuck's stentorian broadsides at the Throwdown, Shocklee began to take Chuck more seriously. "Usually all the MCs at a party is wack anyway, all right," he remembers. "But Chuck came on and did an announcement for the next event that was coming, and his voice just commanded everybody's attention, and that's when I knew. I said, 'Look, I want this guy to do . . . Whatever he does there, I want him do it for my set.'"

"All the systems were kind of sub-par and I had a good voice," Chuck remembers. "I could cut through any system. The thing that got me started to do it was, I was going to too many parties in '79 and the MCs, I thought, were wack. It's just that they had little voices and the little voices sounded terrible over the music and they had no sense of timing. So I used to tell my guys, I used to say: 'Look, man, I just want them to either shut up or I'm going to have to grab the mic to make them shut up,' and one day I did. Hank happened to be at one of those particular events and we got together and we started out on the second phase of Spectrum. I became the primary MC of that particular operation and we stepped up from there to make tapes." Chuck became a pivotal member of Spectrum City from 1979 to 1982. "We had such a big terrain to cover, we immediately got involved with the radio stations from where I went to school, Adelphi University," Chuck continues. "And the fact that Spectrum was on this radio station was a galvanising surprise to the area. People always wanted our tapes, now we had to say: 'Look, forget that, you get our mixes on radio for free, just tape 'em.' That was the beginning of that whole next realm of hip hop."

The link-up with Adelphi's WBAU radio station came via Bill Stephney, who became a DJ after abandoning a promising career as a musician. At Adelphi he had his own programme, the *Mr Bill Show*, before starting work at the *College Music Journal* where he established the magazine's first hip hop column, *Beat Box*. When he became programme director for the station he offered Spectrum its own Saturday night slot, the *Super Spectrum Mix Show*. Chuck, along with co-host Butch Cassidy (assuredly not his real name) and Hank's brother Keith Shocklee as the DJ played the latest hip hop joints as well as inserting their own raps and musical cut-ups – bayonet practice for Public Enemy's later vinyl cavalry charge.

The show won widespread recognition for its role in disseminating hip hop culture to the citizens of Long Island. Russell Simmons even brought Run-DMC over to WBAU to do their first interview, at which Chuck discovered them to be humble and a little overawed by the prospect. As well as playing unrecorded local MC groups including the Choice Five MCs and the Townhouse Three (later Sons Of Bazerk), the station also played a part in breaking records, including T-La Rock's Def Jam single 'It's Yours'. Impressed by Rubin's first rap record, Shocklee and Harry Allen, a local activist and later Public Enemy's 'media assassin' whom Chuck had met at an animation class, arranged to interview T-La Rock and catch his show. They were blown away instead by support act LL Cool J. They obtained his phone number, and Chuck booked him for a show at a Long Island roller rink, thereby establishing a connection with the emerging Def Jam empire.

Others would pop into the radio studios, including the colourful William Drayton, aka Flavor Flav. Drayton, of whom the description idiosyncratic would be diplomatic, was a friend of the Townhouse Three. His reputation preceded him – Chuck had already eyeballed his graffiti 'tag'. "It was actually on a building in Freeport, Long Island. I read something that said, 'Flavor'; and I'd be like, trying to figure out who made that sloppy lookin' graffiti." Flavor was systematically ragged on by the entire WBAU community, though no one can convince him that he didn't get the best of these exchanges. In the end he pestered Stephney into giving him his own, typically esoteric, showcase on WBAU, which at one stage included his recordings of train station announcements. He went on to record comic sketch-songs alongside friend DJ Mellow D (Norman

Rogers, later Terminator X). But for much of the time he was the butt of jokes about his surreal dress sense.

Gradually the elements of the awesome talent pool from which Public Enemy formed fell into place around the campus. Chuck, majoring in graphic design, produced a weekly comic strip for college newspaper *The Delphian*. He also worked the occasional driving shift for his father's V-Haul furniture company, and would invite Flavor along for the ride, the two bouncing rhymes off each other, previewing Public Enemy's inimitable vocal dynamic.

The core members released their first record in 1984. 'Lies', backed by 'Check Out The Radio', was credited to Spectrum City, but this was a conventional old school hip hop record with none of the Black Panther-like radicalism they'd later bring to the table. They enjoyed greater success with their mix tapes, as Hank Shocklee remembers. "We had our mix show, which we called at the time *The Super Spectrum City Mix Show*. That was the first time anybody's ever heard live mixing on the radio. Now, from that we also made what we termed as hip hop tracks, or promos for the radio station that were basically hip hop tracks."

The radio show ended in 1985, by which time Chuck had assembled a demo tape of 'Public Enemy #1', which was used to both intro and outro the show. The title was inspired by the fact that Chuck's previous stature as the top dog local MC was in dispute. A challenger had risen through the ranks while Chuck was concentrating on organising shows and running his radio show. "I couldn't understand why someone would want to battle me," he recalls, "because I hadn't done any of that for a while. So I decided I would write a jam that could serve dual purposes: promote the radio show and let people know that I still had rapping skills." The track, completed in late 1984, was built around a sample of Fred Wesley & the JB's 'Blow Your Head', slowed down and spliced together via two tape decks. It introduced Public Enemy's backstage production team, featuring Hank and Keith Shocklee and Eric 'Vietnam' Sadler in addition to Chuck (who called himself Chuckie D at this stage). By the early Nineties the quartet would take the name the Bomb Squad, becoming one of the most exhilarating musical production houses in hip hop.

Chuck knew immediately what he required in sonic terms. The message he was coming with was hard, so he wanted music to reflect that, in as stark terms as possible. To this end he would road-test his records on his girlfriend. Anything she liked was jettisoned out of hand for being too soft. Instead the putative Public Enemy looked to rock dynamics rather than R&B standards, as Hank Shocklee remembers. "If you noticed, most Public Enemy records never included a bass line. We was very much into guitars, was very much into anything that sounded abrasive, anything that sounded like a sense of urgency, because we thought that the message that we was bringing across had a direct link to the urgency that we wanted to get across to people. And Chuck's vocals was probably the only voice in hip hop that could command the barrage of those frequencies. Mostly everybody else have to tone those frequencies down because it gets in the way of the clarity of their vocals, but Chuck's voice was so big and so commanding, and it's almost like he's the voice of God, so to speak."

Spectrum City started performing with an expanded roster of contributors – including Doctor Dre (Andre Brown) of Original Concept. Norman Rogers, a DJ who worked for Spectrum and also released his own mix tapes, became a semi-permanent fixture. Professor Griff and Unity Force, based in Roosevelt, were martial arts experts who brought elements of Nation of Islam-styled discipline to security operations. As Chuck remembers, "Hank and I both knew Griff the best, so we would tell Griff, 'Bring Unity Force to the gig, and if we make any money, we'll pay you something.'" Their visual presence also made appeal. "We wanted Unity Force to come along with the Public Enemy project because we liked their look," Chuck admits. "Initially, we called ourselves the Black Panthers of Rap, so Unity Force's look fit the concept."

Money was tight, so it was standard practice for those involved to get a cut of the gate money only if the shows turned a profit. Frustrated by these fiscal restraints, Chuck encouraged Hank to shop around for a deal, for the group if not himself. By this time the key participants had left college, and Chuck had taken a job as a film processor, and later film delivery man. Having heard his tapes and radio broadcasts, Def Jam and Rush were on his trail. Rick Rubin, in particular, was excited by 'Public Enemy #1', which DMC had played him. "I heard that song and thought it was the greatest, and knew that he had to be our next artist," Rubin recalls. By 1986 Rubin had given Bill Stephney a position at Def Jam as vice-president of promotion, though his first job would be to obtain Chuck's signature on a contract. Indeed, Bill Adler reckons Rubin threatened to fire him if he didn't bring Chuck on board. But Rubin himself ended up doing much of the legwork in sealing the deal.

Rubin found Chuck resistant. He was concerned that rapping was a young person's pursuit, pointing to the cherubic LL Cool J's breakthrough as corroborating evidence. "He considered himself a grown man, with a family and a regular job," recalls Rubin. "I put his phone number on a post-it note and stuck it next to my phone and I called him every day for six months saying, 'We really have to make a record, it's time to make a record.' I finally tried again in about six months' time and he said 'maybe'." Bill Stephney helped convince Chuck that his ideas could connect with a bigger audience, and that it wasn't undignified for a man of his years (he was 26) to get on the microphone. Chuck's interest heightened just as Run-DMC, the hardest-hitting group in rap, began to get swallowed up in negative publicity after their infamous Long Beach concert. Add the fact that Dre, as part of Original Concept, had joined Def Jam and Bill Stephney was also part of the team, and the choice of label seemed inevitable.

But still Chuck wavered. From interviewing rappers for the radio station he'd heard plenty of tales of artists getting burned by the industry. "We had chips on our shoulders and felt we could run our own record company," Chuck stated in his autobiography. Eventually Stephney set up a meeting, and they took a tape to Rubin's dorm. Rubin immediately asked them to record a full album based on the strength of the demo (which included 'Public Enemy #1', 'The Return Of Public Enemy', which later became 'Miuzi Weighs A Ton', 'Sophisticated Bitch' and 'You're Gonna Get Yours').

Hank suggested changing the name from Spectrum City, but Chuck was still reluctant to isolate himself as lead MC, even suggesting a friend, Obie, who had a similar voice. "I felt I would be a better director than artist, but Rick Rubin was adamant about me being the vocalist in the group. I was in a situation where I received an offer that I couldn't refuse, and I had to do it." If Rubin was won over, Simmons wasn't about to offer them an over-generous contract. The advance was a measly $5,000. "It wasn't an especially lucrative deal. [We were] very frugal in the beginning," remembers Chuck, "because our [royalty] points structure was very, very tight. Myself and Flavor share five artiste points. Hank got two, so I was seven points. It's not much of a role to come in on, but those are the deals that were happening back at that time." Simmons could play hardball because, according to Rubin, at this stage he thought there was no future in what he saw as "black punk rock".

Rubin was still keen to sign Chuck as a solo artist, but on this Chuck held firm. He still loved the 'posse-bilities' of old school tag teams like Grandmaster Flash and the Furious Five, whose performance at the Ritz in 1984 had been such a formative influence. He wanted his whole team on board with him, starting with Flavor Flav, with whom he voluntarily agreed to split his royalties. Rubin could not understand for the life of him what he saw in Flavor, but Chuck had it all worked out. "The simple reason why we work together is just the contrast in our voices. People try to come up with intellectual reasons for 'the noise' and it ain't nothing intellectual. We was just making [W]BAU tapes and needed voices to cut through that shit. Flavor got a powerful, trebly voice, with cut. I got some bass with treble and pitch, which also cuts. So you put me and Flavor together and it's basically like Bobby Byrd and James Brown."

It's easy to downplay Flavor's contribution to Public Enemy. Indeed, he was probably the most accomplished musician within the whole set-up. His uncle had written songs for Nat 'King' Cole while his mother and aunt were both accomplished pianists. Adept at instruments ranging from the oboe to the drums, as Bill Stephney acknowledged to *The Source*, "Flavor is the only member of Public Enemy that could go into a studio and make an entire record by himself. He is probably the most talented member of the group." Or, as Chuck D puts it, "He can play 15 instruments. I can't play lotto." He is also naturally funny. Arriving nearly three hours late at a 1991 shooting of *Yo! MTV Raps*, the rapper whose visual signature was the out-sized timepieces he wore around his neck reasoned, "Yo, my clock broke."

Norman Rogers didn't thrill to Chuck's news he would now be known as Terminator X, but became the group's DJ on a permanent basis. Griff's Unity Force became the S1Ws, or Security of the First World, who would make a name for themselves by square-drilling international stages equipped with replica Uzis rather than merely ensuring order at concerts. Griff also temporarily assumed the responsibilities of road manager. Hank Shocklee, his brother Keith and Eric 'Vietnam' Sadler stayed in the background, but helped Chuck co-ordinate Public Enemy's sonic barrage. From the outset they had mission statements and slogans by the crate. "We're agents for the preservation of the black mind," they stated, with absolute sincerity and conviction. "We're media hijackers."

The formal signing with Def Jam took place in June 1986, with Steve Ralbovsky of CBS present. "No other label would have given us the latitude," reasoned Chuck. "We brought so many ideas to the Def Jam table. They brought the marketing and promotional concepts that made for a perfect marriage." Public Enemy immediately formed its own management company, Rhythm Method, which also oversaw other acts, the best known of which were the Ultramagnetic MCs. Rhythm Method controlled 30 per cent of the management of Public Enemy at the outset. Russell Simmons was keen to get his slice of the action, and bought out 15 per cent of the company. He'd have got more had not Chuck been conscious of the fact that he didn't want to be managed by the same people who ran his record company – a situation which would so compromise Def Jam's previous breakthrough act, The Beastie Boys.

The group spent from July to August 1986 re-cutting 'Public Enemy #1'. However, it was not until March 1987, a month before début album *Yo! Bum Rush The Show* arrived, that it snuck onto the release schedules. By that time others, notably Eric B and Rakim and Boogie Down Productions, had upped the ante. Chuck is still peeved at those delays, believing they dated the album and neutered its raison d'être – to "bum rush the tastes of the industry, that looked upon rap as being a bastard music". But that's Chuck being an over-protective parent – *Yo! Bum Rush The Show* is a fantastic piece of work, matching Chuck's bruising oratory with engagingly tortured harmonics, even if it was widely misunderstood and met with a series of hostile reviews on its release. Certainly cuts such as 'Miuzi Weighs A Ton' and 'Rightstarter (Message To A Black Man)' were not only substantial pointers to Public Enemy's later greatness, but spectacular statements of intent in their own right.

Yo! Bum Rush The Show, featuring guitar and bass contributions by its producer Bill Stephney, remains Rick Rubin's favourite Public Enemy album, though it tends to get overlooked in the rush to garland *It Takes A Nation Of Millions* as the group's most indelible achievement. It was not an instant success – indeed, it was Def Jam's worst selling record at one stage, only picking up sales after Public Enemy joined The Beastie Boys on tour. Hip hop DJs loved the beats, but were scathing about Chuck's booming intonation – a schism later addressed in 'Rebel Without A Pause' where Chuck hit back at those who'd dared to find fault. Among them was influential WBLS DJ Mr Magic (John Rivas), who dismissed 'Miuzi Weighs a Ton' as 'garbage' and broke the record on air. "It was never a plot against anyone," he remembers. "I always knew that Chuck had skills. It's just I wouldn't be easy on muthafuckas who I thought was talented but who didn't give me their best effort." He would have time to repent at his leisure.

Still stung by Eric B and Rakim's brilliant 'I Know You Got Soul', Chuck entered the studio knowing he needed to up his game to compete. 'Rebel Without A Pause', recently voted the greatest single of all time by *Uncut* magazine, was cut in April 1987. It began to transform itself after

Terminator X added his distinctive scratch work, which cemented his position in the Public Enemy hierarchy – though it was only after they'd lived with the recordings for a while that the other participants came to appreciate the weight of his contribution. Incredibly, Russell Simmons tried to block its release, figuring it would damage album sales. Chuck wanted to put it on the B-side of 'You're Gonna Get Yours'. They went to Steve Ralbovski, their A&R contact at CBS, in an attempt to overrule him. They then tried Russell again, about to board a flight to London with Run–DMC, who was non-committal. It was actually his younger brother, Run, who turned round and told them to go ahead (Run would later reckon it was "as exciting as a Run–DMC record", while his partner DMC maintains it's "the best rap record ever made"). Still, according to Chuck, Def Jam knew precious little about its release and it was never sanctioned by Russell Simmons.

Featuring a sample of Jesse Jackson introducing the Soul Children on the 1968 Stax record *Save The Children*, 'Rebel Without A Pause' was an emphatic calling card. The enthusiasm it generated among radio programmers was confirmed by vociferous feedback from live audiences, especially in London, where Public Enemy eclipsed touring partners Eric B and Rakim and LL Cool J – neither of whom made a habit of being upstaged. It helped that Public Enemy mounted the most astonishing live shows; Flavor Flav playing apocalyptic stooge and hype man to Chuck's raging prophecies, while Griff marshalled the S1Ws into the physical embodiment of no-shit-taken-here black pride. Even at this stage Chuck was the fulcrum on which two contradictory forces teetered; the anarchic Flav and his arch-enemy – thematically and often in real life – the disciplined, haughty Griff. "Flavor is how white people wish the black man would be," Chuck once elaborated. "Griff is how they fear we are; I'm in the middle." It was a neat balancing act while it lasted. Both would benefit from Chuck's personal loyalty when the chips were down.

It Takes A Nation Of Millions To Hold Us Back, the album widely celebrated as the touchpaper for a new wave of black nationalism, saw Public Enemy deliver on every promise, immortally framing Chuck D as the chief interrogator of white cultural and social values and quisling-like acceptance of those terms by those in his own community. In so doing, he established a pro-black consciousness that few rap releases of the last decade did not acknowledge. A punishing record, as aurally ferocious as it was uncompromisingly cerebral, its frantic pacing was entirely new to rap, softening up listeners for Chuck's commensurately urgent exhortations.

From being Def Jam's poor relations, Public Enemy were suddenly their most prized asset. *Nation* hardly missed a beat, musically or lyrically, but especially devastating were 'She Watch Channel Zero!?', 'Night Of The Living Baseheads', 'Black Steel In The Hour Of Chaos' and 'Don't Believe The Hype'. The latter's advice that "there's a need to get alarmed" helped re-align rap's compass. However, it's not one of Chuck's favourites. "My God, I didn't even like it at first. Matter of fact, when I heard the mix I threw it across the room. When I got to London, we actually got an acetate of it and we played it. It's like everybody went crazy over it. I was like: 'Well, fuck. I guess this is it.' So sometimes you gotta make records that you don't like. 'Don't Believe The Hype' was simple, clear to the point. It was one of what we call 'expected' records. You can always make an expected record that fits into the trend of the time and 'Don't Believe The Hype' fit in well. The record company says: 'Hey, this would be a great single,' and we didn't argue."

The lyric was written after Chuck was repeatedly questioned over his name-checking of Minister Farrakhan – an association that won the group few fans among the liberal intelligentsia. But Chuck stuck to his guns. "What it boils down to is that Mr Farrakhan is speaking from a Muslim point of view: he's not anti-Christian, anti-Semitic or anti-anything. He may favour the Koran as an interpretation of how we should live, but people shouldn't translate that into a dislike of people – it's just a disagreement of philosophy." Parts of the lyric were also inspired by his outrage at *Village Voice* critic Greg Tate's otherwise laudatory review of *Nation Of Millions*, which upbraided Public Enemy for slighting Jews, women and gays.

The album enshrined Chuck's belief that rap groups should be capable of making an album that was a complete artistic statement rather than a series of singles buttressed by filler, which had undoubtedly been the case to this point. That goal was also addressed by the group's use of video, a medium which played to Public Enemy's strengths. But Chuck remembers the static he received when he first mooted the idea of shooting a promo for 'Night Of The Living Baseheads', his exasperated plea to stop the crack epidemic in black communities. The other members of the group thought it was a licence to throw money down the drain.

" 'Why are we going to make a video? Nobody's gonna play it, and we don't wanna spend any of our money.' We said: 'Look, you know we're going to prove our worth and then get our money back,' which we sorta did. We were saying we ain't spending our money on no video if they ain't gonna show it. Then *Yo! MTV Raps* came out and 1988 was in the middle of [Run-DMC's] Run's House tour. We said they'll show our video and it's feasible now. So we decided to make the video. We said we must do something that's never been seen before. We actually made the video out of a table full of eight people, and came up with a concept that would stand out. Remember, everything we had to do had to stand out. You already had superstars in Def Jam and in the Rush Productions camp, and if you didn't stand out, you was getting lost in the sauce and your ass was staying home." As distinctive as the finished video was, not all the participants were impressed. "Filming in the park, in a studio next to the park, one of these guys was on a park bench. He's got newspaper over him, trying to go to sleep. And Flavor was just on top of him, dancing on top. We was like: 'Leave him alone!' This guy was looking at this character with this big clock and his glasses and his hat and dancing like this on top of him. We laughed for days, man."

Among Public Enemy's fans was director Spike Lee, who asked Chuck to provide a theme song for his superb 1989 film, *Do The Right Thing*. Lee had a celluloid agenda which bore comparison to Chuck's. "I wanted it to be defiant, I wanted it to be angry, I wanted it to be very rhythmic." Lee confessed, "I thought right away of Public Enemy." He contacted Bill Stephney to arrange a meeting with Chuck at an Indian restaurant off Bleeker Street in Manhattan. Having established himself with critically revered low-budget efforts *School Daze* and *She's Gotta Have It*, he wanted to set his next film in Brooklyn, where real life events such as the death of elderly black lady Eleanor Bumpers in police custody had polarised an already explosive ethnic mix.

For many, the resultant 'Fight The Power' is Public Enemy's defining moment. Written on between-show flights while Chuck toured Europe with Run-DMC, it served as the signature song for the ostensibly mute character of Radio Raheem, though it also accompanied Rosie Perez's gyrations as the credits rolled. Its incendiary reclamation of history ("Elvis was a hero to most/But he never meant shit to me") was fighting talk, lunging at white iconography in defiance of rap's previous reputation for battling in its own neighbourhood. Those who assumed the king of rock was the real target were taking Chuck too literally. It was the institutionalisation of Elvis as America's musical figurehead he was lambasting. He wanted to point out the debt he owed to black blues and jazz artists, such as Chuck Berry and Little Richard, who had as much talent and natural charisma as Elvis, but were never going to receive middle America's beatification.

Rick Rubin, the long haired ex-punk from Long Island, who first grasped the limitless possibilities of grafting a punk attitude to the nascent hip hop scene. *(Peter Anderson/SIN)*

Whose house is this? Joseph 'Run' Simmons of Run-DMC, younger brother of Russell, gets the usual affirmative audience response. *(LFI)*

English-born, gold-yoked MC Slick Rick, the walking Fort Knox of rap. *(LFI)*

Kurtis Blow, hip hop's trailblazing star, and the first artist signed to
Russell Simmons' management. *(Peter Anderson/SIN)*

LL Cool J, Def Jam's first breakthrough artist: always on the right-ish side of the tracks. *(LFI)*

Russell Simmons circa 1987: note pre-Phat Farm endorsement of Beastie Boys' headgear. *(Peter Anderson/SIN)*

Top: Young and Useless? The Beastie Boys with Rick Rubin, in 1984, photographed in
Washington Square Park, left to right: Mike D, Rick Rubin, Ad-Rock, MCA;
and below, on stage in the late Eighties. *(Josh Cheuse/PYMCA & David Redfern)*

Clockin' On: Flavor Flav of Public Enemy brings tha noise. *(David Corio/SIN)*

Public Enemies at large; including
Professor Griff (second left), Chuck D (third left) and Flav (fourth left). *(David Corio/SIN)*

3rd Bass – white boys can, indeed, rap. *(LFI)*

That observation echoed Lee's theme brilliantly. The film documented an otherwise personable Italian café owner's reluctance to mount pictures of African-American baseball stars on his walls, before festering resentment spills over on Brooklyn's hottest day of the year. It's an earnest, intelligent and humane meditation on the deep-seated enmities and suspicions at work behind contemporary American multiculturalism, and far less judgemental than some have painted it. Its critics included *New York* magazine, which hysterically claimed it might provoke inner city riots, missing the point by a country mile and positioning Chuck D and Spike Lee as cultural soul-mates. As a thank you, Lee filmed a video for 'Fight The Power', partially shot in Riker's Island Jail, which re-enacted the 1963 civil rights march on Washington. Bill Stephney remembers it as "Public Enemy at their height, Spike at his height, and the height of the hip hop nation's interest in rap and politics."

Some have suggested that if it wasn't for Public Enemy reawakening interest in such figures as Malcolm X, whose biopic he later filmed, Lee may never have got his career as a director off the ground. They number among them Russell Simmons. "The reason that Spike was able to make *Malcolm X* was because we created a climate through hip hop where people wanted to hear it," he cooed, employing the royal 'we' with dubious authority. "There were times where everybody wanted to see who had the biggest gold chain. Chuck D came out and said, 'No, we're going to wear African medallions,' and the whole community wore them."

Not everyone was won over by Chuck, however. Journalists were snapping at Public Enemy's heels, looking for clarification about their reference points, not least the name-checking of Farrakhan. Up stepped Professor Griff, now the group's minister of information (so styled after the Black Panthers' Eldridge Cleaver) to muddy the waters with an interview he gave in which the words "Jews are responsible for the majority of the wickedness in the world" were framed and canvassed before an incensed media.

The group were staying in the Comfort Inn in Washington's Chinatown district when a writer for the conservative *Washington Times*, David Mills, requested an interview. Chuck, who usually conducted such duties, deferred to Griff, because he needed to run over tour dates with promoter Darryl Brooks. Prompted by Mills' references to previous remarks he'd made, Griff not only tipped over the apple-cart but set fire to it. In addition to the oft-quoted 'wickedness' remark, he condemned South African whites for conducting AIDS experiments on blacks financed by Jewish money, and alleged that Jews "have their hands round Bush's throat". All of which infuriated Mills' Jewish girlfriend, who was present at the interview. Mills subsequently requested a follow-up discussion with the entire group to clarify Public Enemy's position. Chuck suspected something was afoot and refused to attend, which he later admitted was a mistake. The second meeting saw various S1W members, among whom there was bitterness at Griff's unelected leadership anyway, attempt to substantiate Griff's remarks. Then Griff arrived and requested he hear the tape of the original conversation. Mills refused, and left the meeting to fax a transcript to various newspapers.

Still, Chuck thought the story would die. It didn't, despite Mills' own efforts to distance himself from the affair. It snowballed after editor RJ Smith ran it in the *Village Voice* on the 14th of June, which prompted protest letters from the Jewish Defence League. According to Chuck, Hank Shocklee and Bill Adler (himself Jewish) were both ready to dissolve the group right there. And Russell Simmons was none too pleased, either, fearing Griff could bring his Def Jam empire crashing to the ground. Though he criticised Griff's statement, Simmons came over as a lukewarm apologist in public. "I let the rappers be what they are," he told *Time*. "I try to choose the most acceptable part of it, but I don't try to change them. These kids are just telling what their realities are. I think it's important that people hear them." In private, Chuck detected a certain amount of blind panic. "He was like, 'So, you're still protecting your man? This shit is about to go down, everything is going to crumble around you.'" As the fur kept flying, some non-combatants found themselves in the firing line. Various studio executives queried Spike Lee over his association with Public Enemy, making it obvious that his career could be in jeopardy.

The sobering voice of Bill Adler tried to convince Chuck that he had a responsibility to sort the mess out. Whether or not he was representing the black perspective, Adler reasoned, his audience included men and women of all colours. It's also worth pointing out that, as Nelson George observes in *Hip Hop America*, Public Enemy were entangled with Jewish friends and business partners at every level of their operation. They were signed by Rick Rubin, had their tours organised by Lyor Cohen, while Bill Adler handled much of their PR. Ed Chalpin and Ron Skuller ran Rhythm Method Productions. All were Jewish. "The central problem was not Griff's anti-Semitism *per se* (his remarks were standard-issue Nation of Islam tripe),"

Adler wrote for the Def Jam box set, "but Chuck's handling of the controversy that erupted over it."

Chuck D's stated intention had been to create '5,000 new leaders' for
the black community. Griff was creating at least as many enemies. His
response to charges of anti-Semitism was founded on the observation that
black people don't view Jewish people as anything other than non-black
people (that may be the case for Chuck, but it certainly isn't a universal
truth amongst sections of the black community). But eventually, in a
manner which recalled Louis Farrakhan's intervention over Jesse Jackson's
'Hymietown' remarks about New York, he was provoked into a revealing
public statement, written with the help of Adler. It followed an angry telephone exchange with *Village Voice* editor RJ Smith, who'd offered him
the right of reply and been rebuked by Chuck thus: "I ain't gonna write
no goddamn white-boy liberal letter to the editor." But Chuck relented,
penning a conciliatory column which attempted to defuse the situation
and explain his feelings, including this self-justifcation: "Black power is
only a self-defence movement that counter-attacks the system of white
world supremacy, not white people or the religious sects they choose."

He subsequently held a press conference at Manhattan's Sheraton
Center, with Mills and other journalists present, something he reckons was
the "craziest, dumbest thing I could have ever done". A prepared statement was read. "The offensive remarks made by Professor Griff over the
past year weren't in line with Public Enemy. We aren't anti-Jewish, we're
pro-black culture, pro-human race. You can't talk about attacking racism
and be racist. Griff's responsibility as minister of information for Public
Enemy was to faithfully transmit these values. In practice, he has been
deliberately sabotaging these values in his interviews for over a year. In the
interest of keeping the group together we tried to deal with Griff's problems internally, but we were unsuccessful. Consequently, as of today, Professor Griff is no longer in Public Enemy, I'm sad to say." That night
Chuck drove over to Griff's house to explain his actions. The gist was to
cool the situation down for a while. In the interim Griff would still get
paid as if he was a performing member, Chuck being conscious of the fact
that he had a family to support.

Chuck's friend, Public Enemy publicist Leyla Turkkan, saw the events
unfold at first hand and has a different take on what happened. "Chuck
and Griff had been close friends since they were teenagers. But Griff was
envious because everyone was looking at Chuck. I know Griff well. I
never thought he believed the things he said about Jews. He just said it to

get attention. Chuck couldn't act on it at first. Even though anti-Semitism was never a part of his thinking, it was really hard for him to diss his friend publicly."

Critic Robert Christgau attended the press conference on behalf of the *LA Weekly*. "Instead of either sticking by Griff or disowning him, Chuck D tried to do both. To an extent this must have reflected genuinely divided loyalties – in the kindest construction, his personal ties pulled him one way and his own beliefs the other." Ultimately, whether kind or pragmatic, this is the only construction that holds water. Those sports and military maxims that Chuck had employed early in the group's career were being sorely tested. And his instinct was to be loyal, to be protective, to pull the wagons into a circle and regroup. Question his judgement if you must, but his misdemeanour, if such it was, had no moral dimension.

Griff, for whom the same cannot be said, continued to tour with the band, appearing on stage and performing his ceremonial duties at several dates. Meanwhile Chuck bobbed and weaved with a suddenly hostile media, claiming to have disbanded the group. "My whole thing is," he stated in his autobiography, "if you're vulnerable, be confusing." The truth is that Chuck was confused himself. He spoke to Louis Farrakhan in Chicago and took his advice to lay low for a month, after which a new press statement was released, admitting Griff had been taken back into the fold. But now he was under orders not to talk to the press. Unfortunately, Griff didn't hold his tongue, or felt he needed or ought to.

On a date in Kansas City, Lyor Cohen advised Chuck that Griff had been seen talking to a reporter. The unrepentant Griff had reaffirmed, under questioning, that what he'd originally said he still held to be true. It was enough to reignite the debate after the reporter broke the story on MTV. That brought more trouble and disharmony to the camp. As Chuck remembers: "I wasn't getting on the bus because the bus was crazy. That bus was hot. It was a silent bus. Everybody had on headphones. The whole bus was quiet." Although Griff kept a lower profile for a while, Chuck encouraged him to hook up with Luke Skyywalker of 2 Live Crew to record a solo album – thereby getting his message out without compromising the parent group.

Behind the scenes, Griff's actions had also scuppered Public Enemy's efforts to leave Def Jam, which Chuck felt they'd outgrown. He'd contacted MCA's Al Teller with the idea of forming his own label – a deal to be negotiated by Chuck alongside Bill Stephney and Hank Shocklee. Then the Griff story broke. Teller had lost his parents in the Holocaust, which ensured a natural degree of sensitivity to anti-Semitism. So Chuck stepped back and allowed Bill and Hank to negotiate their own record deal instead, the ill-fated S.O.U.L. (Sound of Urban Listeners).

Under dark clouds of accusation and counter-claim, Public Enemy returned to the studio in October 1989. *Fear Of A Black Planet* saw Chuck address the ructions head-on, not least in the title, making a far better fist of handling the situation as a lyricist than he had as *de facto* leader of the group. The first track completed, 'Welcome To The Terrordome', its title taken from a *Melody Maker* headline, provided a taut, searingly honest response to the Griff debacle. "We went into the studio and we didn't really know what Chuck was going to do," remembers Eric 'Vietnam' Sadler. "We had the track, we laid down stuff or whatever, and when Chuck does his vocals, I'm usually his guide. So the track comes on and he just starts ranting and raving, do you know what I'm saying? He just keeps going. He was thinking about this Griff shit, he was thinking about a whole bunch of shit. And it just all came out and so it was incredible. He just spewed it all out his guts."

Chuck had written the lyrics while driving to Pennsylvania in an effort to escape all the drama. Its most controversial passage was the line "Crucifixion ain't no fiction, so-called chosen frozen/Apology made to whoever pleases, still they got me like Jesus". Anti-Semitism? Even Bill Adler's not sure if Chuck was playing on the old 'blood libel'. But Leyla Turkkan, who approached him over it, is convinced that Chuck had no idea that his metaphor would be deconstructed in that way. Indeed, she claims he was totally ignorant of the theory that the Jews killed Jesus. The song certainly frightened record distributors CBS, whom the Anti-Defamation League contacted in protest. An internal memo was issued asking employees to ensure that "none of our recordings promote bigotry", without further guidance as to how they should quantify such concepts. Harry Allen, Public Enemy's old friend and hip hop activist, rose to his defence. "This is Chuck's point of view as an African man living on this planet. The notion of saying things to Europeans to make them comfortable is not part of the game."

Pundits on both sides offered dubious opinions. Adeeb Ahmad Shabazz, writing in the *Holocaust Journal*, advanced this statement in an article decrying Griff's treatment. "Despite the overall truthfulness of the statements [made by Professor Griff], the Jews found this to be a fitting time to divide and conquer by levying the charge of anti-Semitism against Brother Griff and Public Enemy . . . After a short time had passed, the group reorganized without Professor Griff as minister of information. The Jews had gotten the most vehemently outspoken music group of the 19Eighties to dismiss a brother for speaking the truth!" If only the black racists and white racists could hold hands. Consider the irony of fascist author Willis Carto's famous 1971 statement that "the Jews came first, and remain public enemy number one."

Chuck's lens zoomed in on the debate intermittently throughout the album, notably on 'Incident At 66.6 FM', where a talk-show caller notes that "White liberals, like yourself, have difficulty understanding that Chuck D represents the aspirations of the majority of black youth out there today." Elsewhere '911 Is A Joke', a track later farcically covered by Duran Duran in one of the greatest point-missing exercises of our time, slammed the race-bias of emergency response times in black communities. But while 'Revolutionary Generation' tackled rap's objectification of women, the put-down of homosexuality on 'Meet The G That Killed Me' showed Chuck wasn't subscribing to a liberal agenda anytime soon.

But the Griff controversy persisted. It was reignited when *Spin* printed an article, *The Repentant Professor*, in February 1990. He'd actually given the interview the previous October when he was still under a gagging order. This time it was Griff who took the decision to walk. He made his final appearance in May 1990 at the Brixton Academy, after a dispute with MS Serch of support act 3rd Bass. As if Public Enemy hadn't experienced trauma enough, there was a further sad incident on that year's Def Jam tour when Heavy D's dancer and best friend Trouble T-Roy (Troy Dixon) died backstage at a show in Indianapolis after falling from an elevated parking lot. Chuck tried to express his sympathy to Heavy's manager and record company head Andre Harrell – only to be told that Heavy should "concentrate on his record sales". For Chuck it was a salutary lesson about what label executives, black or white, really thought about their artists.

The Bomb Squad, meanwhile, used the connections they'd forged at MCA to produce an album with Bell Biv DeVoe – the remaining members of New Edition after Bobby Brown had opted for a solo career. Their hip hop-R&B hybrid, *Poison*, sold three million copies, much of the credit going to Hank Shocklee, who'd brought with him the Public Enemy work ethic, as Michael Bivins recalls: "He wanted it to be right. He [would say], 'Yo, your rapping needs to get better,' or 'Your singing needs to get better.' He was always on us. He worked us the most." By January 1990 the Bomb Squad had put together the rest of *Fear Of A Black*

Planet in four weeks, then finalised Ice Cube's *Amerikkka's Most Wanted* in February.

Ice Cube was involved in his own beef with N.W.A.'s Eazy-E over the fact that he'd written most of the lyrics for a platinum record yet still wasn't "getting paid right". So he kept ringing Chuck, asking him if he'd help produce a solo record. Conscious that he had problems in his own camp and didn't want to get involved in anyone else's mess, Chuck declined, even though he rated Cube "probably the best rap lyric writer ever". But Cube was insistent, and won Chuck over while in town to contribute a typically ferocious section to *Fear Of A Black Planet*'s 'Burn Hollywood Burn'. *Amerikkka's Most Wanted* was completed in five weeks, with the Bomb Squad complemented by Cube's west coast point–man Sir Jinx. By early 1991 *Poison*, *Fear Of A Black Planet* and *Amerikkka's Most Wanted* had all reached number one in the US charts.

1991 brought a further heap of problems. Flavor did little for Public Enemy's credentials by being arrested in Long Island for assaulting his girl-friend Karen Ross, the mother of his three children, an offence for which he would eventually serve 30 days in custody (he was later picked up for failing to pay child support). In April the group's future was again placed in doubt when Stephney and Shocklee split over business differences. By the time Public Enemy entered Record Plant Studios in New York in June 1991, the dark clouds seemed to be taking up permanent residence rather than dispersing. Again, Chuck's indignation was converted to the group's advantage as his frustrations informed the vehement tone of *Apocalypse '91 . . . The Enemy Strikes Black*.

Though not as venerated as either of its forerunners, *Apocalypse* was Public Enemy's most successful album, reaching number four in the American charts. The rhetoric was as fierce as ever. Compare the band's stance on corporate sponsorship to Run-DMC's on 'Shut 'Em Down' – "I like Nike, but wait a minute, the neighborhood supports, so put some money in it." 'Shut 'Em Down' was an exhortation to black communities to grow their own businesses. Conversely '1 Million Bottlebags' decried the victim mentality of those black alcohol abusers who were conspirators in their own downfall. The lyric originally concerned the body bags shipped home during the Gulf War, before a lecturer at Vanderbilt University passed Chuck some statistics that inspired him to address the abuse of malt liquor in the black community (a community deliberately targeted through rap endorsements). When Chuck discovered an advert for St Ides, one of the most popular distillers, was using his voice without clearance, he filed a lawsuit against parent company McKenzie River Brewing Co. He was awarded 'substantial' damages in 1993 after refusing to settle, reasoning that his own reputation was on the line. Left red-faced by Chuck's stand, Ice Cube, who had rapped "Get your girl in the mood quicker, and get your Jimmy thicker, with St Ides Malt Liquor", donated part of his fee to charity.

Chuck's aim took in various manifestations of the injustice of the black urban experience, but he again tackled the part played by his community's low expectations and self-deceptions. 'She Watch Channel Zero!?' berated the dependency on low-grade soap opera as cultural sustenance. 'Bring Tha Noise' was a ferocious broadside at radio's reluctance to play Public Enemy records. 'Black Steel In The House Of Chaos' questioned why so many young black males ended up drafted into the army, or locked down in the slammer, rather than on college courses.

The scarcity of black ownership of their own media outlets provided the subject matter for 'How To Kill A Radio Consultant', on which the closing sample of LL Cool J's 'I Can't Live Without My Radio' saluted the group's Def Jam heritage. Arguably the stand-out track, however, was 'By The Time I Get To Arizona', protesting against the state's refusal to dedicate a holiday to Martin Luther King Jr. The accompanying video, directed by Eric Meza, boasted a fantasy revenge sequence in which those failing to acknowledge the vacation were systematically assassinated. "Decent people do not listen to this kind of trash," responded Arizona governor Evan Mecham.

'I Don't Wanna Be Called Yo Niga' hit out at Uncle Tom-ism just as a group glorying in the name Niggers With Attitude had seemingly misappropriated rap's destiny. He maintained suspicions about the whole gangsta rap movement from its inception, though he was supportive of NWA and even invited them to tour with Public Enemy – choosing not to take sides in their dispute with Ice Cube. "Going round shooting brothers, beating them down – that don't make you hard," he told Simon Reynolds of the *Melody Maker* in 1991. "Gangsta rap is street, but political rap is a level above that, because once you understand the streets then you're political. Gangsta rap has lots of good stories, but it doesn't understand the structure behind those stories. If you don't understand the situation, you're gonna end up victimised by it." While throwing some placatory platitudes in the direction of gangsta rappers, justifying, with reservations, their form and function, Chuck was careful to underline the semantics of what 'hardcore' rap really constituted. Such a construct allowed him to disassociate his group from the negativity of those rappers who take the term on board as an excuse-all. "I think people got a conno-tation that hardcore rap had to have cursing or gangster stories," he told *Time*. "We've got neither. I wanted to show we could make a hard album without those connotations – a positive hardcore record."

The album was promoted by a joint tour with Anthrax, whose guitarist Scott Ian was a huge fan. "They're not just my favourite rap group," he enthused, "they're my favourite group in any kind of music." Together they recorded a ferocious remix of 'Bring Tha Noise' and embarked on a tour that brought Public Enemy to a whole new demographic. "Anthrax was the best fun we've had on a tour," Chuck told *HHC*. "It's been a majority white audience on the tour, but the places we've been [in the US] have been in the middle of white areas. But it was a collaborative music audience – it wasn't straight-out metal heads, it wasn't straight-out rap. It was people who were into both."

While Chuck tied up their joint trek with a series of public speaking engagements, there were murmurs of unrest at such a close alliance with a white rock band, including in-house reservatinos from Sister Souljah (Lisa Williamson), who'd replaced Griff as minister of information in January 1991. But Chuck refused to entertain those objections. He believed Anthrax had done a better job remixing 'Bring Tha Noise' than he had, for a start. And they'd done it without his help, either. Anthrax could never hold Chuck down to a time to re-record his vocals and had to sample them instead, with Scott Ian performing a couple of verses at the end. But Chuck and Flavor did manage to complete a video shoot for the single, at which point the idea of touring together arose. Public Enemy headlined *The World's Greatest Rap Show Ever*, alongside Queen Latifah, Naughty By Nature, MYC Lyte and the Geto Boys, but were soon back working in consort with rock bands. They undertook a further tour with U2, as ever conscious of the kudos an association with 'radical' music could bestow on their own tired guitar rock, including their Greenpeace-sponsored protest against Sellafield's nuclear plant.

With Public Enemy's backing, Sister Souljah signed with Epic and released her literate but dull début album *360 Degrees of Power* in 1992, fea-turing guest spots from Chuck and Ice Cube. But an interview she'd con-ducted in May with *The Washington Post*, ironically a competitor to *The Washington Times* that broke David Mills' Griff piece, came to light. Presi-dent Bill Clinton condemned her for "calling on blacks to kill whites". However, her comments, which bemoaned the pointless and heartbreaking cycle of black on black violence encouraged by gang fiefdoms at the height of the Los Angeles riots, had been entirely robbed of context. Again there was a sandstorm of controversy, proving how intense the media scrutiny on Public Enemy and its camp would continue to be.

Public Enemy's own album release of 1992 was *Greatest Misses*. It featured six tracks from their first four albums in adulterated form, plus six new tracks, the standouts being the Flavor showcase 'Get Off My Back' and 'Hazy Shade Of Criminal'. Chuck remains sensitive to criticism of the record, but the standards he'd set himself ensured disappointment. He was also displeased by Def Jam's handling of the project. "My original dissatisfaction with the whole Def Jam camp stems from my disdain for the trendiness, cliquish-ness, and bullshit we had to deal with on the *Greatest Misses* project," he recalled in his autobiography. "Everyone thought we should do a concept record, and I was like, 'Fuck a concept, this is anti-concept.' I wanted to do some creative shit. Russell Simmons and Lyor Cohen started to take more of a commanding role over Def Jam in decision making, where before they wouldn't question our camp situation." Throughout the group's career Chuck has articulated his differences with Rush and Def Jam as and when they arose. "Even though we're with Rush," he told Dan Goldstein, "they might say, 'Well, this is advisable.' I'll say, 'Fuck that, I'm doin' what I do 'cos I know my audience.'"

Public Enemy were never conventional charges for a record label. While being ferried from hotel to venue to hotel by chauffeur-driven limousine is a prerequisite for most at their level of achievement, Chuck knew that ultimately such indulgences would end up on his bottom line. He immediately realised that such rock'n'roll baloney quickly turns artists into dependent children. But it's only fair to acknowledge the logistical problems Public Enemy caused their handlers, not least Flavor's behaviour, much bemoaned by several staff members at Def Jam. He was soon in trouble again, arrested in the Bronx and charged with attempted murder for shooting at his bizarrely named neighbour Thelouizs English, before he booked himself into the Betty Ford Clinic to try to rid himself of his cocaine addiction. "At that time, I was going through certain pressures in my life," Flavor confessed to MTV.

Chuck stood by him. Again. "Everybody makes mistakes," he told *The Source*. "I asked Flav, 'Yo, are we still family or what? You still down? If you are, then let's work this out.'" Not everyone was as lenient or as patient. Dr Dre of Original Concept, now presenter of *Yo! MTV Raps*, gave air time to the stories. "Flavor asked me, 'Yo, man, why did you want to say that, spreading my business around to the whole world?' I said, 'Flavor, when you do something right, you want everybody to know about it. So all of a sudden, when you mess up, you want me to go hush-hush? No. You screwed up, and I'm gonna tell everybody you screwed up.' " Following Griff's lead, Flavor released a solo album in 1993, this time on Def Jam. But while everyone loved Flavor the sidekick and comic foil, no one was too impressed with Flavor the conceptual artist. Chuck himself moved out of Long Island to Atlanta in 1993, finding himself a peachy bolt-hole (rumoured to have been bought with the proceeds of the St Ides' case) and enjoying the calmer atmosphere – just before the south blew up as the new Klondike of hip hop.

1994's *Muse Sick-N-Hour Mess Age* was the group's first collection of new material issued in over three years. Suffering from one of the worst album titles of all time, it was also an artistic retreat – though not nearly to the extent that it has been portrayed by some. Uneven and sprawling, there were flashes of brilliance where before fans had grown accustomed to perpetual tides of invention and drama. The problem was not so much with the lyrics, but the production, which lacked the tough beats which always fish-hooked Chuck's erudition. "We wanted to borrow from soul, blues, gospel and rock'n'roll elements and blend them into something we can call our own," Chuck confessed at the time. "And make it faster." All well and good, but it didn't work.

Not that there weren't highlights. Flavor enjoyed arguably his greatest moment, or at least one of his most decipherable, on 'Godd Complexx'. 'Thin Line Between Law And Rape', a play on the Pretenders song, and 'Race Against Time', inspired by the Chambers Brothers' 'Time Is Going To Come', both related to Africa, its uncertain future and inglorious past at the hands of European colonisers. A related text was 'Hitler Day', which decried the anniversary celebrations of Christopher Columbus' 1492 voyage. Like much of the album, it was inspired by Public Enemy's tour of Africa, where Chuck observed first-hand the monstrous conditions facing slaves as they awaited transportation from the dungeons of Ghana.

Chuck was sore at scathing reviews of the album by *The Source* and *Rolling Stone*. Rightly or wrongly, critics put his gripes about gangsta rap, lead single 'Give It Up' comparing its adherents to cotton-pickers, to sour grapes at being outflanked and outgunned. Thereafter Chuck wrote his memoirs, a generally impressive, balanced read, and released a solo album, *The Autobiography Of Mistachuck*. It saw him work with Danny Goldberg at Mercury in preference to Def Jam, with whom he still had 'issues'. He also had issues with a couple of other people, too – 'Niggativity . . . Do I Dare Disturb The Universe' saw him pondering who he'd take down first, Bob Dole or Newt Gingrich. The music was of an entirely different hue to that patented by Public Enemy, with contributions from various Bomb Squad alumni while his hero, Isaac Hayes, served as producer. While the host group's sonic crunch was missed, most critics rated it a better package than Public Enemy's recent work.

Accident-prone Flavor continued to get himself into trouble, including a 90-day jail sentence for the neighbourhood shooting incident, before he broke both arms in a motorcycle crash in Milan. There were also charges for, variously, possession of cocaine, a firearm and marijuana. Terminator X bought an ostrich farm in South Carolina and released two solo records. Shocklee joined MCA after his own record label met with little success. Griff worked as a bounty hunter and Stephney, after his dispute with Shocklee, founded StepSun Music, until he got burned by his lead artist Miss Jones defecting to Motown. He sits on the boards of the Urban League and Wade Horn's National Fatherhood Initiative. He has also created his own pressure group — Families Organized for Liberty and Action. Harry Allen, meanwhile, founded the Hip Hop Hall of Fame.

Spike Lee reunited the Public Enemy principals, including Chuck, Flavor, Griff and the Bomb Squad to work on 1998's *He Got Game* soundtrack. The title-track was built over a sample of Buffalo Springfield's 'For What It's Worth' – itself a keynote record in the era of Sixties political unrest. More generous critics greeted the album as a partial restoration of former glories, and the title-track and the KRS-One collaboration 'Unstoppable' spoke of residual creativity to match their reputation. The Bomb Squad's most satisfying piece of work for years, it was also Public Enemy's last album for Def Jam, with whom they would have increasing differences as the label grew from an enthusiast's hobby to a market-domineering monolith. For the first time in a decade, to paraphrase 'Rebel Without A Pause', Def Jam no longer told the public who Public Enemy was.

6

I Can't Live Without Being On The Radio

"When I die, bury me on my stomach and let the world kiss my ass."
— LL Cool J, interviewed in Record Mirror

By August 1987 and 'I Need Love', LL had restyled himself as a ladies man, as he gave the world its first, but sadly not last, rap-ballad. He was an integral part of that year's Def Jam tour that has passed into legend for its excess. While few of Def Jam's acts were figureheads of sobriety, LL topped it off by getting himself arrested in Georgia for public lewdness. Mimicking R&B lothario Alexander O'Neill, he dry-humped a couch while performing 'I Need Love'. Derision also greeted his contribution to Nancy Reagan's Just Say No campaign, when the artist himself was self-evidently answering in the affirmative to every outstretched dealer's hand proffered in his direction. Exactly the sort of thing that Rubin had worried would overtake the young and impressionable rapper as Simmons groomed him for mainstream success. Rubin had been "horrified" the first time he heard 'I Need Love', but LL's ego and Simmons' ambition weren't about to take no for an answer.

Simmons restyled LL for the R&B market by hiring the L.A. Posse, Dwayne 'Muffia' Simon, Darryl 'Big Dad' Pierce and Clarence 'Byrd' Boyce. Formerly members of Los Angeles' Uncle Jam's Army, Simmons had picked up one of their demos and thought they'd make an ideal match for LL. Though the collaboration was certainly successful, it resulted in a hugely disappointing second album *Bigger And Deffer*, mainly because the rapper always sounded more convincing braced against harsher grooves. It was a big seller for Def Jam, but unarguably LL's least durable record. When *Playboy* selected LL as one of the ten sexiest men in rock'n'roll (!) in a 1988 poll, he went up at least another hat size. He was by no means universally popular, particularly among those who resented his embrace of the pop mainstream. Former Treacherous Three MC Kool Moe Dee launched the first significant diss against him on 'How Ya Like Me Now'. The cover of the album that housed it pictured LL's trademark Kangol hat crushed under the wheels of a Jeep.

1989's *Walking With A Panther* and its attendant single 'I'm That Kind Of Guy' hardly narrowed the gulf between LL and the audience that had deserted him, and both single and album were given a wide berth by New York's hip hop community. The perception that he'd sold out the culture reached its apex at a benefit performance at the Apollo Theater for Yusef Hawkins, murdered by white racists in 1989. LL was roundly booed. The emergence of stable-mates Public Enemy had rendered his obsession with the personal largely redundant. Though he tried a couple of half-baked socio-political rhymes on *Walking With A Panther*, his audience had changed in demographic. "The songs that hit were talking about how many women I could do, how many gold chains I had, and how bad I was. I was rapping about champagne, silk shirts, cars, jewellery, girls. I had become the anti-Christ of rap. I was selfish. I was egocentric. People felt like I was not being honourable and that I didn't represent where the black community should be heading." His career trajectory was further compromised by personal issues. He was managed by his father, the very same parent who had shot his mother and grandfather, who did little to atone for previous transgressions and nothing to halt LL's slide into showbiz indulgence. At one point LL even wanted to name his firstborn Alizé, after the French passion fruit and cognac drink. That was, indeed, how he was living.

It came as little surprise when LL hit back with his toughest-sounding body of work so far. *Mama Said Knock You Out* was a forceful if reactionary attempt to deflect accusations that he was merely some sap pretender rather than rap contender. Large parts of it worked brilliantly. A series of MCs were taking pot-shots at his dated style, including old foe Kool Moe Dee, MC Shan, Steady B and Ice-T. This time he hooked up with Marley Marl (Marlon Williams), ace producer to the Juice Crew family. Marley had enjoyed tremendous success through Roxanne Shanté, Big Daddy Kane, Biz Markie and MC Shan (and was brought in despite the fact that Shan had once, among other insults, called LL's mother 'a sleazebag slut' on vinyl). LL's comeback single, 'Jingling Baby' was transferred from its intended recipient, Biz Markie, after Marley fell out with his record label, Cold Chillin'. Dismayed by the escalating misogyny emerging in rap, Marley asked LL to write something pro-female. LL came back with 'Around The Way Girl', a homage to the everyday existence of a

Brooklyn homebody. Their combined efforts sparked a Grammy-award winning renaissance. More importantly, *Mama Said Knock You Out* finally delivered on the promise of those early records like 'Rock The Bells' and 'I Can't Live Without My Radio'.

LL followed up his initial cinematic foray on *Krush Groove* with *Toys*, an unremarkable children's flick starring the ubiquitous Robin Williams. Later he would question whether, given better management, he might have attained the cross-platform stature attained by Will Smith – another Russell Simmons client. The truth is he never had the focus, and didn't scrub up quite as well (Smith would never have been as clumsy as to ask his musicians to 'make it hot for my niggas' as LL did on 1997's under-cooked *Phenomenon*). But LL was still living large and partying hard, until he began to listen to long-time friend and Russell Simmons' associate Charles Fisher. They'd first met in 1985 at Def Jam's offices. Fisher, who discovered R. Kelly and Public Announcement, went on to run LL's fan club. In 1991 he persuaded LL to become the honorary chairman of Youth Enterprises, his programme for deprived youth (motto: "stay in school is the number one rule"). Fisher also handed over a large volume of spiritual literature, which self-diagnosed 'lost soul' LL devoured.

Such 'crossroads' deliberations were distilled into *14 Shots To The Dome*, which made some uneasy concessions to the west coast rap revolution. Though it sold 800,000 copies, it broke a sequence of four consecutive platinum albums. LL's first starring movie role, *Out Of Sync*, also bombed. He was also starting to realise that the terms his father and co-manager Brain Latture had negotiated with Def Jam had been less than advantageous. "The deal basically locked me into the new contract for what seemed like life. I found out that I owed more than $2 million in back taxes." Simmons glosses over the squabble. "LL and I have a love/hate relationship. The bottom line is complete love, but we fight over every contract we negotiate."

It was 1995's *Mr Smith* that revived LL's lost stature, a double platinum till-ringer via the crossover success of singles 'Doin' It' and 'Hey Lover', the latter a saccharine collaboration with Boyz II Men. The finished album could have been much different. LL was unhappy with the original sessions. He confessed his fears to Lyor Cohen, who put him in touch with Chris Lighty, who ran Violator management. Lighty and LL began to rework the songs, though in the end only two of the original selections, the title-track and 'No Airplay', were retained. Lighty brought in the Trackmasters (the hot production duo of Samuel 'Tone' Barnes and Jean

Claude 'Poke' who would later work with Foxy Brown, Jay-Z and Will Smith as well as mainstream artists ranging from Michael Jackson to Mariah Carey).

Once they'd reworked the beats the results were far more appealing – albeit a mile away from the LL Cool J of old. The truth was he'd found a comfortable accommodation between his commercial and 'street' instincts for the first time, and the commercial instincts had won hands down. By the time of the album's release LL had renegotiated his deal with Def Jam thanks to the efforts of the former Los Angeles Lakers' basketball player Norm Nixon, and his new manager was also his spiritual guide, Charles Fisher.

Thereafter LL's acting career took off as he starred in the sitcom *In The House*, directed by Debbie Allen (who'd also directed *Out Of Sync*), playing a genial former footballer who takes in lodgers. Which was somewhat ironic, given that on 1993's 'Ain't No Stoppin' This' he'd penned the line: "I guess I need a TV show to get mine/But I don't feel like kissin' no director's behind". He also began work on *Smithsonian* – a typically grandiose attempt to tell the story of LL's 'life in rap' and the soundtrack to his autobiography. When he told Def Jam about it, Lyor Cohen was delighted. "Hey, cross-promotion!" is how LL reports his reaction. He also formed his own record label under the Def Jam family tree, Illion, with the impossibly conceited ambition of creating "the Motown of the new millennium". But part of his fantasy lifestyle was certainly coming true. He would soon have his own series of Gap adverts and a sneakers company, though otherwise he was a little late on the great rap synergy bandwagon.

By 1996 LL was again involved in contract negotiations with Def Jam. This time there was a little subterfuge involved. Def Jam gave Foxy Brown (who'd appeared on *Mr Smith*'s 'I Shot Ya') the opportunity to re-record 'The Bells' for her album *Ill Na Na*, when LL was about to cut the new version for his *Greatest Hits* collection. "They ended up giving it to Foxy to give me a little wake-up call. I mean, they own part of the publishing rights to it." It was proof that Def Jam was ready to play hardball even with their biggest stars, but for now, LL stayed put.

In the late Nineties LL tried to restore his street cred by inviting Method Man, Redman and Busta Rhymes to join him on his over-ambitious *Phenomenon* venture. But he got into a fresh spat with Canibus, an up-and-coming rapper who contributed a couple of lines to '4, 3, 2, 1' (which featured the hook from the Younger Generation's 'We Rap More Mellow') that LL sensed were disrespectful. LL composed a succinct riposte about "little shorty with the big mouth". Canibus slammed back, claiming that 99 per cent of LL's fans wear high heels in his breakthrough single, 'Second Round K.O.' "99 per cent of your fans don't exist," LL sniffed in 'The Ripper Strikes Back'. Proof that LL's competitive instincts hadn't wilted despite his otherwise mellowing persona. The name-calling was all good clean cat-calling fun, without any of the shadow of violence that had marred the gangsta diss wars running between east and west. But after a while it got equally tedious. Even in 2001 the oeuvre-limited Canibus was still at it, responding meekly with 'RIP The Jacker'.

Run-DMC were never able to stage-manage a comeback as their old sparring partner LL had. By the advent of The Beastie Boys, their appeal was already starting to wane, even though they wrote 'Slow And Low' for *Licensed To Ill* and Run helped out with the beats on 'Paul Revere'. In the interim there was the first of several squabbles with record label Profile, until in 1988 they released the tie-in album and film *Tougher Than Leather*, both of which had Rick Rubin's fingerprints written large on their person.

Spurred on by their dissatisfaction at their experience with *Krush Groove*, Simmons and Rubin had decided to have another crack at the movie industry. Rubin was particularly keen – after all he'd studied film at NYU, and he took another small acting part, appearing as Vic in one film. He also directed, drawing on a storyboard put together by Lyor Cohen and Bill Adler for a "rapping adventure thriller". After having prospered by organising the *Fresh Fest* tours themselves, collective madness dictated that, by cutting out the Hollywood middlemen, Run-DMC and Def Jam would all end up rolling in money. It didn't work out that way.

The lacklustre plot had Run-DMC signing to a production company before their roadie (played by Raymond White) is murdered after witnessing a murder. The idea was to update the blaxploitation format of films such as *Shaft* and *Superfly*, though neither Run nor DMC turned out to be the next Richard Roundtree or Ron O'Neal. Concert performances, the only footage worth salvaging from the enterprise, featured The Beastie Boys and Slick Rick as well as Run-DMC themselves.

The film quickly ran over budget, with costs more than doubling from $300,000 to $700,000. It opened in 50 cinemas but quickly disappeared after receiving sneering reviews. As Run later confessed, "We messed up big time when we decided to make the movie using our own money. I found out the hard way that *nobody* makes a movie using their own money." DMC reckons it was "the worst experience of our lives". And for that he blames Russell Simmons, who insisted on watering down the dialogue and making the group out to be the 'good guys' of rap, which hardly tallied with their B-boy personas. The film only recouped when the rights were sold to New Line Cinema, but by that time the damage to their careers was done. Still, at least there was a neat cameo from Adam Yauch as a Hasidic Jew.

The accompanying album contained some of Run-DMC's finest work, especially 'Run's House', 'I'm Not Going Out Like That' and 'Beats To The Rhyme'. But there were tensions in the camp, exacerbated by Run's desperate efforts to kick his multifarious drug habits. *Tougher Than Leather* sold a million copies, but that was a disappointing figure in relation to *Raising Hell*'s huge impact, and the group were embarrassed to find themselves unable to fill the stadium arenas that had become a second home.

Run-DMC's downhill slide was dramatic. Run became depressed and had a nervous breakdown after he was hit by writer's block, spending much of his time smoking reefer. He hit a particularly low ebb on a summer 1988 tour with Public Enemy and Jazzy Jeff that he'd been coerced into at the height of his personal decline. There's a telling moment in his autobiography where he states, matter of factly, "Two weeks before the tour I told Russell that I didn't want to go out. He sent me out anyway. My behaviour didn't make sense, and there was money to be made." There's no doubt that he got pretty sore at times over his elder brother's conduct. "There was a point in my life when I blamed Russell for anything in my career that I couldn't control. I said that all along it was me out on stage 'tap-dancing' while he had been 'Mr. Businessman'." In particular, when the money stopped coming through, he looked at his elder brother as the successful mogul painted in the magazine features and wondered where his slice was coming from, despite a sneaking suspicion that most of his considerable earnings had disappeared up his nose. Russell then bawled him out over what DMC claims was a genuine suicide attempt. Again, DMC's view of Russell is instructive. "Russell is a guy who always wants more money." Ultimately the brothers resolved their differences: Run even called his son Russell. But for a while their relationship was less than fraternal. Contrast that with Run's (pre-millennium) affirmation that, "Dee, Jay and I have never had an argument. We don't argue. The respect level is so high it's crazy."

1990's *Back From Hell* tried to harness the gangsta zeitgeist, making uneasy lyrical compromises with modish gangsta rap-isms, but words like bitch and ho' sounded awkward falling from the mouths of the two original B-boys, who were always 'street', but never 'wrong side of the street'. DMC admits the album was borne out of desperation. What fewer know is that, prior to its release, Run–DMC were negotiating with gangsta rap's kingpin, Suge Knight, about a record deal with Death Row. Suge's reputation precedes him, and it's probable that they thought it would be enough to scare off Profile from holding them to their deal (he'd acquired a reputation for contract 'resolution', for such as Vanilla Ice, whom it was rumoured was held by his skinny white legs over a balcony, and N.W.A.'s Eazy-E, can attest). In the end, the deal was never done, but it was too late to remove the blot on their copybook that was *Back From Hell*. Trend-cashing tracks such as 'Bob Your Head' were bad enough. But we really didn't need 'It's Like That (Motherfucka)' the '91 remix, which might well have happened had Suge got his hands on them.

Thereafter Run was entangled in a baseless 1991 Cleveland rape charge that his accuser dropped just as it went to court (Russell had brought in some heavyweight lawyers to fight the suit just in case). Despite proving his innocence, his wife left and took the kids. By the early Nineties, after another fight with Profile following the disastrous sales attributed to *Back From Hell*, and their threat not to record another album, their financial problems overtook them. Run was the first to file for bankruptcy, but DMC wasn't far behind. Profile tried to argue that their clients were attempting to use bankruptcy as a screen to renegotiate their contract. Nope, they really were broke, but they did indeed leave the courts with an improved contract.

1993's *Down With The King*, was far more satisfying, at least for the Pete Rock-produced title-track, though some of the cloying, po-faced Christian lecturing was irritating. Run, after having been 'found' by the Zoe Ministries, spent increasing time with his 'flock' after taking the title Reverend Run in 1994, and also attempted to head up Def Gospel, a ghastly idea if ever there was one. In his autobiography he explains the short shrift the idea received from his brother: "What does God have to do with money and prosperity," was Russell's reply. Run, who'd completed the journey from self-righteous but immensely talented MC into self-righteous preacher of dubious authority, committed his pious self-help lessons to print in the form of an autobiography. Among the gems were 'Run's House Rules' like, "Think back to one activity that you really enjoyed as a kid. If you can, today do it just for fun. If not, try developing some new hobby that you've perhaps thought about but never gotten around to trying." Run will never be a sucker MC, but he's developing strong credentials as a sucker in any other idiom.

DMC had his problems with alcohol, eventually developing pancreatitis after he took to a liquid diet when his weight ballooned. The result was a three-week hospital stay and a life of abstinence. He temporarily joined Run in the Zoe Ministries, but was always a little more querulous. He now confirms he is distrustful of organised religions, his pseudo-pantheism making him highly unusual in God-fearing hip hop circles. Jam Master Jay was involved in a serious car accident (and by the new millennium was to be found advertising 'DJ lessons' to any takers on internet auction site E-Bay) as well as starting his own label. Always a more stoical and contemplative presence in the group, DMC has committed his own memoirs to print in a book that is eminently more humble and readable, though like many rappers he has a quixotic, slightly naive view of any country that isn't America. He also confessed that nowadays he never listens to rap, preferring classic rock.

Run-DMC finally got away from Profile, the label they'd never seen eye to eye with throughout their career, but only migrated to its purchaser, Arista. Russell could have brought them to Def Jam if he thought for one minute it was worth the effort. Profile were keen to hand their potential saviours a viable product – and the best they had was the promise of a new Run-DMC record. However, DMC was out of action, having strained his vocal cords. So Profile bought off Run, encouraging him to demo studio tracks on his own for which he'd receive desperately needed advances. When DMC found out by accident, the first real schism developed between the long-time partners and friends. DMC staged a tactical retreat, and continued with the group only on sufferance. As he recalls, "When I look at Run these days, we only connect when we're together during a live stage performance. Because that's something that we did together for so many years that it's unchangeable, unbreakable. But there comes a point when it's time to move on." The Sam and Dave of rap had reached the end of the pier, but DMC remains part of the show, for now.

A new generation of fans were reminded of Run-DMC's achievements when New York house producer Jason Nevins took a remix of 'It's Like That' to number one in Britain in 1997, though he did his best to take the credit for himself. Run was indifferent, but more than pleased to take the money. "Now I have the Mercedes, the Rolls-Royce, the customized limo, the diamond Rolex, but this time it's different," he proposed in his autobiography. "Those things don't control me." How much wisdom does it take for a man to learn that he only needs one car? To paraphrase the younger Run at Madison, I beg your pardon – the world is not your muthafuckin' car showroom.

As LL and Run-DMC experienced career downturns and resurrections, there were plenty of other Rush clients to take up the slack, not least Eric B and Rakim, the duo featuring the purists' favourite MC. In the mid-Eighties Eric Barrier was an established DJ for New York's WBLS. William Griffin Jr, the nephew of R&B legend Ruth Brown, responded to his search for 'New York's top MC'. He pestered his friend and room-mate Marley Marl, founder of the Juice Crew and a fast-rising production star, to let him use his home studio on 12th Street. Marley agreed, though he had few expectations that his laid-back room-mate would use the time constructively.

The first track they worked on together was 'Eric B Is President'. Marley recognised immediately that the rapper Eric had brought him was "hot", and handed over one of his increasingly celebrated backing tracks to work on. When they were through, he ran off a cassette of the track, with the intention of mixing it later in the week. Instead, Barrier took it straight to radio. Within five days it was blowing up on the airwaves, leaving Marley Marl incredulous that his work had been mastered off a cassette. Released on Harlem's tiny Zakia label, 'President' became the hit jam of New York in the summer of 1986 and set Eric B and Rakim on their way.

The lyric to 'Eric B Is President' related to Rakim's Five Per Cent Nation beliefs, but it was his comfort at the mic, intuitive understanding of phrase and fable and his stoic delivery, a stark contrast to Run-DMC and LL Cool J's chest-beating ways, that electrified listeners. He was also a comparatively bashful and media-shy personality, preferring to let his lyrics do the talking, while both he and Barrier were disdainful of alcohol and drugs. Importantly, at a time when artists like the Fat Boys were turning hip hop into a bawdy comedy routine, they were deadly serious about both the music and message. The single alerted Russell Simmons to the duo's presence, and they were soon signed to Rush, though Island got there first with a recording contract.

The duo settled into Manhattan's Power Play studios in early 1987 and began work on *Paid In Full*, their début album and magnum opus. *Paid In Full* saw Rakim "hold the microphone like a grudge", splintering expectations with a dazzling mix of Muslim theology and street-smart realism, delivered in his timeless, unhurried tones. Eric B's tough and eclectic vibe-watch melded James Brown samples with 808 drum kicks to show-stopping effect (though Rakim later suggested to journalists that he'd also played a major part in producing the music). Highlights included the Bobby Byrd-sampling 'I Know You Got Soul' and 'Chinese Arithmetic', but this was one of rap's first flawless albums.

By the time of 1988's almost as riveting follow-up, *Follow The Leader*, they'd switched to MCA subsidiary Uni. "In 1990, we were about to sign with Island for $400,000," recalls Barrier. "But one night I talked with this guy who used to work at MCA. He said they wanted to fly me to LA, to talk about a deal. I told our manager Russell Simmons about this, and he said, 'Look, Eric, we got $400,000. Let's not fuck it up. MCA could be blowing smoke up your ass.' I said, 'Cool. That's still what I want to do with my life.' So we flew to LA and went back and forth between Warner Brothers and MCA. Stayed out there a day or two, signed a multi-album deal with MCA. The initial commitment was about $1 million. One of the first big rap deals." None of the duo's subsequent efforts approached the majesty of their opening salvos, though both *Let The Rhythm Hit 'Em* (1990) and *Don't Sweat The Technique* (1992) betrayed flashes of musical and lyrical genius. Disappointed by the commercial failure of the latter, the duo split, each party recording poorly received solo albums which heightened rather than alleviated the sense of loss felt throughout the hip hop community at the demise of the duo.

Philadelphia's DJ Jazzy Jeff (Jeffrey Townes) and the Fresh Prince (Will Smith) existed at the opposite end of the rap spectrum. One of the power-house turntable wizards, Jazzy Jeff advanced the stylistic repertoire of the Bronx originators by gifting his fellow DJs such innovations as the transformer and chirp scratch, founding a technical library at which today's vinyl-worshipping turntablists study. But his role would quickly be eclipsed by his clean-cut partner Will Smith, the black Cary Grant. The duo landed a record contract in 1986 after Townes won the New Music Seminar DJ Battle for World Supremacy. Word Up Records, via Dana Goodman's Pop Art Records, released *Rock The House* in 1987, which housed the crossover hit 'Girls Ain't Nothing But Trouble', featuring a prominent sample of *I Dream Of Jeanie*.

Their success led to a complicated legal tangle with their original label, from which Simmons, who'd signed them to his management company because he appreciated their sense of humour, would extricate them. Afterwards he put them on tour with Run-DMC. But their troubles had disheartened the duo. "When Russell told us that he was going to put us on tour with Run–DMC in two months, we just knew it wasn't going to happen," Smith wrote in his introduction to Darryl McDaniels' auto-biography. "Everything had been going wrong, and we were absolutely positive everything was going to continue to go wrong. So going out on the road with the hottest rap group in the world didn't seem possible." But Russell was as good as his word.

Both Eric B and Rakim and Jazzy Jeff and the Fresh Prince toured in consort with Rush's other headline acts, Run–DMC, Public Enemy and LL Cool J. All five demonstrated (at least until Eric and Rakim fell out in 1992) the tenacity of Russell Simmons' chokehold on the rap industry. A world his old friend and business partner Rick Rubin was about to back out of.

7

Produced A Man Just To Watch Him Get His Muse Back . . .

"I never had the feeling I ever had to make a dime doing anything."
                                                              – Rick Rubin

Tensions within Def Jam accompanied the label's late Eighties triumphs. Rubin wasn't especially pleased with the direction Simmons had taken LL Cool J in. He had little time for his partner's increasing diversions into R&B, either. Simmons had signed Oran 'Juice' Jones, whom he also produced, as an attempt to imbue the sounds of the Stylistics and Chi-Lites with a Harlem hustler aesthetic (Jones had also written songs for others, such as 'Day Dreamin'' for Kurtis Blow). To that end Simmons inaugurated a new Def Jam subsidiary OBR, dedicated to 'vintage soul'. Jones' 'The Rain' may have displayed melodic niceties, but its worldview was as bleakly misogynist as anything gangsta rap belched out – the song's protagonist strips his girlfriend of the gifts he's bestowed on her after he catches her cheating, before she's unceremoniously kicked to the kerb. A hugely successful record reaching the top 10 of the pop charts, it caused a small bush fire in R&B circles, and generated a series of reply records from disgruntled female vocalists in the manner of the old 'Roxanne' song cycle (inspired by a similar women-baiting diss song early in hip hop's history).

Simmons began working with a slew of R&B singers, including Alyson Williams, Chuck Stanley and Tashan – each collaborating on the other's albums without securing a breakthrough single between them. Blue Magic were a Philadelphia vocal trio active since the early Seventies giving stardom one last shot, while Don Newkirk, who worked on a series of projects with Stetsasonic's Prince Paul and 3rd Bass, was temporarily promoted as Def Jam's very own Prince, lacking only the talent, sex appeal and the hits to justify the comparison. But Simmons' big experiment – to marry classic vocal R&B with contemporary rapping in an approximation of the style former colleague Harrell was pioneering at Uptown – was not the direction Rubin was looking in.

The further the music steered towards R&B, the less interested Rubin became. He'd never lost his love of loud rock bands, and throughout the late Eighties regularly caught shows from breaking alt-rock groups, especially The Pixies. In 1987 he signed on as musical director on *Less Than Zero*, a shoddy adaptation of Brett Easton Ellis' bleak portrait of drug addiction, male prostitution and adolescent vacancy in Los Angeles. The soundtrack featured Public Enemy's 'Bring Tha Noise' and LL Cool J's 'Going Back To Cali', the song on which Rubin returned as LL's production partner after a two-year hiatus. Rubin and LL enjoyed the reunion so much, Rubin agreed to shoot an engaging black and white promo for 'Cali', easily LL's finest four minutes since his début album. The video wound up on rotation on MTV, though the movie itself was justifiably mauled by critics. More conventional rock fare from Slayer, Aerosmith, Joan Jett, Danzig and the Bangles dominated the film soundtrack though, ironically, Oran 'Juice' Jones also made an appearance.

The Bangles' hard-kicking update of Simon & Garfunkel's 'Hazy Shade Of Winter' charged to number two in the charts early the following year when it was released as a single by Def Jam, only mall goddess Tiffany preventing Rubin from securing his first number one. But the finished version did not meet his approval, members of The Bangles having returned to the studio to record overdubs and tweek the tape, trying to re-establish the 'folk vibe' from Simon & Garfunkel's original. Rubin was aghast at the changes, and asked for his name to be removed from the producer's credits. As The Bangles Vicky Peterson recalls: "He hated the finished version, thought it was too 'homo'. That's his favourite word, homo, for anything that ain't macho enough for Rick Rubin."

The experience reminded Rubin that oranges were not the only fruit, and that he really wanted to work with a rock band again. Initially, he saw no reason why he couldn't bring such a project to Def Jam. As strange as such a marriage would seem to contemporary fans of the label, Rubin had inaugurated the imprint for his own rock-based releases long before he'd met Simmons. But his efforts to sign Orange County hoodlums Slayer provoked a furious response from Walter Yetnikoff of CBS. Yetnikoff, the "high-handed vulgarian" who later sold CBS to Sony, considered the sentiments on *Reign In Blood* to be anti-Semitic. He was especially offended by the track 'Angel Of Death' and its amoral depiction of Nazi butcher Dr Joseph Mengele. Single-handedly pioneering the speed metal idiom, *Reign*

In Blood is an equally inspirational artefact for another torrid sub-genre, death metal – variations of the term 'death' occur in the album's lyric sheet no less than 56 times in its brief 28-minute song cycle, giving some clue as to Slayer's thematic breadth and philosophical scope. Yet it remains one of Rubin's most memorable productions, cleaning and sharpening the band's previously muddy clatter into sharp gouges of over-driven ultra hard rock. Public Enemy were quick to recognise fellow shock troopers at the height of their craft and employed a sample of 'Angel Of Death' on 'She Watch Channel Zero?!'. Slayer guitarist Kerry King also provided guitar on The Beastie Boys' '(You Gotta) Fight For Your Right (To Party)'.

Irritated by Yetnikoff's intervention, Rubin brokered a distribution deal for Slayer with Geffen. Russell Simmons, utterly disinterested in his partner's tinkering with heavy metal rednecks, let him get on with it. But as Simmons confirmed in his autobiography, he could see trouble coming. "Slayer and Oran Jones had nothing in common," he states. "If we'd been a huge label with many divisions, it would have been fine. But at a small company like Def Jam, it was apparent that a real cultural and creative separation was taking place." But Rubin saw in Slayer the same germ of excitement and danger he'd loved in rap. "To me it made perfect sense," he remembers. "When I heard Slayer I just thought that I had to sign them because they were just as extreme and relevant as, say, Public Enemy."

Rubin had long been troubled by Lyor Cohen's increasing power within the Rush/Def Jam power structure, and his efforts to make the label a mass-market, corporate entity, rather than a haven for the cutting edge radicalism he admired in music. The last Public Enemy album had also convinced him he'd done everything he could within rap. He first heard *It Takes A Nation Of Millions* on a tape Chuck had sent him shortly before he flew to Los Angeles. "I was on the airplane listening to it and I remember I cried. I was so proud. Because to me it just took it to a whole new level, and I remember crying, thinking that this is just such a beautiful thing that's evolving and growing. But for me it felt like that was the last one like that. That's what I always wanted from music, and I wasn't getting it from rap at that time."

He followed Slayer's début by working with The Cult on 1987's *Electric*, "the first rock'n'roll record I made". Singer Ian Astbury had hunted Rubin down after being impressed by The Beastie Boys' Def Jam début, 'Rock Hard'. Though a fan neither of Billy Duffy's ostentatious guitar playing nor Astbury's vocal histrionics, Rubin got involved after he agreed to remix tracks recorded with Love producer Steve Brown. His attempt to reduce the group to its rock'n'roll essentials were not entirely coherent, however, given that effects and affectation were always a huge constituent of the Cult's muse. Dismissed as 'retro-moronic' by one critic, *Electric* includes an awful version of 'Born To Be Wild', though 'Love Removal Machine' provided a quantifiable hit. It was recorded in Jimi Hendrix's Electric Ladyland studio on 8th Street. The group have since disowned the album, claiming it was more Rubin's record than their own. If that is true, it's a mistake he would not make again.

In 1988 he started talking to his contacts at Geffen, with whom he'd struck up cordial relations since working on Slayer's distribution. The fact that *Reign In Blood* had sold half a million copies helped convince them that Rubin was a viable commercial proposition. For his part, Rubin was ready to do something different. Geffen granted him his own imprint, Def American. But though he kept the prefix, this was intended as a more eclectic concern than its rival.

Def American allowed Rubin to escape the straitjacket of being viewed solely as a rap producer. "I like doing different kinds of stuff and I always have," Rubin later told David John Farinella. "As soon as I started making rock records after making rap records, I was unanimously told: 'You're a rap producer and you shouldn't be making heavy metal records.' Then it was: 'You shouldn't be making rock records, because you make heavy metal records.' I've been labelled a lot of things over the years and I just try to make records I like." The perception of Rubin as a fan is something he is keener to encourage, and his track record bears him out. "It's really in the job description to have taste. Because an artist is usually very close to the material that they're working on, and it's almost like being a professional fan – it's really what the job is."

Rubin has emerged as one of the most thoughtful producers in contemporary music, proving particularly adept at encouraging musicians to "come to themselves" rather than imposing a sonic template that can be traced across his catalogue. Ironically, while his reputation was built on his discovery and nurturing of 'new' music, most of his productions are united by a spare, uncluttered aesthetic that could be described, and indeed has, as 'retro'. His heroes include George Martin and Mutt Lange. Rubin credits Lange's contribution to AC/DC's *Highway To Hell* as axiomatic in getting "as good sounding a rock record as you can get". He also prefers to let sessions develop organically rather than rush the creative process, even if this plays havoc with his own release schedules. "We're just experimenting and having fun, and seeing what comes out. We do this over a long enough period of time where we have enough things to choose from to really see what the best is. We don't say, 'go write ten songs, and that'll be your album.' It is more of a search."

Rubin didn't entirely disassociate himself from rap, which would feature prominently on Def American, especially in its early years. He cut a deal with NastyMix to distribute Seattle's Sir Mix-A-Lot (Anthony Ray), an artist whose oeuvre, limited as it was largely to the discussion of female anatomy, is usually dismissed as 'booty music'. His take on adolescent sexual urges was informed by humour and self-parody rather than the more hateful instincts of those other deifiers of the derriere, 2 Live Crew. "I think Mix-A-Lot is a tremendous artist," responds Rubin. "He's a great entertainer. From the first time I ever heard him, I just loved him." They enjoyed considerable success together, too. Taken from Sir Mix-A-Lot's 1991 album *Mack Daddy*, 'Baby Got Back' gave Def American its biggest hit, selling over two million copies and procuring a Grammy Award after becoming the biggest selling American single of 1992. Rubin also continued to help out as executive producer once Mix-A-Lot established his own Rhyme Cartel imprint and moved to Warners.

Rubin also worked with Houston's Geto Boys, a wild bunch even by the hair-raising standards of gangsta rap. Indeed, they would have felt honoured had they read his assessment that they were "the most offensive group I've ever worked with." After hearing their *Grip It! On That Other Level* album (credited to the Ghetto Boys), Rubin encouraged them to rework the material, add new cuts and remix other tracks, signing a deal with James Smith's Rap-A-Lot Records to distribute the results. But after releasing the Ku Klux Klan-baiting single 'Do It Like A G.O.', Geffen refused to have anything more to do with the album due to the inflammatory lyrics of tracks like 'Assassins' and 'Size Ain't'. Geffen president Ed Rosenblatt's dismissal of it as "the worst thing I ever heard" mirrors Rubin's own remarks about the group, but Rosenblatt was coming from an entirely different headspace. As was pressing plant Digital Audio Disc Corporation, who balked at any involvement. In truth it was just the sort of project Geffen should have anticipated after employing Rubin, who had always been synonymous with 'difficult' artists. The group itself was unapologetic, their label head suggesting that, "This rap shit is the biggest challenge to the government in a long-ass time. It's bigger than Martin Luther King and all them." Rubin finally found someone who could live with the album's contents in the shape of Giant. Thereafter the Geto Boys held it down for uncompromising lunacy; group member Bushwick Bill forcing his girlfriend to shoot him while threatening their baby. He lost an eye in the process, and a picture of him, mobile phone in hand, being pushed through a hospital ward with half his head missing, graced the cover of 1991's *We Can't Be Stopped*. Rubin was well out of it.

Further notoriety surrounded Rubin's work with Andrew Dice Clay – the oafish Brooklyn stand-up. Sample joke on Dice Clay's eponymous 1989 début album for Def American: "How can Japanese people drive with their eyes three-quarters shut. You can blindfold these people with dental floss." Clay, like the Black Crowes and Slayer, was initially signed by Rubin to Def Jam, but seemed better placed to join Rubin's roster in Los Angeles when he made the decision to relocate.

Rubin hired former Profile executive Dan Charnas to talent scout further rap acts for Def American. The first item he brought to his employer's attention was a demo by The Art Of Origin, a duo featuring Kern Chandler and Chino XL – who became the first rappers signed by Rubin since Public Enemy. "It made perfect sense," remembers Charnas. "The Art Of Origin was musically a hip hop group, but they had the visual imagery of a metal group like Slayer. Rick was the only person who could have understood them." However, they turned out not to be the new Public Enemy after all, and despite recording two albums' worth of material, just a brace of singles emerged; 'Into The Pit' (1992) and 'Unration-Al' (1993). The latter's ghastly Eric Clapton reference, "I'm trowin' that ass out the window like Eric Clapton's son," dignified absolutely no one involved with it.

The group broke up but Chino, a talented rapper with a gift for metaphor, remained with Rubin for his 1996 début *Here To Save You All*. Quincy Jones declined sample clearance because the lyrics slighted some of his pals, including Russell Simmons, though Rubin loved the line, "My company is fucking me/Like Arsenio does Eddie Murphy", even though he was the intended target. Chino was due to release a second album, *Poison Pen*, but his deal with American collapsed. Eventually he created Ill Records, an under-achieving dance and rap-themed imprint whose best known artist was Native Tongues-influenced Queens rapper Kwest Tha Mad Ladd. It also premiered would-be gangsta rapper Pretty Tone Capone, who used his own New York State parole record and police sketch as promotional material.

But the majority of Def American's roster was drawn from the rock world – albeit the extremes. Despite flitting between musical genres, even Rubin had to concede that making rap and rock records necessitated an entirely different approach. "[Rap]'s more of a producer-driven format where it would be my responsibility to actually come up with the tracks." Later, he admitted that rap music had lost much of its enchantment. "I'm not feeling rap records, where at the time I was doing them, it was really a different time. It was an exciting movement for me at that time. It was a new exciting community that I was a part of. I don't feel rap now. I still like it, but I don't have the same relationship to it that I did before."

If there was a single act that established Def American's identity in its infant years, it was the Black Crowes. At one time tipped as natural successors to The Rolling Stones, they were more accurately direct descendants of The Allman Brothers-Lynyrd Skynyrd southern boogie protocol. *Shake Your Money Maker*, released in 1990, became a fixture of the album charts and eventually sold over five million copies, while its successor, *Southern Harmony And Musical Companion* (1992), débuted at number one on the US album charts.

They were signed by Rubin's long-standing friend from his NYU days, George Drakoulias, who'd been involved in a peripheral role on many of the early Def Jam projects. "Rick was the DJ at the dorm, and I had started dating an old girlfriend of his," he recalled in an interview with Bud Scoopa. "She introduced us, and I started helping him with the parties. He said he was starting this label, and I said I'd try to get an internship and get credit, and I would work with him and we'd do something." Drakoulias was with Rubin when he took his first steps in the studio. "I didn't know what I was doing and Rick didn't know much more, I don't think. He was just paying for the studio time and kind of had a vision . . . I really have nice memories of it. You never knew what was gonna happen."

When Rubin headed west, Drakoulias followed him, later lodging in his cellar. "Actually, I use Rick's house as an office," he confessed. "He uses that as an office and I use it as my office, too. If we need to do something there or go over something, we do it at his house." In a mirror image of the relationship Andre Harrell had forged with Russell Simmons, Drakoulias migrated from protégé to the standing of respected industry professional in his own right. His nominal A&R role doesn't take account of the creative input he had as producer working alongside each of the groups he signed. They included Minneapolis' Jayhawks, led by songwriters Mark Olsen and Gary Louris. Often held responsible for the growth of alternative country, The Jayhawks, alongside Uncle Tupelo, instilled the once-ridiculed genre with contemporary modulation whilst retaining reverence for its dustbowl songwriting traditions. Adored by critics on both sides of the Atlantic, the current popularity of Americana can be traced back to the group's 1991 Def American début *Hollywood Town Hall*, after which they effectively imploded.

Drakoulias later played a hand on Tom Petty's *Wildflowers* (1994), where he was credited with being "consultant on anything really important" in the liner notes. He has subsequently worked with everyone from Dan Penn to post-grunge acts Screaming Trees and The Afghan Whigs, as well as former Lone Justice singer Maria McKee and British alternative rockers Primal Scream, Ride and Reef. But he's a New York boy at heart and, as You Am I's Timothy Rogers observed, "George Drakoulias had spanokopita sent by his mother in Long Island, sent in freight. He got it delivered to Rick Rubin's house. We were doing vocals there, and Rick Rubin has his own personal chef who was put out because Mrs Drakoulias' five trays of spanokopita took precedence over anything she was making."

Alongside The Black Crowes, the other mainstay of Def American's early years was Danzig, named after its eponymous lead singer. Rubin had long admired Glenn Danzig from his days in legendary hardcore splatter punks the Misfits, whose combination of ghoulish imagery and sonic savagery comprised just about everything Rubin loved in rock music. His interest revived when he saw Samhain, then Danzig's current band, play at the New Music Seminar (Rubin had signed Slayer at the previous year's event) while still working at Def Jam. "He came backstage," Danzig recalled to Steven Blush in *American Hardcore*. "I didn't even know who he was. Here's this guy with a long ZZ Top beard going crazy backstage – I'm like, 'Who the fuck is this guy?' He's telling me people he knows, people who know me." Indeed, while Def American delighted in signing scary acts, nothing was quite as likely to startle as Rubin's own appearance – prodigious hair, sunglasses and facial growth that would have pleased a Grateful Dead camp follower with pro-Taliban sympathies.

Rubin had a vision of the ultimate extreme rock band. To that end he suggested Danzig recruit former DOA, Black Flag and Circle Jerks drummer Chuck Biscuits, rightfully regarded as hardcore's foremost percussionist. The new guitarist was the previously unknown John Christ, who'd been a jazz-playing heavy metal kid at college and hated punk. It was Rubin who persuaded him to come aboard. "After the first audition, I met Rick Rubin and he took me down to Electric Lady studios in Greenwich Village, where Hendrix recorded," remembers Christ. "We talked for a few hours, and after I had hung out in Hendrix's studio for a few hours, I was like, 'I want this gig!' " Retaining bassist Eerie Von, Samhain became Danzig and signed with Rubin. "I was looking for a label," remembers Danzig, "and we had interest from Elektra, Epic, and of course Rubin's label, which was Def Jam at the time. I decided Rubin's label would be the best to go with. That became a whole other nightmare, but he did get the band out there." Rubin's 'perfect' rock band, two parts metal to one part punk, brought Def American consistent success but interminable cat fights.

He also signed another of his former heroes, the drug-addled San Franciscan punk beatniks Flipper, whose 'Sex Bomb' had been the 'Louie Louie' of the mid-Eighties hardcore generation. Indeed, Rubin's first band, Hose, was practically a Flipper tribute band, and supported them on their first New York appearance at the Mudd Club (a gig also attended by The Beastie Boys). Sadly *American Grafishy*, their first studio album in eight years, with John Dougherty replacing the much-missed Will Shatter, failed to restore past glories, though the single 'Flipper Twist' was a hoot. Flipper remained too inherently unstable to deliver the goods.

As well as running Def American, Rubin also worked as a freelance producer. In 1991 he began a fruitful working relationship with funk-rock party animals The Red Hot Chili Peppers. "I remember with the Chili Peppers' *Blood Sugar Sex Magik* album, we rehearsed for that record nine months. We wanted to cut it very quickly, but it was that advance time that really made the record what it was. It's more about working out the details, the transitions, and the arrangements. This way you have a very good draft before you go into the studio, so you're not trying to write the song in the studio."

The sessions were an exercise in catharsis for the band, who had just said goodbye to old friend and original guitarist Hillel Slovak who'd died from a heroin overdose – a loss contemplated on 'My Lovely Man'. Singer Anthony Kiedis was himself trying to kick the habit. "I was a completely dysfunctional self-destructive drug addict and that was a huge failure for me, but what getting off it led me to was the most beautiful feelings in my life and the most beautiful creation of music in my life." It was Rubin who encouraged Kiedis to commit his ballad, 'Under The Bridge', a despairing song about his addiction, to the album, even though it was atypical of the group's sound to that point. It became their biggest single, peaking at number two in the US charts and cementing their status as MTV hombre-perennials.

The Chili Peppers assignation was the first of several projects that won

Rubin praise for kick-starting seemingly moribund careers. "Because they had made either four or five albums before that in their career," Rubin reflected, "and just to take away the feeling that, 'Oh, we're making another album, going into the studio doing the same thing we've done every other time,' we rented this big old house, that was empty, kind of like a haunted house type of thing. We set up everything there, and had the band live there. It was an adventure just making the record. It was different than all of their previous experiences recording. I think there's an energy to it that we wouldn't have gotten had we just gone into a studio the way they had in the past." The results were staggering – *Blood Sugar Sex Magik* sold five million copies while the band's previous four had averaged 500,000 each.

The Chili Peppers have remained loyal to Rubin ever since. "Rick turned out to be the best producer we could ever have hoped to have," Kiedis said in 2001. "He's very intelligent, very emotionally in tune with hardcore, soulful music. He knows how to extrapolate the best and most relaxed natural performance of a band without changing them . . . He makes subtle, little, well-focused, well-thought out changes in the arrangement in songs and basically lays there and lets you do your thing."

A queue began to form for Rubin's services, leaving him to cherry-pick his workload throughout the Nineties. For Mick Jagger's 1993 solo album *Wandering Spirit*, he assembled a stellar cast including Lenny Kravitz and the Chili Peppers' Flea. Most noteworthy, however, was the presence of bass player Doug Wimbish, who'd appeared on all those old school Sugar Hill hits. While a Jagger solo release hardly sets everyone's pulses racing, Rubin again garnered acclaim for getting the best out of his subject – it's widely considered Jagger's finest solo project, even if the competition isn't too hot. However, there were difficulties between the pensionable icon and upstart producer. "We had very different musical tastes," Rubin conceded to the late Ben Fisher. "We were both going in different musical directions a lot of the time. There was some tension. I think Mick is used to being in a tense atmosphere when recording, so to him it was normal. To me, it was kinda weird. I also don't think Mick's used to people telling him what they really think."

Jagger eventually had to make it clear who was in charge of proceedings. "Certain things that he'd wanna do that I didn't like, I'd really make it obvious that I didn't like it, and get all cranky, and he said, 'Look, if you don't like something that I wanna do, just go out and get a veggie burger or something. But don't make everyone feel uncomfortable.' So I started getting a lot of veggie burgers." Barry Rudolph was working on the project. Though the track he engineered, 'Sweet Thing', was eventually rejected, he has one abiding revelation about Rubin during the sessions. "I think I know why Rick wears those dark sunglasses: without them he has the most cherub-like face you could imagine. With them he looks like a tough hombre. Amazing! He knows that in the entertainment biz, it can be all about perceptions. However, he's not that bothered about his celebrity." That's a statement that Rubin concurs with. "I just don't really pay attention too much to the industry. I just make my records and do my own thing. I'm not really part of the Hollywood scene that much. I have a lot of friends who are interested in music for the right reasons. It's not that hard. You just be true to the things you love. If you're really a fan of music, it's easy."

On 27 August 1993, coincidentally the anniversary of Brian Epstein's suicide, Rubin removed 'Def' from American Recordings, giving the prefix an honourable burial with a New Orleans-styled funeral procession to a Hollywood cemetery. The legend 'Def' was placed inside a coffin and interned. All of which served to provide a good news story, but also to distance both American and Rubin from preconceptions about what they did. The prefix was now an anachronism, an echo of an earlier age, and Rubin wanted to situate his label at the cutting edge. And indeed it was. In 1994 Jermey Welt was employed to head the company's website, one of the first at a major label. Featuring streaming audio and artist communities, it also housed the original Ultimate Band List, a concept that grew in popularity during the Nineties and was eventually folded into Artists Direct.

1994 brought another collaboration with a musical veteran Rubin held in high regard, Tom Petty, whose 1989 album *Full Moon Fever* he'd loved. The sessions spanned nearly two years and 30 songs, testimony to both contributors' refusal to rush proceedings. On release it became Petty's best-selling album, achieving triple platinum status thanks to a series of successful singles including 'You Don't Know How It Feels' and 'It's Good To Be A King'. The understated production brought the best out of Petty, undoubtedly one of rock music's great craftsmen, after the over-expansive Jeff Lynne had helmed his two previous releases. The sessions allowed Rubin to meet another of his heroes, Ringo Starr, who drummed on three tracks. "I'm a huge Beatles fan," he enthused. "I was thrilled to be sitting and looking through the window, and seeing him play." If anyone still doubted Rubin's assertion that his role was that of a fan, you need only compare a list of his collaborations with his record

118

collection. It's impossible to escape the impression that, for Rubin, each producer credit on an idol's work is a notch on his bedpost that surpasses the allure of any sexual conquest.

In 1995 he got to match his skills against another of his heroes, Mutt Lange, by working with AC/DC. The veteran Australian rockers completed sessions for 1995's *Ballbreaker* with Rubin in New York but decided the sound quality wasn't satisfactory. Rubin persuaded them to travel to Los Angeles to complete the album. In the process he found a band whose instincts were as perfectionist as his own. Malcolm Young's obsession with getting the optimum guitar tone is a memory that will stay with him. "The first day we worked together he told me that before he came to the studio he tested 100 different Marshall heads before he selected the one that was right for him." A less likely, but ultimately more rewarding Rubin assignation saw him record with neglected British folk troubadour Donovan, a childhood favourite. On 1996's *Sutras* he encouraged his subject to go back to basics. "Like a coach, he would play me my own records and say, 'Write me a song in this style,'" recalls Donovan, an unlikely case for career salvation. But to his credit, the vagaries of hipness have never intruded greatly on Rubin's agenda. He admired Donovan's spiritual purity and ranks *Sutras* among his greatest achievements.

American Recordings, meanwhile, continued to offer succour to the wilful, the fanciful and the commercially untenable. 1996 saw A&R director Dino Paredes sign Chicago's Wesley Willis, fighting off competition from Beastie Boy Mike Diamond's Grand Royal Records. Diamond backed out because he thought recording Willis, a diagnosed schizophrenic with a child's eye view of society, might be seen as disrespectful to the mentally ill. His sagacity was doubtless informed by previous run-ins with the tabloids over The Beastie Boys' 'abuse' of terminally ill kids, though his own claims that he was born without legs, and The Beastie Boys would peddle 'handicap rap' in early interviews hardly constituted moral authority on the subject. Rubin and American were vilified for what some saw as exploitation, a criticism that escalated when Willis' long-term friend and sometime collaborator Dale Meiners told the *Chicago Reader* that American paid Willis only $5,000 per album. As Robert Levine noted: "If American *is* trying to cash in on Willis, the company certainly isn't doing very well at it; Willis' first release for the company in August has sold less than a thousand copies so far."

Of more import in 1996 was Rubin's collaboration with Nusrat Fateh Ali Khan, the beloved Pakistani Qawwali singer, which took place shortly before his death. *The Final Recordings*, completed posthumously after Khan's health failed, saw Rubin win universal praise for the sympathy afforded the singer and his musicians, leading one otherwise impressed world music reviewer to insert a horrified exclamation mark after noting that previous Rubin production subjects included LL Cool J. Rubin would also work with Khan's nephew and successor, Rahat Nusrat Fateh Ali Khan. As Gavin McNett noted: "Rubin has an indisputable talent for wringing the best possible performances out of the artists he works with, and for pushing flattened-out careers over the brink of stardom."

Rubin's greatest achievement came as producer of Johnny Cash's 1996 Grammy Award-winning Country Album of the Year, *Unchained*. His relationship with Cash dated back to 1994 and the solo acoustic set *American Recordings*. Cash had recorded a string of largely unsuccessful albums for PolyGram-owned Mercury Records and was touring in California when Rubin approached his manager, Lou Robin, and suggested a move to American. Cash was bemused, describing his first impression of his prospective label head in his autobiography. "I thought it all pretty unlikely. He [Rubin] was the ultimate hippie, bald on top but with hair down over his shoulders, a beard that looked as if it had never been trimmed (it hadn't), and clothes that would have done a wino proud." Later, though, Cash would compare Rubin to Sam Phillips of Sun Records. Rubin, in turn, reckons Cash is "one of the nicest people I know".

The man in black was won over by Rubin's no-frills approach as he attempted to get back to the essence of Johnny Cash, the artist. "No echo, no slap-back, no overdubbing, no mixing," recalled Cash of their first sessions, "just me playing my guitar and singing. I didn't even use a pick; every guitar note on the album . . . came from my thumb." The sessions were conducted in Rubin's house with the aid of a single microphone and a DAT machine. "He'd made like a hundred albums before we ever worked together," Rubin recalled. "I think somewhere towards, maybe starting in the Eighties, maybe the whole Eighties and some of the Nineties, I think [he] was kind of going through the motions of, 'Oh we're supposed to make another album, so we're going to make one.' But I don't think the care might of went in. So with him, it was more of a matter of us spending time and realising just how important the record should be."

As good as *American Recordings* was, it was *Unchained* that really hit home, partially due to unlikely covers of Soundgarden's 'Rusty Cage',

Danzig's '13' and Nick Cave's 'Mercy Seat', Rubin again proving that disparate musical forces could be reconciled. But then, as Quentin Tarantino noted in the liner notes for Cash's *Love, God, Murder* box set, there was little thematic or moral distance between gangsta rap's "tales of ghetto thug life" and Cash's "tales of backwoods thug life". Indeed, Cash's fatalistic storytelling had already connected with a number of rap practitioners; The Beastie Boys sampled his *Live At Folsom Prison* on *Paul's Boutique*'s 'B-Boy Bouillabaisse', while the title of De La Soul's *3 Feet High And Rising* was inspired by a Johnny Cash song. By the advent of the third chapter in the Cash trilogy, *Solitary Man, American Recordings III*, promoted by Rubin as a collection of material "you'd always wished you could hear Johnny sing", the singer's poor health was beginning to show.

If Johnny Cash and Donovan had been childhood heroes, the Pixies were one of the few contemporary rock acts to catch Rubin's attention during the late Eighties, when he was (supposed to be) preoccupied with rap. Indeed, he had a relationship with group leader Frank Black stretching back to 1988. "I was wondering why this guy I didn't know was calling me at 2 a.m.," recalls Black, of the fan who turned out to be Rubin. Afterwards they stayed in touch, and seven years later Rubin had his opportunity to sign Black after he'd recorded two unsuccessful post-Pixies solo albums for Elektra.

The deal was consummated in bizarre circumstances. Black got another call. "Rick says, 'Hey, I just found out about this UFOlogy meeting happening today. Do you want to go?' So, before I know it, I'm in a hotel banquet room somewhere in Burbank with the head of my new record company, sitting in the middle of 400 people who're talking about their UFO abductions!" Unfortunately *The Cult Of Ray* was not enough to restore Black's standing in the alt-rock community. American passed on his next project, *Frank Black And The Catholics*. "The Catholics tape was what precipitated my battles with American," Black says. "They're obligated under my contract to put it out, but because I opted for a rougher, liver sound, they balked." Early in 1997, American closed briefly as Rubin straightened out his financial problems. That meant the project was further delayed. "It's the usual record company baloney," Black observed at the time. "I'm staring into the trickle down of American Recordings' troubles. I've been talking to Rick Rubin through my lawyer."

More of a name producer than a label magnate, American often took a back seat to Rubin's production roster. Sometimes the two careers overlapped, as on 1998's *Chef Aid: The South Park Album*, which Rubin executive-produced alongside Trey Parker and Matt Stone for American. But not everything on the imprint was a rousing success. Dan Baird, former leader of the Georgia Satellites, recorded *Love Songs For The Hearing Impaired* in 1991, and while charming many critics who appreciate his puritanical rock muse, won over few new fans. Raging Slab's attempts to reconcile blues and country with punk fell between at least two stools, while the Red Devils, a bar band from LA's King King Club, were unable to replicate the fire of their live shows, which won converts including Mick Jagger and David Bowie. Other tax losses included Fresno's Supreme Love Gods, who tried to affect an American Happy Mondays style in a musical climate hardly disposed to club music played on guitars, while Black Sabbath-worshipping Chicago rockers Trouble released a brace of nondescript albums for the imprint in the early Nineties before being dropped.

Of more import were the high-level defections that took place towards the end of the Nineties. Linchpin artist Glenn Danzig finally threw his voodoo dolls out of the cot, prompting a spate of finger-pointing exchanges in interviews, a situation repeated with the label's other key act. The Black Crowes, according to Rich Robinson, were disorientated by American's ownership passing from Geffen to Warners to Columbia. He was less than flattering in his appraisal of Rubin. "When they went to Columbia, really their only bargaining chip was us," he protested. "And so, we just said, 'Hey, we're not really gonna record for Rick again unless you pull us away from him, 'cause we can't stand him.' And so they did. And they assumed our contract from American, but they took Rick out of our daily lives and took any sort of decision-making away from him."

Other bitter comments followed in a *VH1 Behind The Music* special, where the band intimated that Rubin had tried to shape their image against their wishes and taken creative credit for processes he wasn't involved in. "It didn't make me feel good," Rubin confessed to *Rolling Stone*, "but knowing who was saying what and what they're like and what they've said about other people, it's almost like there's nobody safe. So I didn't feel like I was singled out. I've heard the brothers say things about each other that were as unpleasant or worse than what they said about me."

But Robinson's assertion that American was in financial peril was accurate. Other mainstays, such as the post-Bauhaus English goth rockers Love And Rockets, also headed for the exit, as did Skinny Puppy. The latter, one of the more inventive acts spearheading the industrial-rock movement, were caught up in numerous drug-induced personal problems of their own. But that didn't stop them from lambasting Rubin in print after they split up in 1995, just before their intended major label début. Love And Rockets also presented Rubin with a rather nasty leaving gift. They'd invited former Throbbing Gristle member Genesis P-Orridge over to Rubin's Laurel Canyon house, which doubled as a studio, in 1995. P-Orridge was forced to jump from a second-storey window and land on concrete after a fire broke out. He broke ribs, a wrist, and shattered his elbow. A subsequent negligence suit cost Rubin $1.5 million, plus $250,000 interest, after P-Orridge claimed he was now unable to play keyboards or guitar following the injury. "Rubin turned to his insurance company and [they] decided to counter-sue Love And Rockets," David J of the band told *Rolling Stone*. "At the end of the case, we were proved to be innocent, Rick Rubin and American Records were judged responsible, because the house was not approved for commercial use, and Mr. P-Orridge was awarded nearly $2 million in damages. We were left with a big fat bill to pay. But at least we were found not responsible for the fire."

That story doesn't coincide with one told off-the-cuff by Pete Murphy, their former bandmate and friend. "Not wanting to mention names, but somebody was burning candles to 'get the vibe up', and they burned the studio down, apparently." Whatever the truth of the situation, it was very un-punk rock of Rubin's house guests to sue, especially seeing as Genesis was at that time on the run from (entirely false) charges of child abuse which kept him out of the UK. Add the fact that the mansion formerly belonged to Harry Houdini and you have all the elements of a TV mini-series.

By July 1997 Rubin had moved his operation to Sony's Columbia division rather than pursue a new deal with Warners, and was therefore out of jail financially. The first artist he signed to the new deal was System Of A Down. "The thing about Rick," recalls bass player Shavo Odadajian, "even when we had doubts about signing with American, he still came to our shows as a fan; in fact, he even came to our show in New York (at the CMJ convention) when we were falsely labelled as Universal/Cherry recording artists. Rick really believed in us and seemed to have a special interest in our music."

Rubin the producer, meanwhile, is still going strong. Recently he executive-produced Macy Gray's *The Id* and worked with Neil Young and has worked with former members of Rage Against The Machine and Soundgarden. There was even a bit part on Spice Girl Mel C's solo début, though an intended collaboration with Limp Bizkit lasted barely a week before the sessions were halted. He regularly juggles about ten projects at any one time, though he now dedicates several hours a day to yoga and meditation, having long since studied Eastern theology and become a vegetarian. In 2001 he recorded an album of Hindu devotional chanting, or *naam raam*, with 50-something celebrity magnet Krishna Das, friend and spiritual advisor to the likes of Madonna and Sting. Conversely, or perhaps appropriately given Rubin's love of contrast, he also owns the franchise for a Southern wrestling circuit.

Despite everything he's witnessed over the last 20 years, Rubin still believes in the same essential methodology. "I always wanted to take music down to its most basic and purest form," he once said, and that continues to hold true. To that end, the Krishna Das sessions represented music that was as rock'n'roll to Rubin as the System Of A Down album he interrupted to record it. "It's no different than when the Beatles sang about love," he told *Pulse* magazine. "Those are devotional songs. That's the reason why, 35 years later, they're still number one. It's their ability to connect. Music that has that spiritual connection in it appeals to people, whether they recognise that's the reason or not."

As someone who believes in karma, Rubin must have been thoroughly amused by the summer 2001 announcement that American Recordings was moving once again – and this time it was joining Universal's Island/ Def Jam Music Group, headed by Lyor Cohen. Universal/Vivendi had purchased Columbia's 50 per cent stake and thereby secured the label's entire catalogue and roster, which at that time featured the Jayhawks, as well as Slayer, Johnny Cash and new signings Saul Williams and American Head Charge, with the exception of System Of A Down, who were retained by Columbia. But the fact that Def Jam and American were bonded together revealed nothing more sinister than the machinations of a hopelessly centralised music industry, whose control of the distribution of America's art needs to be checked, or better, challenged. Hopefully by another dorm-based kid with the balls and the beats to take on the world.

8

Business As Usual

"Def Jam in the Eighties was the most reliable label, it found a way to allow artists expression and creative control, first and foremost, and still wind up selling like a million, two million records. And that is so rare. And it's so rare that a label in the Eighties or the Nineties that puts out rap records could be as dependable as Def Jam was."

— DJ Bobbito

LL Cool J, The Beastie Boys, Public Enemy – by the late Eighties, often cited as 'the golden age', Def Jam was undoubtedly the pre-eminent label in hip hop. But this was rap's most artistically fertile period, and Def Jam also signed three more unique, groundbreaking acts – Slick Rick, EPMD and 3rd Bass.

Ricky Walters was born in Wimbledon in 1965 to Jamaican parents. The family moved to America in 1972, chasing the land of opportunity carrot, though their son never quite lost his accent. The family washed up in the Bronx four years later. Walters started hanging out with local B-boys the Kangol Crew, named after the famed hip hop headwear. The group, organised around studies at La Guardia College of Music and Art, featured four guys and two girls, including later rap star Dana Dane. They traded rhymes together and had their own distinct uniform, comprising shirts, ties and the hats that gave them their name. Walters started wearing the eye patch that became his visual signature. As Ricky D, he competed in venues like the Funhouse and the Roxy, with a style predicated on traditional party themes, but occasionally introducing harsher narratives and more vulgar vernacular.

The most memorable of his early efforts was 'La Di Da Di', which eventually migrated to vinyl when released in 1985 as a double A-side with 'The Show'. The record was credited to the Get Fresh Crew, after Walters teamed up with Doug E Fresh, the self-styled human beatbox.

The song married bawdy humour with reassurances that the protagonist was not here "to cause trouble", and introduced Walters' unreconstructed English accent. Both tracks blew up in New York. The end of 'La Di Da Di', in which Walters dismisses the enticements of the mother of one fan with a put-down of her "wrinkled pussy", established the comic-nasty agenda which he'd pursue over subsequent recordings.

Doug E. Fresh was signed to Reality Records, but the union with Walters was never permanent and they parted in 1988. Ricky D became Slick Rick (one of the names he was addressed as in 'The Show'), signing to Def Jam after both Rick Rubin and Lyor Cohen decided he warranted headlining status in his own right. "At the time other labels were interested in me, so I went and did my own thing," Slick recalls of his time with the Get Fresh Crew. "Plus, there was money conflicts. I wasn't too into it for the money, but I felt I wasn't being dealt with fairly so I went my own way. We're still friendly, but I didn't grow up with Doug E. Fresh, I met him at a club." The only problem was that the initial negotiations between Rubin, Simmons and Walters had to take place in a mental ward, where Walters had been consigned after partaking of a little too much angel dust. Warning signs that Simmons and Cohen chose to ignore.

Slick wasn't an immediate success for Def Jam – the sessions for his début album took close on 18 months, in which time he'd completed only one track he was content with – 'The Ruler', produced by Jam Master Jay. In the end Public Enemy's Bomb Squad came in and wrapped the project up within 10 days, though Rick was canny enough to keep production credit on five of the songs. Released in 1988, *The Great Adventures Of Slick Rick* featured the hits 'Mona Lisa' and 'Hey Young World' and sold 1.5 million copies. While critics rebuked the author for 'Treat Her Like A Prostitute', Robert Christgau dismissing the album as the creation of a "man [who] hates women", there was more to Slick Rick's appeal than blunt, misinformed misogyny. The keynote track was 'Children's Story', a prophetic tale of youth going off the rails, with Rick Menello's Keystone Cops meets Bugsy Malone video being one of rap's finest early promo clips. 'Children's Story' had supporters proclaiming him as rap's finest natural lyricist, though both Rakim and Chuck D may have had something to say about that.

His reportage, always too engaged with events to be simply voyeuristic, was rooted in what he claimed were everyday experiences, establishing a defence plea that has been much abused by rappers since. Few, however, equalled his ability to build narratives that married grim authenticity with humour. "It was like back in the day when there was no TV and people listened to the radio," he recalled to *HHC*. "You would have to visualise everything with the help of sound effects to help you see. I just put that to a hip hop flavour. It's a state of mind where you want to rap and compete to see who's the best, most complex rapper. Then there's the other side where you take your idea and thoughts and go different places, and you put your vision onto paper." But what really differentiated Slick Rick was his easy, unhurried, uniquely accented flow as an MC, a sing-song, intuitively melodic style which greatly impacted on later practitioners, Snoop Dogg (who covered 'La Di Da Di' on *Doggystyle*) and Notorious B.I.G. He was frequently described by Simmons as "the rapper's rapper" and widely celebrated as the *de facto* urban storyteller, preferring matter-of-fact narration over metaphor and simile. But bad luck and bad choices interrupted his ascent.

The problems started in 1990, after completing tours with De La Soul and LL Cool J to promote *The Great Adventures Of Slick Rick*. He hired his cousin Mark Plummer as a bodyguard, whom Rick claims "got greedy and wanted more". Summary justice was meted out. "I have relatives that are from Jamaica and I was trying to put everybody that was in the family under the business. Mark Plummer was like a bad seed in the family, he made his living doing illegal business. To make a long story short, he wanted to take my belongings from me and that's what led to the whole ruckus. He was having other people do it on his behalf so it wouldn't look like he was doing anything. And when they failed the word got out Mark was really behind all the stuff and eventually he was fired. From that point, he just wanted to have me robbed. I was wearing a lot of jewellery, so that's instant cash. So he was trying to have me robbed and intimidated."

Walters' jeep was shot up outside a club and he considered Plummer the prime suspect. "I was kinda scared at the time because I knew what to expect from this guy," reckons Rick. "I knew he already had a reputation of robbing and killing. That was the kind of bad seed I was involved with. And me not being the type with no killer mentality, I'm confronting someone who doesn't give an 'f'. So I felt I had to beat this person at their own game. I got a gun and prepared for the final confrontation."

He was shopping in the Bronx in July 1990 with the mother of his son to be, when he spotted his adversary at a known drugs spot. He reacted by shooting at Plummer – a doubly reckless act given his partner's condition.

And his aim wasn't much better than his judgement. A bystander, Wilbert Henry, received gunshot injuries in the foot. Plummer himself was hit in the leg and thigh. After crashing his car into a tree during the subsequent high-speed police chase, Slick was found guilty of attempted murder and two lesser felonies. The sentence was three and a third to ten years in prison (the police found no less than six firearms in the trunk of his car). His lavish lifestyle was instantly forfeited for a humble cell at the Bronx House of Detention, the first of several penitentiaries he'd inhabit, including the Gouveneur Correctional Facility on the Canadian border. Accidental victim Wilbert Henry supported his petition for parole after agreeing a financial settlement on his civil suit for damages. While Rick was in prison, Plummer was shot and killed in 1992 in the Bronx after allegedly beating a man's wife and stealing her husband's valuables. But that was little solace to his incarcerated cousin.

Def Jam and Russell Simmons did what they could to help their new star. Bill Adler set up the 'Free Slick Rick' campaign, which garnered thousands of signatures and letters of support from fans (though quite what the justification for his release was, given the nature of his crimes, is a mystery to this writer). Simmons posted an $800,000 bail bond in 1991 to allow him to cut a new record. On a hectic work schedule, anticipating a long, unproductive stay in the slammer, he recorded five videos and 21 new songs. These formed the basis of *The Ruler's Back*. Ultimately, however, the album betrayed the haste of its construction and the lack of supervision from the artist, such a key ingredient on the protracted sessions that produced his début.

Still, Simmons was keen to make the most of his investment in Rick – especially given that his run-in with the law lent him added kudos in the post-NWA rap market. In 1993, due to his 'impeccable' behaviour, the New York State parole board assigned Rick a work release programme to allow him to complete a new album. He sifted through the leftovers from those 1991 sessions to put together *Behind Bars*, whose title suggested Simmons didn't exactly intend to downplay Slick's predicament. But five months later the parole board interjected, deciding that he'd shown "no remorse" for his crimes. As a result he wasn't able to supervise properly the finishing touches applied to the album.

At this point he contacted Simmons, their conversation within prison confines recorded in the 1994 film *The Show* – ironically also the title of the single that first brought Slick Rick to public prominence. On the drive to the facility, Simmons betrays his own discomfort with the situation. "I don't wanna come visit no rappers in jail. I'm saying, for what? You sold a million-two. I'm not no role model or nothing, I'm not trying to be. But if you got all that success . . . I always tell artists it's all right to be real. Real is – everybody says I wish I got to where you got. If I got to where you got, I wouldn't be throwing no guns in nobody's faces or robbing nobody, or none of that. If someone got a beef with me, believe me, they can go. I'm only going to see Ricky because of the movie. That's the only reason."

This instructive soliloquy continues as Simmons passes through the prison gates. "I'm 37 years old, I want to travel round the world, chase famous models. I'm always going to be ghetto, I'm too old not to be. I'm who I am, but I'm not broke, so I don't have to throw no guns in nobody's faces for nothing. I don't even wanna see no guns . . . I don't want nobody near me with no kind of drama. The only drama I want is Naomi Campbell."

After Simmons updates him about the progress and release date of *Behind Bars*, he informs his charge that people are still "waiting for your music", before delivering a lecture, which you can't help but think is for the benefit of the camera. "Kids, they've got this gift, they make these records, they get success. Instead of taking that success and doing the right thing, a lot of them take that success as a green light to go to hell and do all the wrong shit. That to me is a shock, but I keep seeing it more and more." The discussion is interspersed with earlier footage of Rick at the height of his pre-incarceration arrogance. Now, he is more thoughtful. "The world is bugging out as it is, you know, brothers are just talking all type of mad stuff, that's the way they feel like expressing themselves. But then when they have their shows and stuff, they have to live up to that image."

It was only in 1998 that, finally free of incarceration, Rick was able to deliver *The Art Of Storytelling*. "I wanted to reintroduce the art form by making an album that included many different variations of stories and rap styles," he mused. Collaborators included Snoop Dogg, Big Boi of OutKast, Nas and Raekwon of the Wu-Tang Clan, a testament to the breadth of his influence. But his prison stay had short-changed fans. His powers had not waned as such, but they definitely belonged to a different era. At least he had learned some lessons. "Everybody is not street, even the hardest artist has a soft spot." His child was born while he was in jail, and that prompted a more sober outlook. "I don't promote the ra-ra non-sense. I'd rather say you've just got to grow out of it. Sooner or later, when you get old like me and shit, you've got to think about family, and house and raising kids and happily ever after. Sooner or later, we all get old."

In September 2000 Slick Rick donated the throne he employed on his 1989 US tour to an exhibition, *Hip-Hop Nation: Roots, Rhymes, and Rage*, at the Brooklyn Museum of Art. The curators can probably mothball it for now: Slick doesn't look like he'll be needing it anytime soon.

In his absence EPMD had become Def Jam's pre-eminent 'keep it real' artisans. Erick Sermon and Parrish Smith were using Zapp and P-Funk bass lines long before Dr Dre made an industry out of doing so. Operating in a stylistic cul-de-sac, they did so with such flair it was easy to overlook their reliance on patchwork samples, un-modulated delivery and a limited worldview – the topics of their songs rarely moving beyond those classic rap staples; women-chasing and money-making. In keeping with this thematic imprint, their name was an acronym for Eric and Parrish Making Dollars. But though the "two cats in fishermen's hats" were never intuitive MCs in the manner of Slick Rick or Rakim, with whom they shared an aloofness when they stepped to the microphone, their wordplay was clever, playful and often startlingly incisive. Most of all it was 'real', as in the concept pioneered but later abandoned by Run-DMC. As Smith put it, "Hip hop should just be straight-up rawness, grit, street." Witness 'Crossover', their biggest hit commercially, taken from 1992's *Business Never Personal*, which berates rappers for switching to R&B as "brothers sellin' their soul to go gold".

Nevertheless, EPMD themselves had a thing about filthy lucre, reflected in their choice of album titles. "EPMD is a business," confessed Parrish. "We market ourselves like a business, and it works fine that way." Their endless deliberations on the practicalities of remuneration over old funk grooves were an obvious precursor to gangsta rap, as well as later Def Jam artists such as Jay-Z. And those who didn't note that the Notorious B.I.G. modelled his action on Erick Sermon's stuttering enunciation are missing a page in their text book. Ironically, their worship of Roger Troutman's Zapp and George Clinton's Parliament, and their elongated travelogues annotating the hustler lifestyle, led many to believe they were from California. In turn they became one of the most sampled acts in hip hop. Pop may eat itself, but rap dines out on its own flesh on a weekly basis. Hence EPMD's chops were revived on huge hits such as Warren G's 'I Shot The Sheriff', DMX's 'Get At Me Dog' and Jay-Z's 'Ain't No Nigga'. All three were Def Jam releases.

Raised in Long Island suburb Brentwood, the duo began collaborating after Smith had already released a 1987 single for Tommy Boy as DJ with Rock Squad. The début EPMD recording, 'It's My Thing', was cut in three hours and despatched to various labels. Chrysalis licensed the song, before EPMD signed to Sleeping Bag Records and released their début album, *Strictly Business*. It went gold on the strength of the title-track, also released on single, and the classic 'You Gots 2 Chill' – recently voted the greatest song of all time in *The Source*'s 100th issue.

Their début was followed by *Unfinished Business* in 1989, before Sleeping Bag went belly up and Simmons bought out their contract. EPMD quickly got their feet under the table. 1990's *Business As Usual* featured a fantastic house-warming collaboration with LL Cool J, 'Rampage', and a somewhat less appetising put-down of women who go after men's assets post-divorce in 'Gold Digger'. *Business Never Personal*, which included two of their most authoritative statements in 'Headbanger' and 'Crossover', was the last in a quartet of albums that are still revered throughout hip hop circles – though few would contest that their finest work came prior to their tenure at Def Jam. Despite their hardcore reputation, it was only on their Def Jam début that they began to use curse words, Parrish admitting: "For our third album, in order for that kid who was having problems to understand the cassette, we had to go low. We had to go down to a level where he's at." Otherwise, as Havelock Nelson surmised in his review for *Rolling Stone*, they weren't doing much different, but that wasn't the point. "EPMD does what it does very well, thank you, and a large part of the group's musical magnetism is owed to how Erick and Parrish manage to run the same formula – a funky joyride through a gangster-fantasy universe – without running it into the ground."

They also unveiled their extended family, a practice which later became the new orthodoxy for rap artists who'd made it and wanted to demonstrate their largesse and pay their dues. EPMD's Hit Squad comprised K-Solo, Keith Murray, Redman (who featured on *Business Never Personal*'s Joe Pesci-namechecking 'Headbanger') and double-time tongue twisters Das-EFX, who initially overshadowed the other Hit Squad members. Redman later became a high-profile Def Jam client in his own right. However, in 1992 EPMD split over money issues, despite desperate attempts to heal the wounded egos involved. Run-DMC, Russell Simmons and then platinum-selling Hit Squad members Das-EFX all issued public statements encouraging the former partners to heal the rift. "I understand where they're all coming from," said Sermon, "but I want them to know it wasn't something we were planning to do. It wasn't a publicity stunt, it was just something that happened, something personal happened between us. There's no way to mend it so fast. It'd been going on for a long time." Chris Lighty led Def Jam's mourners: "They're better as a team. They were very hot. They'd just put out Redman and Das-EFX. It looked like they were going to be the Baby Face & Reid of rap. Everybody misses EPMD."

Both Sermon (1993's *No Pressure*) and Smith (1994's *Shadé Business*) released solo albums. Sermon, who titled his album due to misinformed perceptions that he was the duo's weak link, had a dig at his former partner on 'Stay Real', itself a minor hit for Def Jam. The label passed on Smith, and he took his underwhelming album to RCA instead. Sermon also enjoyed success as a songwriter working with, amongst others, George Clinton and Ice Cube. The duo reformed in 1997, releasing *Back In Business*, followed two years later by *Out Of Business*. Both did well, without scaling previous heights. The warmth afforded their comeback was tribute both to the substantial fan base they had acquired and their prevailing influence on the culture.

It's sad, but you can't talk about 3rd Bass, one of Def Jam's most technically brilliant acts, without bringing the race issue to the table. By the late Nineties, when white rappers MC Serch (Michael Berrin) and Pete Nice (Peter Nash) were on the comeback trail, questions on that subject elicited caustic treatment from the veterans. In response to an interviewer on *Sonicnet*, the ever droll Serch posited: "I personally believe that Marion Jones is the fastest woman on Earth. And if you wanna talk about Michael Johnson? I'll tell you, that motherfucker is quick. That's what I think about the race issue."

Initially, 3rd Bass, named after their first composition '3 The Hard Way', did their best to behave as if accusations of race theft didn't perturb them. Both grew up in areas where black culture dominated. Nice, a formidable basketball player, attended high school in South Floral Park, before affecting a statesman-like demeanour accompanied by a walking stick and Havana cigars. Serch, the son of a trained opera singer, was an authentic wordsmith, citing James Joyce and Arthur Rimbaud among his influences, who'd grown up in the Hammel and Redfern communities of Rockaway. After perfecting his rhymes in the cafeteria of the High School of Music and Art, Serch recorded a solo single for Warlock, 'Melissa', then switched to another famed old school

132

imprint, Idlers. Serch and Nice eventually met while hanging outside Latin Quarters, the Manhattan club frequented by The Beastie Boys with a reputation for great music but also regular violent muggings. They clashed immediately. But their mutual acquaintance, producer Sam Sever, believed they should work together.

Lyor Cohen offered them parking lot space with Def Jam after they'd won over his boss. Serch's recollection of meeting Russell Simmons goes something like this. "It was the summer of '88, the club was The World, and I was the only white boy in the house [Simmons, if he'd had any sense, should have been alerted to the potential of any unattached white boy in a black enclave by now]. Russell was by the bar, Newport in one hand, mix drink in the other. I spout some street jargon and begin to James Brown across the floor into his focus. Russell looked at me a little confused, and I said to him, 'I'm the next kid on Def Jam to get you paid.'"

Their song 'Steppin' To The A.M.', originally intended for Eric B and Rakim, provided their début hit. Produced by Keith and Hank Shocklee of Public Enemy's Bomb Squad, it became a summer anthem in 1989, and featured samples of no less than three Def Jam artists – The Beastie Boys, Public Enemy and Slick Rick. It announced *The Cactus Album*, which also housed Prince Paul-produced single 'The Gas Face', whose 'Elroy' reference was actually a nod to Cohen. The rather less flattering MC Hammer references had the loon-panted one's posse threatening extreme repercussions, a potentially ugly situation averted by Russell Simmons personal intervention.

By 1991's *Derelicts Of Dialect*, another gold album, the uneasy relationship between Serch and Nice was beginning to unravel, though producer Prince Paul has fond memories of the sessions. "Working with 3rd Bass is pretty wild. Serch would run up and act a fool. Do spins on the ground and crack corny jokes. Pete Nice, he did this impersonation of Colonel Sanders, putting masking tape on his face to make a beard. That was kind of awkward, 'cause he's usually so cool."

By exaggerating their distance from other white interlopers, 3rd Bass did as much as anyone to pigeonhole themselves by reacting with a zealot's outrage at what they saw as inauthentic pop-rappers. The Beastie Boys and Hammer had already been cudgelled before they performed their ultimate diss on *Derelict*'s Vanilla Ice-baiting, Pete Gabriel-sampling 'Pop Goes The Weasel' (the accompanying video featured them beating up on a Vanilla Ice impersonator played by Black Flag's Henry Rollins).

Once the duo had imploded, Serch pursued a career as an opinionated and outspoken A&R rep for Wild Pitch, leaving 3rd Bass to be remembered as the white rap duo who hated white rappers more than anyone in the black community. In justification, Serch posted this on Davey D's bulletin board in the late Nineties. "I can only speak for myself when I say that we went after the ones who we thought were violating the culture. Both Pete and myself dissed the Beasties because they came out first with Latin Quarter bangers and then went on to pour beers on themselves and tour with dangerous animal bands. We felt that we were in it for the streets and that was our angle. We later realized that they are innovators and we were short sided in many of our positions and we kept it moving. Everlast [formerly of 'shamrock rappers' House Of Pain] never came into that fold because he was down with the syndicate and was street, just LA not NY, hence why he did not get dissed. We had personal beef but that was ego and not skill. I look at that as embarrassing for myself as well. We all need to eat humble pie as long as we can still back it up with skills . . . I love that Em [Eminem] brings it 'cause he wants it as much as any MC from our era wanted it. Fuck everyone, bring it. But notice that me and Pete never get mentioned. It is because we worked hard for the values that Em and some others savour still in this culture. We all don't go after each other, it's just that the ones that want to be the best will always fight those who think they can take us down."

The altogether less complicated Nice 'N' Smooth were brought aboard by A&R man Jordan Wild, the son of singer Helen Reddy. Old school beat-boxer Greg Nice (Greg Mays) and Smooth Bee (Daryl Barnes) belonged to an earlier tradition of block park parties and throwdowns. Their freestyle-honed raps graduated from the Strange Family independent label after the duo achieved significant radio play by dint of personally distributing début single 'Skill Trade' to New York record shops in 1987. Following an introduction by Boogie Down Productions' Scott La Rock, they released a début album for Sleeping Bag that did good business after the single 'Funky For You' took off. But after the label filed for bankruptcy leaving them penniless, Russell Simmons pounced, as he had done with EPMD, and convinced them to drop the awful suits and dressed them instead in Timberland threads. The result was 1991's *Ain't A Damn Thing Changed*, and their best single, 'Hip Hop Junkies'. The video featured friend and later hip hop big cheese Fat Joe, and a Spanish-language version was released. 'Sometimes I Rhyme Slow', meanwhile, was underpinned by a sample of Tracy Chapman's 'Fast Car', and hit number one on the rap charts early in 1992. They also contributed 'Cash In My Hand' to John Singleton's *Poetic Justice* and collaborated on Gang Starr's single 'Dwyck'.

A third album *Jewel Of The Nile*, featured collaborations with Bobby Brown (for whom Barnes had written lyrics and later sued for non-accreditation), Slick Rick, Everlast of House of Pain and K-Ci of Jodeci. But Nice 'N' Smooth faded quickly, largely because they operated in an obsolete dimension too closely implied by their name. Blame too Greg Nice's not-destined-for-longevity lyrics on cuts such as 'How To Flow' ("Found out she liked to eat noodles/For her birthday, I bought her a French Poodle").

Def Jam's late Eighties and early Nineties output had been practically flawless, as DJ Bobbito, who worked for the label during the period, notes. "He [Simmons] put out LL in '85, The Beastie Boys in '86, Public Enemy '87, Slick Rick in '88, '89 was 3rd Bass, then '90 was EPMD and Nice 'N' Smooth. So for six years they were putting out joints, and every single one of those records was either going gold or platinum, or double platinum."

Like many Def Jam graduates, including Dante Ross, he started out as a humble messenger, but then benefited from Simmons' fast track promotion regime, one of the rare meritocracies in the music industry. He was working in promotions within three months, then became an A&R representative two months later. He found Simmons' management style to be open, frank, and receptive to opinions. A family atmosphere that he'd also created at Rush, which boasted its own all-star basketball team featuring Bill Adler, LL, Andre Harrell and others, prevailed. "Russell was very loyal to his artists and the people that he worked with," reckons Bobbito. "He was very personable. You could see him in a club and sit down, have him check out girls, and you'd be in an office with him the next day. That always made an impression upon me. I liked how he always appreciated my honesty. The first meeting I ever went to as a messenger, LL Cool J's *Walking With A Panther* was about to drop, and the first single was 'I'm That Type Of Guy', which I thought sucked. I thought it was wack . . . So everyone's talking about – 'that's dope, that's dope, that's dope . . .' I raised my hands – I know no one's really asking my opinion, but I was like: 'Yo, if I heard that on the radio, I wouldn't even tape it, in fact I'd change my radio station. I think the record is wack.' And Russell looked at me, this little kid talking, but he respected me. And afterwards he always asked my opinion, because he knew he'd get an honest response from me."

135

One of the few artists to be signed personally by Russell Simmons was Nichele Strong, or Nikki D, the first woman to be awarded a contract with the label. She'd made her name by working with Ice-T in her native Los Angeles, but moved to New York in 1986 and initially had to sleep in the World Trade Center while trying to make ends meet. She eventually hitched a ride with the L.A. Posse while they were working on LL's *Bigger And Deffer*, and persuaded them to produce a demo tape for her, which won over Simmons.

Her first recording was a cameo on Alyson Williams' 'My Love Is So Raw' before her own début, 'Lettin' Off Steam', produced by Sam Sever. *Daddy's Little Girl* followed in 1991. The title-track, a feisty pro-abortion narrative which sampled the popular DNA remix of Suzanne Vega's 'Tom's Diner', topped the rap charts for two weeks in the spring of 1991. But she then switched to Queen Latifah's Flavor Unit Records (though she stayed on Simmons' books at Rush) and lost momentum. She enjoyed little further success, despite forming the Underdogs – a female MC group and support unit – with Heather B and Lady of Rage in 1998.

After a period of unchecked growth, by the turn of the Nineties things were looking a little sticky for Def Jam. First, NWA, Dr Dre and their gun-toting ilk had seduced hip hop fans away with their misanthropic urban 'realism'. Meanwhile Def Jam was beginning to have problems with Sony. Simmons had renegotiated their deal in 1988, giving up 50 per cent of Def Jam in return for money to expand its staff and marketing, and access to Sony's infrastructure. Sony in turn insisted that Def Jam review its internal organisation so that its structure matched that of the parent company. The internal reshuffle was conducted by Carmen Ashhurst, a former film-maker and activist who'd originally been recruited as Bill Adler's assistant and quickly rose to become president of the label by 1990.

The new deal was basically a production contract, which meant that Sony ran the risks in terms of product but kept most of the potential rewards. It allowed Simmons to set up RAL (Rush Associated Labels), though the indulgence of artists (including Chuck D, Jam Master Jay and Ed Lover of *Yo! MTV Raps*) in effective vanity publishing exercises proved to be a financial disaster. Several promising acts were stymied in the confusion, while established Def Jam stars had their fingers burned when their deals were eventually squashed. In addition, the start-up costs pushed Def Jam deep into the red.

The saddest example was Dew Doo Man Records, Prince Paul's imprint, which spent a protracted period of time going nowhere, cost both parties a fortune and turned one of the nicest guys in hip hop into a near depressive. The irony was that it was never Prince Paul's idea in the first place. He'd been approached by Cohen and Simmons after De La Soul's *3 Feet High And Rising* made him one of the hottest producers in rap. "I was like, quote, this up-and-coming producer that crossed a lot of quirky rap over to pop audiences," Prince Paul recounts of their overtures, "[and they were] pricing dollar signs, ching ching . . . 'Paul, do this label. We have RAL, whatever you want to call it.' I said, 'No, I don't want to do it.' I just want to produce records. I'm just so happy, I was like a really naive kid, I want to produce records, don't want to do nothing else. Then I was getting the calls at the house: 'Paul, why don't you think about doing the label?' 'No, I don't want to do the label.' At the time I had Russell managing me, and then my lawyer starts calling me: 'Russell's calling me up and wants to know if you want to do the label.' So I'm like, 'OK, I'll do the label, fine.' "

So he dutifully set about rounding up some neighbourhood friends, including Resident Alien and Mic Tee Lux, before producing a series of demos. According to Prince Paul, Simmons thought they were "dope" and green-lighted the project. But when it came to releasing the records he demurred, which hit Paul straight in the pocket because he'd financed most of the recording costs and had been turning down other production work in the meantime. "I just lost a whole lot of time and when everything was said and done, it was like, I got jerked. You know what I'm saying, it wasn't Russell's fault. I mean I could get mad at him all day, but I was just dumb and young and I just went, crawled [out] under the pressure."

With Simmons starting to explore TV deals and other media outlets, several members of Def Jam's staff were concerned that the label was being left behind in a rapidly evolving marketplace. Though Public Enemy went platinum and 3rd Bass and EPMD gold in 1991, their sales were outstripped by those of NWA's *Efil4zaggin*, Heavy D, Ice Cube and pop-rappers Kriss Kross and Hammer. Def Jam was in grave danger of losing its status as a market leader, and surrendering the sales that any product bearing its name once guaranteed. Which is where Lyor Cohen stepped in, stressing the importance of re-establishing Def Jam as a brand. Its reputation had been forged, after all, by unique artists who set their own agendas rather than chasing the latest trend. Def Jam badly needed some genuine pace-setters rather than production line R&B vocalists or second generation LL-wannabes to claw its way back. Luckily, Newark's

Redman had deranged charm in buckets.

Reggie Noble aka Redman, aka Funk Doctor Spock, was spotted by A&R executive Tracey Waples after guesting on EPMD's *Business As Usual* posse cut 'Headbanger' as a member of the Hit Squad (he'd also checked in on Hurricane G's 'Tonight's Da Night'). He made his solo bow in 1992 with *Whut? Thee Album*, though EPMD's concurrent split may have stifled its rightful impact. Produced by close buddy Erick Sermon, with whom Noble lived for a couple of years pre-fame, the album announced Noble's out-there personality and propensity for the comic-absurd aside – he seemed able to convey a lifetime of experience in a single stanza. Both his advocacy and intake of marijuana, meanwhile, rivalled that of Cypress Hill. "It's not important for me to get blunted," he insisted. "It's just that I like to get high. I handle my business in the day and get fucked up at night."

A succession of albums including *Dare Iz A Darkside* (1994), *Muddy Waters* (1996), *Doc's Da Name 2000* (1998) and *Malpractice* (2000), proved how well he managed that trick, even if he did miss the odd deadline. Each achieved gold sales or better while establishing Redman as the most satisfying of the new breed of MCs, his surreal preoccupations and steady-rolling delivery beautifully framed by Sermon's head-bobbing, bruised funk, which occasionally equalled his best work with EPMD. He was also one of the most adept 'skitters' in rap, a pastime introduced by De La Soul that others explored to largely dreadful effect. Funniest was his Uncle Quilly characterisation of an old-skool know-it-all who wasn't about to give props to these greenhorns. Gold records are all very well, but arguably his greatest honour came when he was featured on the cover of the pro-cannabis legalisation, counter-culture magazine *High Times*. The fact that he's not actually pro-legalisation aside, they couldn't have picked a harder working advocate of the weed. "I'll smoke anywhere, as long as it's comfortable and the police aren't around. I smoke when I'm brushing my teeth, and rinse my mouth out with smoke when I'm done."

Sure, Noble's not a great one for progression. As he stated in 2001, "I'm sticking to the same format, and I ain't changin'. It's the only thing I know, man. I ain't gonna venture off into something I don't know anything about and then lose it, so I got to stick to what I know." But anyone who can give us lyrics like "I sparkly like Colgate/My dick's name machete/I stab much hoe-cake" ('Watch Yo Nuggets') or "When Reggie Noble's sprung, we stick nuns that got funds/Bomb niggaz like they did in Oklahoma" ('Case Closed') is hard to take entirely seriously.

Meanwhile, a more direct riposte to the east coast gangsta phenomenon was being readied by Def Jam. If Compton and Oaktown could thug it out, so could New York City, reasoned Sticky Fingaz, Suave Sonny Seeza, Fredro Star and Big DS, the quartet comprising hardcore rough-necks Onyx. Formerly a Jamaica, Queens breakdance troupe, they were signed and groomed by Jam Master Jay, who had just launched his own Def Jam-affiliated JMJ imprint, following a brief stay with Profile. *Bacdafucup* was released in 1993 after the group splattered itself all over the sidewalk with 'Throw Ya Gunz In The Air', a macho inversion of the old DJ imperative to get busy on the dancefloor. The album went platinum after a second single 'Slam', which sampled The Mohawks' 'Champ', did just what it said on the tin. When Def Jam took the video to MTV they were told it was way too scary, which infuriated Simmons, who couldn't see the difference between it and the alt-rock groups the station was only too happy to give air time to.

Onyx were the first hip hoppers to colonise rock's moshpit, especially after a remix version of 'Throw Ya Gunz In The Air' was given a new twist by metal extremists Biohazard – the sort of terrain you'd more readily associate with Rubin's American Recordings. Which could also be said for the low-rent, post-*Porkies* sexual bragging on their infamous 'Black Vagina Finda'. All were set in a musical context they christened 'grimy'. The best things about Onyx, however, were their visuals – from their all-black dress code and crew cuts to their video posturing and distinctive logo, an appropriation of Milton Glaser's 'I love New York' heart sub-verted by a decidedly non-smiley expression. All of which readily con-veyed their ethos of cartoon malevolence. Unlike his English namesake, Fredro Star and company were not here to eat your hamsters; it was your babies they had designs on.

After they ditched Big DS as well as Jam Master Jay's production wizardry, they were never the same proposition. *All We Got Iz Us* (1995) and *Shut Em Down* (1998) were the dying embers of a one-trick career. The former album in particular upped the violent black/white rhetoric with its exhortation to "point the guns in the right direction", and came up with the mathematically indisputable logic that if blacks killed enough whites, hey, blacks would be the majority ('2 Wrongs'). Similarly 'Ghetto Mentalitee' was as wrong-headed as it was wrong-spelt. Its dubious lyric, "Fight, a nigger and a white, if the nigger don't win then we all jump in," actually paraphrased an old 1993 rhyme from the equally repugnant Apache.

Sticky Fingaz, who once assaulted a fellow flight passenger who asked him to turn his walkman down, didn't exactly ooze the milk of human kindness. "The world is doomed. You're doomed. You're a walking corpse. Me, too. To me, truthfully, life is a big waste of time." Nevertheless, he did pluck up enough motivation to have a stab at a solo career, while various former Onyx members took to acting. Their enduring legacy can be felt in the testosterone-fuelled locker room jock-rap of Limp Bizkit, Korn, Kid Rock and their peers, in eternal servitude to the puerile fantasy world of bored suburban teenagers the world over.

Onyx served their purpose, but what Simmons really wanted was a toehold on the frontline of gangsta rap. In 1993 he launched Def Jam West, a Los Angeles-based subsidiary which set about rounding up NWA's leftovers. "The move reflected our understanding of how hip hop was evolving," Simmons contended. "We followed the growth of the culture itself." Ah, but didn't you once *grow* the culture itself? The first act that Def Jam West threw its weight behind was female MC Bo$$, but she never truly justified Simmons' faith or the marketing hyperbole she earned as the first 'hip hop gangstress'.

Def Jam's record with women was hardly encouraging, Nikki D being the first to work for the label after it had been in existence for more than five years. Her gangsta-bitch aesthetic was shared by the next female incumbent at Def Jam. Bo$$, born Lichelle Laws in Detroit, also made play of having experienced tough times, sleeping rough till her career got off the ground when she was spotted by DJ Quik. After a guest appearance on AMG's 'My Sista Was A Bitch', Simmons signed her because he believed "the same women who buy Ice Cube or NWA will buy hardcore female rap if they're given the opportunity." He got that one wrong.

For a while the ruse worked. Bo$$'s début album *Born Gangstaz* was a surprisingly accomplished affair. Lifted from it, 'Deeper' topped the rap charts for three weeks in the summer of 1993, though Def Jam had to stump up $10,000 for the privilege of clearing the Barry White sample. But it all went wrong when some mean-minded journalists discovered her endless, expletive-ridden references to guns and cheeba (the 'f' word comprised exactly a quarter of the opening stanza of 'I Don't Give A Fuck') belied a middle class background and part-completion of a business studies course. Turned out homegirl's only connection with the Tupacs of this world was that she, too, had studied ballet. That put the kybosh on her career, though she later took a job as a DJ on Texas radio. More sophisticated, and more authentic, hardcore female rappers would eventually take up the slack.

Def Jam West also signed the four-MC, twin-DJ South Central Cartel from Los Angeles, readily dismissed by some as NWA clones, though they'd actually been together for six years and released a début album for their self-formed independent GWK Records. The deal with Def Jam came about after the super-assured MC Havoc, whose father was a member of Simmons' favourites, the Chi-Lites, pushed himself in the mogul's face. "I met him at Jack The Rapper [the black music convention]," he told *HHC*. "I just saw him sitting on the chair, and all my buddies were going, 'Hey, there goes Russell Simmons, man, why don't you go holler at him.' So, I went over there and hollered at him!"

The resultant *'N' Gatz We Truss* was less sensational but arguably even more brutal than standard gangsta fare – Prode'je's warning, "Don't be another nigga on my shitlist" set the tone and sounded worryingly authentic, though the rest of the lyrics were rote gangsta cliché. If Def Jam wanted a slice of the west coast action, they also got a share of its hinterland of trouble when a young buck shot an officer and blamed the incident on listening to gangsta rap – as was briefly fashionable with cop-shooters at the time. South Central Cartel and *'N' Gatz We Truss* were in the frame. The album eventually went gold on the back of 'Gang Stories', whose video used graphic footage obtained from the police. It is also probably the only gangsta rap record in existence to name-check footballer Pele. Ultimately South Central Cartel caused Def Jam more problems than they solved. Though the shooting case went nowhere, so too did their subsequent album *All Day Everyday* (1997), after which Def Jam relegated them to the independent labels from whence they'd risen. But they weren't totally washed up. Prode'je's production talent was utilised by a series of artists including LL Cool J, MC Eiht and Spice 1.

DJ West made a more substantial breakthrough when Lyor Cohen persuaded honey-voiced Shawn 'Domino' Ivy, one of Snoop Doggy Dogg's homies, to join the label. Having released his début album for Long Beach's OutBurst, a brief bidding war ensued over his talents – the greatest of which was an effortless rhythmic sensibility, honed by his service in gospel choirs, and a quasi-country twang informed by his childhood in St Louis. Def Jam won his signature because "we ended up going with the best". His seductive delivery, which he always maintained inspired Snoop Doggy Dogg rather than the other way round, counterpointed gritty urban fables. This dichotomy was noted by one critic who suggested he

141

was "a soft spoken businessman who will make an excellent bank manager when he gets sick of making records". Domino himself put his attraction down to his pouring of a little sugar on gangsta rap's dietary roughage. "I think it's the melodies in my songs that have made me more successful. Nobody wants to hear just a beat all the time, nobody wants to hear the same monotone voice all the time, there has got to be some soul."

Domino also maintained that there was more to ghetto life than guns and drive-bys, implicitly criticising his former friend Snoop for exploiting a desperate situation. "I don't consider myself a gangsta, and I feel that if you come from the place that I come from and you really know what's up with gangsta life, that's not something that you're gonna come out with on a record." He only hit pay-dirt for Def Jam twice, but spectacularly so. The jazzy 'Geto Jam', which had first alerted record executives to his talent when circulated on demo, topped the rap charts for six weeks at the start of 1994, and 'Sweet Potatoe Pie', which adopted the vice-presidential spelling of the popular root vegetable, also sold by the bucket-load. Def Jam had every right to expect more of the same, but his career faded as the public appetite for such thoughtful vocalists ebbed, even as their thirst for hardcore rappers increased. Still, he used his fleeting fame to the public good, launching his own condom range titled after his safe-sex themed song, 'Raincoat'.

Def Jam West's biggest coup came when they went to the heart of NWA's success and brought in a member of golden goose Dr Dre's immediate family, step-brother Warren 'G' Griffin. Dre remembers him coming through while he was overseeing the sessions for the epochal *The Chronic*. "He started fucking around with the drum machines and shit, cranking on that, learning the shit. I would come down and show him some things now and then, but he basically picked it up on his own. It's not like I was telling him. If I'd have known the motherfucker was going to be two million copies a couple of years later, I'd have been down there a little bit more."

Lyor Cohen was impressed by the video for Mr Grimmm's 'Indo Smoke', taken from the *Boyz N The Hood* soundtrack. Warren both produced and guest MC'd on the cut, and was self-evidently its star turn despite the song's billing. He also had a strong track record as producer, having worked with Tupac and MC Breed. After catching a plane to LA to meet him, Cohen legendarily moved into his house and over the course of three days persuaded him to join Def Jam as an artist, rather than merely a producer.

He was an instant success, his reputation rubber-stamped by connections to the white-hot G-funk cliques of Dre and Snoop. His début single, 'Regulate', featured smooth piano from former Doobie Brother Michael McDonald's 'I Keep Forgettin' (Every Time You're Near)' that belied the subject matter – in which Warren is the victim of a car-jacking before exacting his revenge on his perpetrators, with the help of friend Nate Dogg. Afterwards they chill and chase girls, replicating the nonchalant attitude towards violence that informed so much west coast rap. "I had just bought the Michael McDonald album and really liked the soulful beat on that song," Warren recalled in an MTV interview. "So Nate Dogg and I flipped the beat on it and then worked off one another for new lyrics. That's how the song was created and how my career jump-started."

It turned out to be Def Jam's biggest single, defining the Long Beach G-Funk sound and reaching number two in the pop charts after it was prominently featured on the soundtrack to Tupac's *Above The Rim*. The accompanying album, *Regulate . . . G Funk Era* sold three million copies, though critics carped at the paucity of good songs on offer apart from the title-track and accompanying single, 'This DJ'. Back in 1994 there was conjecture that stealing Warren from under Suge Knight's nose had caused the much-feared Death Row founder some disquiet, and that Simmons and Cohen were consequently in danger. Warren was signed to the label only after conflicts with Knight, including an incident where he was publicly 'slapped'. He also claimed to have had his lyrics amended to reflect 'pro-Bloods' sentiments, in tribute to the gang with which Knight, and consequently Death Row, was heavily affiliated. Later, while attending the release party for Snoop's *Doggystyle*, his friends were beaten and thrown off the boat at Knight's direction.

Def Jam did hire extra security for Cohen, just in case. In fact, Simmons was able to co-exist with Knight much more happily than many west coast label execs, later securing Tupac's release for his *Gridloc'd* movie. While the fur was flying in the east-west coast diss war, Simmons did at least try to calm the feud by writing to *Vibe* magazine and criticising them for hyping up the tensions that would eventually lead to the felling of Tupac and Notorious B.I.G. More recently Simmons expressed regret that he didn't do more to get in between the warring factions – as a friend of both Suge Knight and Puff Daddy, the two main protagonists, he was well positioned to do so. It's the type of soul-searching that many in the industry – but not nearly enough – were doing after it all went down.

In the event Warren G's career never quite took off as Cohen and others had intended, and subsequent effort *Take A Look Over Your Shoulder*, three years in the making, was poorly received. He left Def Jam after he got caught up in the merger between Universal and PolyGram. "I went to Russell and Lyor and asked if I could find someone to buy me out," recalls Warren, "would it be OK to leave? At first, they was like, 'Nah. We ain't going for that.' But then I just keep telling them that I got a family, I got things that I've got to take care of. Plus I'm not trying to come out in 2000. Finally they said OK. They let me get bought out [by Restless Records]. But we still got a good relationship."

In 1994 hip hop's slate was wiped clean by Staten Island's impenetrable Wu-Tang Clan, whose *Enter The Wu-Tang (36 Chambers)* confounded convention with its taut and tall stories of inner-city claustrophobia. The tight-knit brotherhood of MCs that lay behind it spouted Kung Fu flick philosophy, chess strategy, mystic arcana and other meaningless but engaging gubbins, over production values that offered the acoustic equivalent of quicksand. Def Jam missed its chance to sign the core group, who'd created a huge buzz with the independent release of début single 'Protect Ya Neck', but chief producer RZA (Robert Diggs) was shrewd enough to institute a provision in their RCA/Loud contract allowing individual members to record separately. Def Jam went after both Method Man and Old Dirty Bastard prior to the release of *Enter The Wu-Tang*. Old Dirty Bastard opted for Elektra, which was probably just as well for Def Jam, given a subsequent reputation for waywardness that makes Flavor Flav seem like a beacon of social propriety.

They were pleased enough to have Method Man on their books instead. The deal was brokered by Tracey Waples, who had to fight off stiff competition from the group's parent label, Loud. Method Man, aka Clifford Smith, was the most vital MC presence on *36 Chambers*, introducing himself on the track that shared his name with a rush of stark but hilarious threats. Chris Lighty thought he was a perfect match for Def Jam, combining the label's reputation for hard-hitting hip hop with an affable, aloof charm that helped make him the most photogenic Wu-Tanger. "Besides," he revealed in the Def Jam anniversary sleevenotes, "his name is so def. It just felt like Method Man should be on Def Jam with Redman, like Superman and Batman both belonged on DC Comics." To torture the analogy a little further, while other rappers boasted of their lineage to masters Kent and West, Method Man and the Wu-Tang came across like rampaging mutations of Swamp Thing.

At first it appeared as if the Wu-Tang's central exploits would over-shadow those of its extended network of contributors, as seemingly every-one with even a passing connection to the mothership won their own solo contract. But as subsequent Wu-Tang efforts fell a long way short of their début, it became increasingly apparent that the group's star performers (RZA, Old Dirty Bastard, Gza, Raekwon and Method Man in particular) were doing their best work as solo artists. Certainly Method Man's *Tical* (1994) underpinned his reputation as the group's pre-eminent MC, with his husky, slack-jaw delivery marrying shades of menace with high comedy. Roots' drummer DJ Ahmir's description of it as "the stinkingest, dirtiest album I've ever heard" gives some idea of the gauze-filtered pro-duction job RZA performed on it.

The highlights included 'All I Need', a huge summer hit, while 'Release Yo' Delf's update of Gloria Gaynor's 'I Will Survive' worked brilliantly, against all conceivable logic. Elsewhere there was depth as well as swagger, including Islamic subtexts on 'Sub Crazy', where Method announced he could "drop bombs like Qur'an". The next year his hit duet with Mary J. Blige, 'I'll Be There For You', a Grammy Award-winning performance, delivered on the promise Def Jam had first detected in him as someone who could crossover to the pop market without leaving hard-core fans behind. The first of several collaborations with the like-minded Redman, 'How High', which they would later develop into a film script, was almost as successful.

Promoting Method Man would always be a delicate balance which Def Jam's staff deserve credit for getting more often than not. Although there would be concessions to the pop market – his second album *Tical 2: Judge-ment Day* is the only record in history to boast cameo appearances from both Donald Trump and Janet Jackson – he remained rooted in the Wu-Tang's blunted realism. However, the inconsistency of production approaches, some wearisome skits and the over-emphasis on guest collab-orations diminished the impact of its few truly great songs, not the least of which was 'Judgement Day' itself.

Also signed in 1994 was Montell Jordan, who would become the most successful R&B act on Def Jam's books. Cutting an imposing figure at six foot eight, Jordan had been searching for a deal for over half a decade before Russell Simmons took notice, tipped off by Paul Stewart of RAL-PMP Records. His 1995 début featured astutely interwoven blues samples, principally from B.B. King, in sharp contrast to the prevailing fixation with west coast funk or jazz. His lyrics, too, were more forward-thinking and celebratory of life in South Central, a panacea to the negativity embraced by gangsta rap. The title-track, 'This Is How We Do It', sold more than a million copies when released on single, but set a benchmark he found difficult to match. The opening lines of his second album, *More . . .* roundly boasted that he was the king of hip hop–soul, but while that was once briefly true, the statement now fell into the category of misplaced optimism.

However, his subsequent recordings for Def Jam have never sounded anything less than classy. "Everybody talks about the lack of creativity, individuality, excitement and lyrical depth in modern R&B," he confirmed on the release of his third album, *Let's Ride*, "and I want to bring those qualities back to music." That failed to justify the inclusion of a monologue by Pastor Clarence McClendon on the finished recording, though its presence pointed to Jordan's efforts to promote himself as a God-fearing R&B role model.

Through this new clutch of artists, Def Jam was getting back on track, even as their deal with Sony/Columbia was dissolving. The exchanges had been curt for some time. In particular, Simmons' relationship with Sony's Donnie Ienner had deteriorated to the point of antipathy. By now Def Jam was $17 million in the red and Simmons was forced to close labels, creating bad feeling among those artists who'd invested time and faith in them. Simmons was horrified to find out that Sony used the impasse as leverage while sniffing around some of his bigger acts, Public Enemy and LL included. To the credit of both, those advances were declined.

Simmons put the label on the market and eventually negotiated a new deal with PolyGram's Alain Levy. On a 50-50 equity split, Def Jam received a $35 million advance, which after paying off the $17m they owed Sony, put them back in the black. Sony did their best to secure the rights to Def Jam's back catalogue, but Simmons held firm – knowing it was hard to put a price on the intellectual property that albums by Public Enemy, LL Cool J and The Beastie Boys constituted. Simmons was jubilant when the new deal was signed. "Alain Levy believes in hip hop as a global lifestyle and he believes that I'm the guy to make PolyGram the company that can exploit that." Eventually that relationship would sour, but for now Def Jam concentrated on repaying PolyGram's investment. Warren G's *Regulate . . . G Funk Era*, released shortly after the deal was finalised, sold three million copies, and both Montell Jordan and Method Man achieved platinum sales with their débuts. Despite appearances to the contrary and wide-ranging speculation about the label's viability, 1994 was Def Jam's most successful year so far.

The dark days were behind them. Chastened by the problems that Def Jam encountered when he took his eye off the ball, Simmons took Lyor Cohen on as his partner. The turnaround was achieved, to some extent, by following industry trends rather than initiating them, and a combination of record company politicking, brinkmanship and an astute retrenchment of the value of Def Jam's trademark. It was Cohen who takes much of the credit for the latter. As he confessed in the sleevenotes to the Def Jam 10th Anniversary box set, name recognition and brand identity was key to the label's stature. "We can't out-clout, outspend or out-finance our competitors. The only thing we can do is out-taste them, guard our logo and our art."

The brand was being rebuilt. As Dave Tompkins wrote for *Rap Pages* while reviewing Method Man's *Tical*, "Remember that Def Jam mystique? Those jackets and ill-billed tours? Remember the times when we bought records based on the mere criteria of – better sit down for this one – logo recognition?! With a haughty air of elitism, Russell and Rick would annually unveil an act that in retrospect would define that particular year in hip hop: LL Cool J, Public Enemy, Beastie Boys, Slick Rick." It was now Russell and Lyor, of course, but Method Man's album, alongside Redman's *Dare Iz A Darkside*, did a lot to resurrect the 'elitism' that Tompkins refers to in the early Nineties. While first Oran 'Juice' Jones and Montell Jordan had significant success, their value to Def Jam, symbolically, was minimal. R&B was never the label's forté and merely served to dilute its identity. Whatever Simmons thought, the future for Def Jam lay in the same raw hip hop aesthetic with which it had started.

The changes left Def Jam stronger than it had ever previously been, and better placed to regain its status after Death Row had temporarily usurped its crown as rap's premier record label. At this juncture Def Jam's acts didn't necessarily measure up to those of the competition, nor to previous cycles in the label's own history, but that situation would soon be rectified, leaving Simmons' hands free to ingratiate himself in other areas of the entertainment industry. In the process Lyor "the cheque writer" Cohen became the label's anchorman, his stoicism complementing Simmons' more distracted outlook, a wandering eye syndrome that extended beyond ogling supermodels to canvassing business opportunities on a daily basis.

Simmons trusted him to get on with day-to-day operations while he took his latest hobbyhorse to the gallops. Cohen not only had motivational skills, but a drill sergeant's bark to match his bumper sticker logic. "If you're a baker, you make your living off of baking," he once pointed out. "If you're a construction worker, you make your living doing construction. If you're a rapper, rap, motherfucker." The match was perfect because Cohen was as single-minded as they come. "I'm frightened of defracted focus," admitted Cohen. "I can't stay up at night. Russell can't go to sleep. He loves talking to billionaires. I don't know what to say to them."

9

The Type Of Businessman Who Has Several Plans

"Life is pretty simple: You do some stuff. Most fails. Some works.
You do more of what works. If it works big, others quickly copy it.
Then you do something else.
The trick is the doing something else."

– Thomas Peters

"He [Simmons] established the paradigm of how to make it in the business of hip
hop. There are two types of people in this world – the ones like Berry Gordy and
Russell, who can take something from nothing and create something – and then there
are people that are great executors."

– Anne Simmons of Drush

While Simmons wasn't the first boss in hip hop to become synonymous with his label, Sugar Hill's Sylvia Robinson having started the phenomenon, by the time Def Jam was established, the path was set for a number of 'personality execs' – such as the late Eazy-E at Ruthless, Suge Knight at Death Row, Sean Puffy Combs at Bad Boy, Master P at No Limit and Jermaine Dupri at So So Def. For many of these, Simmons had blazed the trail. "If it weren't for Russell Simmons, I wouldn't be in the game," stated Combs. "He gave the blueprint for hip hop. For our generation, the baton was taken by Russell Simmons. He knows how to break down colour barriers without compromising who he is. He never took off his Adidas or turned his hat from the back, even though he was doing business with white people. He's taught us that you can go out there, get your money and be yourself, and you don't have to throw on your tap dancing shoes." Dupri similarly venerated Simmons the businessman. "I want to release more artists, of course, and brand my label a little more. I'm learning from Def Jam how important that is."

But Simmons always had objectives above and beyond music. With Def

149

Jam and Rush sailing under their own wind, he embarked on a series of allied projects, all of which shared a hip hop inflection. His role in the now mature businesses he'd founded grew increasingly marginal the more they became self-supporting. As an instinctive, boot-strap entrepreneur, he wanted to start building from the bottom-up again. As Nelson George notes, neither Def Jam, nor any other Simmons business, has ever been 'textbook'. "At least since the late Eighties, its leader has spent as little time as possible in the offices of his label, management company, or any of his other enterprises. First via fax machines and later through cellular phones, Simmons was a mobile executive way before it became fashionable, a man who is as likely to conduct business on a StairMaster, in a Russian bath-house, or at the Village's Time Café."

But while his zest for new ideas was legend, at heart Simmons was not some tearaway fiscal fire-starter, and his personal values remained rooted in prudence and caution. As he wrote in, of all things, a testimonial to his accountants, "While the entertainment industry is extremely speculative and my demeanor is casual (I always wear my Phat Farm clothing), my orientation to managing and financing my companies and personal hold-ings is very conservative." His investments were invariably medium to long-term, and he was capable of stomaching a loss in the early stages if he thought the idea remained viable. The trick is knowing when to cut your losses, something he would also prove adept at. The Nineties saw Simmons spread himself pretty thin, get his fingers burned on more than one occasion, but still emerge as someone who inspired confidence in his bank managers.

Confident that he'd left Def Jam in the ultra-competent hands of Lyor Cohen, while Rush Management was safely ticking over under the super-vision of Carmen Ashurst-Watson, Simmons took time out to diversify his interests. He was surplus to requirements, as he admits in his auto-biography. "The truth is, the more I got away from Def Jam on a day-to-day basis, the better the company did." Which is a pretty blunt admission, but credit the fact that he had faith in his employees commen-surate with his willingness to delegate to them. A trait that is too often a rare commodity in ambitious businessmen of his ilk.

But Simmons isn't your regular businessman. He's often cited that his experience "comes from necessity. It didn't come from school or formal training of any kind." The trademark hooded tops and baseball caps hardly signify the cut and thrust of Wall Street, but he was beginning to move in those circles. In true buppie style, by the mid-Nineties Simmons was taking extended holidays in the Hamptons, the beach towns at the east of Long Island favoured by the seriously rich, where he could park his bullet-proof white Rolls-Royce without fearing for its hubcaps (bought despite the fact that he didn't pass his driving test until his early Forties). He and Andre Harrell, who shared a house there, organised baseball parties to which the fabulous and wealthy flocked. There's no six degrees of separation with Russell Simmons; he just knows everyone. And no pretence either to keeping it real or staying in the ghetto, those bare-faced lies peddled by the more craven gangsta rappers. Simmons was quite happy for anyone within hearing to know how large he was living.

Simmons' attempts to ingratiate himself in the business world earned him a reputation as one of the greatest living name-droppers. But while those of greater privilege may have been in the Hamptons to shoot the breeze or basketball hoops, Simmons was networking away like a rogue search engine. Part of the appeal lay in the fact that Simmons likes nothing better than to bask in the warm glow of celebrity skin, and throughout his career his validation by the great and good seemed inordinately important to him. But he also measured his acquaintances by their potential usefulness. His circle boasted such industry luminaries as Walter Yetnikoff of CBS (the streetwise Brooklyn lawyer whose reputation was openly questioned in Frederic Dannen's damning survey of the American music industry, *The Hit Men*, and the man who started the tiff that led to the end of Rubin's participation in Def Jam), publicity-shy billionaire Ron Perelman, fashion designer Tommy Hilfiger, and Quincy Jones, the most universally respected figure in the black music industry, and the first black executive of a major record label. Later they were joined by property tycoon Donald Trump (whom Simmons claims he sometimes speaks to two or three times a day, though it's hard to imagine for what earthly reason). He also befriended a series of Hollywood figures including Jon Peters and Peter Guber (whose partnership yielded films such as *Flashdance*, *Rainman* and *Batman*), as well as Jeff Wald (*2 Days in the Valley*), whose son Jordan was given an A&R post at Def Jam.

Thus fortified by his new social circle, the business expansion began in earnest in 1992. Phat Farm, a wholesale and retail clothing company focused "on the creation, production and distribution of classically styled merchandise with an urban perspective", was his attempt to take a cut out of the pervasive influence hip hop was exerting on mainstream fashion. It was an idea Chuck D had already latched on to by launching RappStyle, some two years previously. Chuck, in his turn, had bought clothes from the Queens boutique IV Plai, its lines designed by Christopher 'Kid' Reid of Kid 'N Play. However, while Chuck's ambitions were to bring business back into the community rather than see it exploited by third parties, Simmons' motivation was less altruistic.

He recalled the inspiration behind Phat Farm on *The Show*: "It started out with tall skinny bitches. I was looking in magazines, saying, 'She's fine, I want to meet this ho'.' Then, next thing I know, I'm hanging out at parties. At one party there'd be 60 girls and they'd all be six feet and fine . . . After that I met the clients and all the people who run the department stores and buy all the clothes. And then I start looking at the fabrics of the clothes and how they make them. I start seeing how hip hop niggas influence all the shit they try to do anyway. I go to a Chanel show, and Karl Lagerfeld got a big gold chain around a bitch's neck, I was like, 'How fake is that?' Phat Farm became like a hobby. I started making clothes, I looked at the fabrics and started to understand the business through all the designers, the editors and the models. It became a real serious hobby. The hobby became more serious as we began to put more money into it. When I first started hanging out with these tall girls, they wasn't playing hip hop music in the parties. I had to have a reason to be up in that spot besides from some tall bitch, because my job is to get money." He then goes on to qualify this assessment of 'bitches' as women who are "super-powerful, independent, successful – bitch. Not at all derogatory. Because I love women." Hardly enough to win him an invite to dinner with Andrea Dworkin, all the same.

Starting out of a flagship store on Prince Street in Soho, New York, Phat Farm's influences were clearly designers like FUBU (For Us, By Us), who used LL Cool J as their spokesman and whose head, Daymond John, came from Simmons' old hunting ground, Hollis. Cross Colors, launched in 1989, saw designer and owner Carl Jones stencil political slogans on his shirts and rose to sales of $160 million by 1993. Then his biggest retail customer filed for bankruptcy taking Cross Colors down with it – as well as Jones' own stint in the spotlight as a celebrated African-American entrepreneur with a media profile to rival Simmons.

Other hot urban retailers included April Walker's Fashion in Effect and Tommy Hilfiger. All were already hugely popular in the rap community from which, with the exception of Hilfiger, they'd organically grown. Before the big cheeses moved in, hip hop fashion had enjoyed an independent period analogous to the development of its parent culture, as stores like Brian McDaniels' Uncle Ralph's in Brooklyn opened their doors to reflect what was happening on the streets around them. But it was

Tommy Hilfiger who truly capitalised, with artists including KRS-One and Snoop Doggy Dogg endorsing his range. "There are no boundaries," Hilfiger opined. "Hip hop has created a style that is embraced by an array of people from all backgrounds and races." Other prominent rappers, including Q-Tip of A Tribe Called Quest and the Wu-Tang Clan, celebrated Hilfiger in rhyme. When, in 1994, Snoop performed on *Saturday Night Live* bedecked in Tommy labels, it was estimated that the association helped push annual sales ahead by $90 million. Soon every major urban fashion line was beholden to a rap star as walking billboard. Karl Kani signed Dr Dre, Mecca backed Ma$e, while Ecko hooked up with Busta Rhymes.

As Ifé Oshun notes, "The more popular and lucrative the rap industry became, the more profitable it was for companies to offer the same looks you saw on your favourite rap celebrities. This undeniable link between music and fashion, along with the streetwise entrepreneurship that fostered it, was the foundation of what we have now – a billion dollar industry whose life blood still flows through the soul of the urban community . . . Bottom line, hip hop celebrity generates dollars. Rap mogul, Russell Simmons, understood the equation of fashion plus rap equals celebrity."

As well as patronising these established urban designers, Simmons had also been outfitting his coterie of girlfriends at Mark Beguda's shop on West Broadway. After a mild contratemps over whether he could afford the clothes, Beguda became Simmons' friend and partner in Phat Farm. Simmons' initial investment was half a million dollars, though he claims to have pumped 20 times that amount into the coffers until the line finally reached profitability in 1998, a timescale delayed by the 1994 bankruptcy of distributor, USA Classics. Unlike Cross Colors, Phat Farm had the finances and resources to push through such a setback.

Initially the clothes, hooded sweatshirts, overalls, snorkels and sweaters, and eventually silk pyjama pants and boxer shorts, were stocked by chains such as Dr Jay's, Up Against the Wall and Jimmy Jazz, but also small, specialist boutiques like Hollywood's Fred Segal. Simmons fought against the most obvious schematic – having his clothes placed in the 'ethnic' departments of department stores, fearing that would ring-fence their potential appeal – which turned out to be worldwide, with as much as a third of Phat Farm's sales coming from Asia.

Designers were hired or licensed, including a cast of Simmons' favourite tailors, such as British family-run concern John Smedley, beloved of Paul Weller and Liam Gallagher. Former Staten Island graffiti artist and high school drop-out Kevin Leong, meanwhile, became Phat Farm's lead in-house designer. He met Simmons in an elevator, and was prompted by his friend into introducing himself. So he paid a compliment to Simmons on the model he was using for Phat Farm, Kimora Lee – wholly unaware that Simmons and Lee had just become engaged. Simmons challenged Leong over his comments, before asking about his clothes. "I remember asking what kind of jeans were those," remembers Simmons. "He's like, 'These are from my exchange, but they never came out. These are from a sample sale. The niggers never made these.' Then he said, 'I'm a designer.' He was perfect." Leong seized the moment and gave Simmons a presump-tuous imperative. " 'You need to give me a call.' That's what I said to him. Exactly." Simmons did indeed call, the next day, and offered him a job. Leong's first Phat Farm range of T-shirts were an instant smash, and by his early Twenties he was presiding over Phat Farm as chief designer.

The group's president was the devoutly obsequious Marcie Corbett. "Phat Farm reflects the style and philosophy of our founder, Russell Simmons," Corbett deferred, "who has unerring instincts for design and what's hot." More accurately, she pointed out that, "Fashion trends have always originated on the street. It's a question of who is smart enough to figure out what's hip first. And what's hot on the street will continue to pave the way for future fashion trends."

Simmons' first love was 'fly' clothes, and he has maintained a personal connection to Phat Farm. He insists on running it on a day-to-day basis, managing the licensees and ensuring the label never loses its cachet – a burden he was only too pleased to relinquish at Def Jam. His hands-on involvement has undoubtedly diminished his input into other business spheres and prompted critics to question his priorities. He won't be seen dead in photo shoots without his Phat Farm logo clearly visible, and hypes the brand at every conceivable opportunity. His cheerleading for the clothes line seems to dwarf any pride in his contribution to the Def Jam legacy. And his secret to Phat Farm's success? "The plan has to be adhered to. It's really about focus." Which might surprise, or possibly even flatter Lyor Cohen, who'd spent years trying to get his business partner to do just that at Def Jam. Baby Phat, its female equivalent, eventually headed by Simmons' wife Kimora Lee, was established in 1993 with a fitted T-shirt range that proved immediately popular. It went on to equip the modern home-girl about town with slip dresses, skirts, bikinis and lingerie.

Of course, having your own clothes range is now a prerequisite for any rap star who wants to hold their head up in the 'hood, denoting "I've arrived" status. It's a phenomenon that shows few signs of abating, with Puff Daddy's Sean John label being chased down the catwalk by Master P's No Limit and the Wu-Tang's Wu-Wear. One of the most recent entrants is Jay-Z's Roc-a-Wear. Jay-Z's partner Damon Dash had this simple rationale. "I mean, why shouldn't we capitalise, when everyone else is capitalising off our lifestyle, why shouldn't we? You know, we just got to learn the business, make it lucrative to us, and just go about it right."

Meanwhile mainstream design houses such as Ralph Lauren, Donna Karan and Calvin Klein all launched jeans collections designed to appeal to the 'urban', aka hip hop consumer. Much to Simmons' chagrin, Lauren's Polo jeans even lured one of Phat Farm's designers away. This type of co-opting of black cultural success has long been a feature of both music (from jazz and blues becoming white man's rock'n'roll) to fashion. In 1957 Norman Mailer's essay 'The White Negro' founded the concept of 'black radical chic'. It's never really gone away.

Writer Amy Alexander makes a connection between Mailer and the current preoccupation with 'ghetto fabulous', a term first coined by Puff Daddy (though some credit it to Andre Harrell) to describe his own out-landish lifestyle, and notes the way it has slowly invaded mainstream fashion spreads and commentaries. "Obviously, most of us in the media think we know what the term means: to be 'ghetto fabulous' is to engage in a lifestyle, expressed primarily through one's fashion choices, that cele-brates new money, personal independence, and a distinct lack of interest in whatever the mainstream style mavens identify as 'good taste'. It suggests a kind of 'hood-bred reverence for flashy, Mack Daddy-*Superfly*-type clothing . . . It also suggests a fashion agenda based on the earliest dreams of an inner-city youngster who longs for what he imagines is a plush lifestyle, a world in which the champagne flows freely, all the cars have shiny rims, and the only thing thicker than the platinum chain around his neck is the wad of cash in his pocket. And where the term 'ghetto' once carried heavy negative overtones . . . it now seems as if that word, paired with the suffix 'fabulous', has become not only acceptable but downright desirable within the context of hip-ness and hip hop." Things have come a long way since Run-DMC rubbished Calvin Klein or Grand Puba, renowned for his patronage of Tommy Hilfiger, stated, "If Tommy ain't givin' loot, I'll be the fuck if I wear it."

In fact, as Lauren Goldstein discovered in an article for *Business 2.0*, the celebrity link was often more important than the quality of the goods. "The fact is, urban clothing is hot not because it's designed by African

Americans ('Style has no colour,' one inner-city consumer explained), nor even because of its revolutionary design ('Our camp shirt is no different than anyone else's,' admitted an urban-apparel executive). Urban-wear companies have ridden in on the coat-tails – and jacket backs, and baseball caps, and shoes – of rap musicians." Which is why you can never find an editorial piece in a US hip hop magazine without thumbing through a dozen pages of glossy menswear ads first.

Certainly Simmons hated any discussion of what he was trying to do in terms of 'black business'. "I have not let race limit me. Although there is still a real racial issue in America – very strong racism still exists – rap has done a lot to alleviate that amongst young people. But I have not accepted the role of a black producer or a black record executive or a black clothing designer or a black advertising agency or a black film producer. None of that shit! I'm an American, I want American money, and I won't let them marginalize my work."

By the late Nineties, Phat Farm's product range had expanded to include jewellery, lingerie, shoes and perfumes – which raised the tantalising prospect of further synergies with his Def Jam roster and, who knows, 'Eau d'Redman'? In fact, Simmons had signed a licence agreement with Stern Fragrances, the company that develop fragrances for Oscar de la Renta, Perry Ellis and even Cher.

Simmons even produced a shirt featuring prints of his wife, Kimora 'she's a supermodel' Lee, for commercial sale. He opened a further flagship store in Harlem, which also carried Puff Daddy's line, as well as Polo and Versace. Adding shopkeeper to his ever expanding curriculum vitae, Simmons promised it would be "the first of what should be many, many stores." It's also indicative of his desire to own not only the means of production, but also distribution – something that is harder to achieve in the more centralised music industry structure.

1992 was Simmons' 'busting out' year. As well as Phat Farm, he also launched *Russell Simmons' Def Comedy Jam* in March, syndicated on the HBO cable channel. The inspiration came from his first extra-curricular venture at Def Jam – *The New Music Report*, a short programme of videos and sketches that promoted the label's latest releases, but also featured comedic interludes. *Def Comedy Jam* was inaugurated in partnership with Stan Lathan, a sage Hollywood TV player. Lathan introduced Simmons to the Bernie Brillstein and Brad Grey management team who would serve as producers (the quartet's initials leading to the production acronym SLBG).

The intention was to broaden the reach of black comedy, whose potential had stalled following the breakthroughs of Richard Pryor and Eddie Murphy. But the new artists they found belonged to a different generation, microphone gun-slingers who were readily comparable to gangsta rappers in their belligerence and intensity. The most popular performers were often straight-up dirty talkers whose lewdness drew on the chitlin' circuit repartee of Red Foxx and his ilk. Every week for 30 minutes they rapid-fired jokes backed by DJ Kid Capri (David Love, whose father once played trumpet with Miles Davis) spinning the latest Def Jam joints – no stone was left unturned in Simmons' determination to cross-promote. This time, though, he had judged his audience's mood perfectly. The show was an immediate hit.

The original intention was to give comedian Robin Harris a TV showcase. A personal favourite of Simmons', Harris was a veteran who'd made a name for himself at the Comedy Act Theater in Los Angeles, his routines including one on how to repair a car with an oil leak using the grease from a Jheri curl, before appearing in movies such as *House Party*. A sitcom pilot was prepared, but Harris died in 1990 from a heart attack, thereby scuppering the format. But Simmons was hooked on the idea of a stand-up show, having seen a variety of performers at venues such as the Comedy Act and Harlem's Uptown Comedy Club. He believed, rightly, that they could connect with hip hop audiences, who had never bought into the 'white' alternative comedy revolution and been left primed for more visceral entertainment by the advent of 'reality' rap.

SLBG successfully pitched HBO a four-show series featuring a roster of 16 comedians. Martin Lawrence, later star of hit movie *Bad Boys* alongside former Rush client Will Smith, was chosen as the host, at the suggestion of Eddie Murphy. Lawrence played an effective hand as compere and ringleader, encouraging the audience participation that lent so much atmosphere to the series (and even covered for some of the comics' deficiencies). The show instantly became a bankable commodity. Later taken under the wing of Russell Simmons Television (RSTV), *Def Comedy Jam* showcased a new generation of black comics including Bill Bellamy (whom SLBG also managed), Steve Harvey, Reggie McFadden, Chris Rock and Chris Tucker. Initially, many faced approbation for their 'foul-mouthed' routines, while critics scoffed at their over-reliance on parodies of prominent black community figures such as OJ Simpson and a tidal wave of dick jokes. Sidney Poitier and Bill Cosby were among those to express concern at the excesses of their language. While it's easy to over-emphasise the parallels between gangsta rap, which had developed its own tradition of X-rated skits, and *Def Comedy Jam*'s in-your-face burlesque, the one certainly paved the way for the other.

Equally, despite its critics, the show featured several quality acts, not all of whom lacked subtlety or invention. The finest was the genuinely funny Chris Rock, whose observational gambits – poking around in his audience's discomfiture with racial and gender politics and exploding the tiny nuances he discovered – made him rap's Bill Hicks, or the hip hop Alan Bennett with swear words. His choice of material was also hugely significant, because it openly challenged the black community's more inward-looking platitudes. "The taboo he shattered was exposing the secret, closeted discourse among black Americans about their own," commented cultural critic Michael Eric Dyson. "Rock signifies an unwillingness among the younger black generation to abide by the dirty-laundry theory. That theory suggests you don't say anything self-critical or negative about black people where white people can hear it. But the hip hop generation believes in making money off the publication of private pain and agony." Ironically, it made Rock hugely popular with white audiences too. "The white media chose pieces of Rock's performance that made them feel comfortable," reckoned Simmons, "and they wrote about it and they loved him."

By 1993 the popularity of the acts was such that Simmons was able to put a touring version of *Def Comedy Jam* on the road. Indeed, the format was so successful that two separate line-ups crossed the country simultaneously. The show itself ran for seven years and was one of HBO's great success stories, its biggest rating weekly show until *The Sopranos*. But in the end, Simmons claims simply to have got bored with the audience demographic, protesting that nobody 'cool' revered the show any more towards the end of its run. All the really good comics had moved on, many making the transition to film careers just as their rap peer group had – though too often in hugely predictable and rarely funny buddy cop movies.

Rush Management was valued at $34 million in 1993, boasting seven record labels, management, fashion and broadcasting interests. With so much to supervise, Simmons increasingly became a figurehead rather than a manager, responsible primarily for the ethos of the umbrella company: "My only real purpose is managing and directing,' he stated. 'I sacrifice all the time for my artists. It's my job to make sure they have rich black babies." He was dubbed 'a hip hop mogul' by *The Wall Street Journal* and crowned 'The Rap Impresario' by *Time* magazine, plaudits he lapped up like a greedy tomcat.

He also dusted off his best 'good guy' hat by founding The Rush Philanthropic Arts Foundation with his brother, artist Daniel Simmons. Although some criticised him for attempting to brand his conscience, the foundation has done impeccable work within urban communities, providing disadvantaged children with access to the arts and exhibition opportunities for emerging artists. He was also involved in a series of scholarship funds, a fresh air campaign, and raised money to build a children's wing inside Brooklyn Hospital. In 1998 he was awarded the Moet & Chandon Humanitarian Award for his support of inner city youth. Some saw this in terms of a back-door attempt by that most exclusive champagne house to get down with the hip hop community, having been outflanked as the bubbly of choice for the new rap generation by Louis Roederer Cristal, at $250 a bottle a heady indicator of status and spending power.

Simmons' success with comedy led him to believe he might have another crack at conquering Hollywood – especially after he was flattered by friend Jon Peters, who offered him a development deal with Sony prior to that corporation's bust-up with Def Jam. He'd had some fraught experiences with *Krush Groove* and *Tougher Than Leather*, but dipped another toe in the water with the sprawling performance documentary *The Show*. His next major project also went sour, however. He was one of the first to see the script for John Singleton's *Boyz N The Hood*. But while Simmons was trying to work a deal, Singleton instead signed with Columbia's president Frank Price. That was "some scumbag shit he did," Simmons later fumed.

His next film was intended to be a launch-pad for one of his more photogenic, teen-friendly stars, Will Smith, but this time neither Peters nor Columbia were biting, and the project was stillborn. Shortly thereafter, Benny Medina and Quincy Jones nipped in to offer Smith the lead on a new TV sitcom entitled *The Fresh Prince Of Bel Air*. Simmons had just missed the boat on hip hop's holy grail – a rapper who could transfer to the screen and in the process broaden his appeal rather than diminish it. Ironically, the format echoed one Simmons had been developing as early as 1992, *The Clown Prince*, a comedy about a white youngster growing up in a black ghetto.

In *The Fresh Prince Of Bel Air* Smith exhibited a persona that was at once rebellious and streetwise, but never threatening enough to scare parents and guardians, either on set or out in TV-land. In the process Will Smith established himself as the hip hop Bill Cosby, the rapper you could take home to meet your folks who wouldn't push crack to your little sister.

Kurtis Blow, Simmons' first client, had long coveted a similar career path, but was forced to surmise: "The Fresh Prince [Smith] did what I couldn't do. He took the ball and ran with it." Other old school rappers like Doug E. Fresh were equally impressed. "Will Smith always made funny records like 'Parents Don't Understand'. So it was that whole kinda vibe that he had, when you seen him on TV. I knew he had talent, but when I seen him get on TV and act, he was a natural. And he kept it hip hop. He even introduced slang on TV. Like, 'Yo, that's hot, that's phat, that's butta, yo yo, watchudoin', stop trippin'." Simmons got a cheque for $250,000 in return for releasing Smith from his management contract which Smith, as honourable as ever, didn't fight over. But with the series a hit, and Smith about to turn into box office gold, that signalled a disappointing return on his investment.

Undeterred, Simmons hooked up with Hollywood veteran and Imagine Entertainment founder Brian Grazer, who'd enjoyed a series of commercial successes with films such as *Splash* and *Kindergarden Cop*. Together they hatched the idea of remaking Jerry Lewis's *The Nutty Professor*. Martin Lawrence was originally mooted as the lead, until Eddie Murphy was recruited to turn in one of his finest performances for years as the multi-persona lead. After Grazer acquired the rights to the film, which was co-produced by Simmons (Jerry Lewis also took an executive producer post), it became one of the biggest-grossing movies of 1986, taking $125 million at the box office and receiving the People's Choice Award.

But then, once again, Simmons found himself frozen out by Hollywood. He claims Grazer started bad-mouthing him for his lack of on-set involvement (criticising his work-rate was one of the few barbs never previously thrown Simmons' way). This was resolved when, with a sequel in the offing, Glazer took sole producer credit in return for Def Jam getting the soundtrack – Lyor Cohen securing the co-operation of a succession of major label artists – and Simmons a repeat fee. But the experience clearly still rankles.

Simmons also gravitated to a director who resided in a world at the polar opposite of that inhabited by Eddie Murphy and the Hollywood set. Considered by many to be a visionary, by others to be a talentless upstart poking his fingers into the dirt of human existence to no useful end, Abel Ferrara built his name through bleak, violent narratives such as *Driller Killer* and *Bad Lieutenant*, the latter featuring a particularly vicious depiction of humanity in Harvey Keitel's title character. It saw some dub him the low-budget Scorsese, while others reviled him as a man of 'uncompromising perversity'. His best-realised film was *The King Of New York*, a turf war morality tale which had a big impact on a generation of rap artists. Simmons originally met Ferrara at Manhattan drinking spot Save The Robots and befriended the notoriously bumptious director. His trust won, Ferrara passed him the script to *The Addiction*.

Revolving around the contemporaneous vampirism of NYU student Kathleen Conklin, played by Lili Taylor, the film's themes were self-evidently analogous to the half-life world of heroin addiction, though the joy of the film resides in its characters' idiosyncracies. *King of New York* star Christopher Walken employed meditation to police his hunger for blood, while Taylor's character stoically completes her thesis before the film's end. Shot in black and white over just 20 days, it's undoubtedly the least commercial project that Simmons ever involved himself with. Certainly the box office takings were minimal. Undeterred, Simmons also associate-produced *The Funeral*, Ferrara's meditation on revenge in the Thirties underworld, again featuring Walken alongside Chris Penn, who won the best actor trophy at the 1996 Venice Film Festival for his portrayal of Chez Tempio.

In 1996 Simmons and Stan Lathan, his Def Comedy Jam partner, founded Def Pictures, its scope announced with the typically Simmons-esque proclamation "ain't no black film company". Lathan was a little more measured. "Def Jam's records and Def Comedy Jam appeal initially to the young African-American audience. That's where our collective expertise is." That was an advantage Simmons also stressed. "White studio execs are not bringing me anything we don't see already. I can give them shit they don't know anything about. I know everybody from Ron Perelman to Leonardo DiCaprio, in terms of what they're about, more than they know about where I come from. And they certainly don't know where Snoop Doggy Dogg comes from." Their first movie followed in 1997. *Gridlock'd*, a co-production with Interscope starring the late Tupac Shakur and Tim Roth, was a satire released through Grammercy Pictures. Though the film – a thinly plotted but energetic take on the buddy movie, as the protagonists try manfully to quit hard drugs – is uneven, its redemptive glory lies in the two central performances and some diverting gallows humour. Nevertheless, it was not a major box office success. *How To Be A Player*, a co-production with Island Pictures, featured comedian Bill Bellamy in a less appealing romantic comedy about the protagonist's chronic infidelity and eventual come-uppance, replete with accompanying Def Jam soundtrack.

Simmons also sponsored the early career of Brett Ratner, like Rick Rubin a film student at NYU, who talked his way into Simmons' circle via his friend, photographer Glen Friedman. His hip hop credentials came from running his own label, whose most notable release was the *Big Men On Campus* compilation, which featured Jon Schecter, later the joint founder of *The Source*. Chuck D was the first to take him seriously, asking him to shoot a public service short for the *Rock the Vote* campaign. Thereafter he was used on a variety of Def Jam projects, including promos for Pete Nice and Foxy Brown, before freelancing for artists including Madonna, The Wu-Tang Clan and Mariah Carey. Since then Simmons' 'Jewish son' has racked up one of the great modern film franchises in *Rush Hour*, the hit comedy featuring Chris Tucker and Jackie Chan, that seems set to run and run (generating a huge amount of money for Def Jam via its attendant soundtracks in the process). Ratner is just another former Def Jam intern doing the business.

As if Simmons didn't have enough problems with the film world, he walked into further controversy when he attended the 1996 Academy Awards, boycotted by Jesse Jackson because of Hollywood's poor representation and recognition of blacks. The award show may have been produced by Quincy Jones and hosted by Whoopi Goldberg, but of the 166 nominations, only one was black, while less than 5 per cent of the academy's voting panel were non-white. All this in a year when Morgan Freeman, Angela Bassett, Laurence Fishburne and Denzel Washington turned in acclaimed performances. Jackson sent a letter to studio executives stating that, "We seek not to embarrass the entertainment industry, but to educate the public that the standards of fairness should also be applied to the film and television industries." Simmons' rationale for walking past the pickets, alongside companion Veronica Webb, who'd made her name as Vera in Spike Lee's *Jungle Fever*: "They got to do what they got to do from the outside, and I got to do what I got to do from the inside."

Some might say that's idealised, egotistic or just plain simplistic. The gulf between the music and film industries is immense. Technological advances mean that recording a group or MC and releasing the results constitutes a process so straightforward that it can be accessed by people regardless of economic circumstance – developments which brokered hip hop in the first place. The barriers to entry are few, and retreating. For all the concurrent progress in video-photography, a film still requires a huge budget and a team of specialists answering to an invariably monied producer. If you get that far, you'll require studio backing, and preferably a studio-approved star, to get the film screened to a mass audience. While Hollywood remains implacably racist, aspirant black music-makers can bypass or even ignore such economic structures. Film-makers, however, have to make compromises if they want to get anywhere beyond a show-reel. Which is why African-American directors consistently rail against their films being stigmatised as 'ethnic' when they address universal themes but happen to employ black faces. Many of the best black producers and directors, such as Kasi Lemmons (*Eve's Bayou*) and George Tillman Jr (*Soul Food*) have had to claw their way up through independent film-making. As *30 Years to Life* director Vanessa Middleton notes, "The talent and material is out there, but Hollywood isn't trying to tell our story." What Simmons sees as personal perfidy in relation to his sole hit movie, *The Nutty Professor*, resonates against the experiences of fellow black film-makers like a thousand glass ceilings. But the lure of the red carpet will out, and Simmons was never going to turn down the chance to party with A-list celebs for the sake of a little ethical harmony.

Chastened, Simmons temporarily abandoned the world of celluloid, doubtless convinced that even bigger sharks than he'd encountered in the music industry were not going to surrender their feeding grounds. But it would have been a surprise if his ego allowed him to accept a reversal so readily. So the February 2002 announcement that Universal Pictures, alongside Misher Films, had acquired the rights to Simmons' autobiography in order to make a film of his life (the second, following *Krush Groove*) should have surprised no one. "This project is the story of the American dream," producer Kevin Misher proposed. "Guys who set out to get paid and wind up at the leading edge of great cultural change, taking rap from being a street commodity and making it a cultural force."

Co-founded in 1996 alongside his unrelated namesake Anne Simmons, who later defected to UrbanMagic.com, Rush Media was an advertising agency established to lend hip hop style and invention to corporate partners who desired such an association. The company's objective was to provide clients with access to 'the American youth culture market'. Simmons filmed his first Coca-Cola commercial shortly after founding the company, Brett Ratner's *Father And Son*. In it, a middle-aged father listens to Marvin Gaye and Tammi Terrell's 'You're All I Need To Get By', before the camera cuts to his offspring, similarly drinking 'the real thing', though his head is bobbing to Method Man and Mary J. Blige's update of the same song. Other Rush clients included Esteé Lauder and Tommy Hilfiger. But what, some inquired, did hip hop have to do with

Coca-Cola? "Hip hop likes to buy the stuff they see on TV," reasoned Simmons. "They like to buy the things that are established and big and successful. They like the Coca-Cola. They don't want no un-cola."

That rationale of linking hip hop to successful, household name products was extended in 1999 when Rush Media became dRush in partnership with Donny Deutsch, the head of the largest independent advertising agency in the US. The idea was to create marketing synergies that would offer clients a fully integrated service. Simmons gained Deutsch's resources and infrastructure, while his new partner shared his ambition to break down barriers between mainstream and urban marketing – a concept that would be anathema to many in the hip hop community, who abhorred any such ideas of convergence. Simmons argued that any reservations are irrelevant, given that, largely by his own hand, hip hop culture was nearing the point at which it *was* the mainstream. He was simply marketing the culture, not adulterating it. The distinction, as *Time* magazine noted, was that Simmons 'moved' rather than 'modified' hip hop.

For his part, Deutsch saw Simmons as a means to harness hip hop's ability to engage consumers creatively, an argot that most American companies could neither understand nor address. "Youth culture dominates every trend," Deutsch admitted. "If you look at all the awards shows, music, clothes – they all reflect that. Russell Simmons is the epicenter of that urban youth culture movement." In a separate statement he issued further eulogies to his new partner. "I have tremendous respect for Russell as a business person. The opportunity is huge. No one has cracked this code as far as the youth market."

Simmons still wanted to broaden his media base further, and after discussions with mentor Quincy Jones, set up meetings with *Source* publisher Dave Mays about taking a stake in his pre-eminent rap magazine (as early as 1992, Jones and Simmons had talked about creating a magazine entitled *Volume*, which they immediately trumpeted as the "*Rolling Stone* of the 19Nineties"). Jones brought on board Time-Warner's financial muscle, but they were asking for a bigger slice of the magazine than Mays was willing to part with. Instead, Quincy launched his own magazine, *Vibe*. It was Simmons' task to audition an editor, but Time-Warner were keen on Jonathan Van Meter, later a *New York Times* reporter. Simmons was unnerved by the fact that Van Meter was gay, and in turn hired a chief reporter "who knew hip hop but who people in the community suspected was gay." Simmons clarified his objections in his autobiography. "If Jonathan had been editing *Harper's Bazaar*, this sexual orientation wouldn't have been an issue. But hip hop is absolutely the most homophobic, macho culture that's influenced mainstream America in a lot of years. In painting, dance, fashion and theater the gay perspective is respected and valued. Gay people are generally accepted in all forms of art in America. But homosexuality is a real issue in hip hop. It's unfortunate, but it's absolutely the truth."

Simmons is a pragmatist rather than a bigot – plenty of evidence suggests he worked quite happily with gay businessmen and colleagues in various business spheres and there's certainly more hostile attitudes to be found elsewhere within the rap community. Indeed, he helped sponsor the career of Caushun, the celebrity hairdresser turned rapper whose clients included Jennifer Lopez before he became a 'personal stylist' to Simmons' wife, Kimora Lee. "During this whole time, I was like, 'Honey, I'm rhyming, and this is what's happening,'" Caushun later recalled, "and I always got her support. When Russell would come home, she'd be like, 'Russell, listen to this honey, this boy can rhyme.' So I told him I had this one record called 'Gay Rappers D-Lite'. A lot of people were like, 'Oh, that's going to be controversial.' But Russell was like, 'All you gotta do is say this is only entertainment at the front of your album. It's all about peace, and you should be fine.' After Russell told me that, I was like, 'All right, I don't care what nobody says. The grandfather of hip hop told me that my shit is the bomb.'"

Simmons ended his involvement with *Vibe* when the editorial staff produced a promotional brochure which, to his thinking, equated hip hop culture with Madonna – even though the material girl was a self-confessed Public Enemy fan (using their beats on 'Justify My Love') and had Stephen Bray, whose brother was a prominent rap video director for Brand Nubian, Big Daddy Kane, Eric B & Rakim and Cypress Hill, author several of her hits. Simmons to this day believes that his quarrel with the *Vibe*'s direction resulted in the magazine being hostile to Def Jam and its product thereafter. Meanwhile, *Vibe* still boasts gay editorship in the form of Emil Wilbekin, and it doesn't seem to have done it any harm.

Simmons' other ventures included a TV show that attempted to give viewers the inside track on rap's big willies. Again, it came with Simmons' own name prefixed to it. *Russell Simmons' One World Music Beat*, though it hardly broke new ground, and included far too many "we just try to keep it real" ersatz interviews (the rap equivalent of rock's "we do what we do, and if anybody else likes it, that's a bonus" numbskull rhetoric), it did showcase rappers as something more rounded than their, often self-sought, caricatures. The comperes included Washington actor/comic Pierre, Simmons' girlfriend and later wife, Kimora Lee and Puerto Rican rapper Angie Martinez.

This being the Nineties, there also had to be a website – 360 Hip Hop.com. Although Simmons got dot.com fever late, he caught a bad case. For once, he was also a late entrant. Heavy-hitters such as BET.com and Urban Box Office had already taken a toehold on the on-line hip hop community – estimated to number 40 million-plus. But his prior business success gave him the financial muscle and reputation to make a big splash. And a big loss. However, he was never going to share the fate of the Silicon Valley net heads who won and lost a fortune within months – one thing he'd learned from *Tougher Than Leather* was not to invest too large a portion of his own fortune in any venture. So he carefully selected his new business partners, using his own reputation as collateral. As Morgan Stanley software analyst Chuck Phillips commented, "Not many people can stay cool for 20 years. That's worth a lot."

To start the website he sought backing from Seagram and Sony, plus rap stars Will Smith, Queen Latifah, Jay-Z and others. "We are confident that 360 Hip Hop.com will be the leader in delivering hip hop culture on the internet," Simmons waxed for his publicity machine. Simmons hyped his target audience, estimated to be 80 per cent white, incidentally, as "the most important cultural group in America. People say, 'You keep hip hop, and we'll keep the rest.' But they're giving me all of young America! The rest of it is old and out of date." The slogan for the site was, "The #1 destination for hip hop and culture on the internet." He spelled his goals out in an accompanying mission statement cum press release. "By launching the site, we hope to bring together people with common interests. With the increased popularity of urban culture, our goal is to offer a site that appeals not only to the African-American community, but to all people interested in the hip hop cultural experience."

Simmons gathered a talented cast to support the spiel. "Hip hop has become the vernacular for an entire generation of music fans," concurred Rick Holzman, the CEO of 360. "We have not pigeonholed ourselves as another music site. It's a hip hop lifestyle site. It's primarily a content site, and we have a strong editorial group." The scribblers were spearheaded by former *Source* editor Selwyn Hinds, while designer Ola Kudo opted for 'futuristic' visuals – with content including streaming music, video, and far too many adverts for Phat Farm clothes and *Def Comedy Jam* videos. Other ideas were ambitious, even grandiose. The iPix technology made it difficult to download on a 56k modem, the equipment with which most users without broadband could access the site. That meant that some ideas, like the virtual subway station where graffiti pieces could be submitted, or the interactive 'battle rhyme' arena, never obtained the 'traffic' that was envisaged. Even where these elements worked, there was too little attention paid to the swingeing truth that escaped the whole net generation: where does the money come from?

With a launch date set in June 2000, the staff was only finalised in January, leaving precious little time to pull the various strands together. And it showed. The website was quickly in trouble, débuting just as the high-tech economic meltdown got into full swing. In a medium he did not truly understand, Simmons, like many others, left expensive fingernail marks on a bandwagon that was rolling too fast and ultimately went straight over the cliff.

But he moved quickly to counter the site's haemorrhaging cash-flow just as other African-American themed websites, such as BlackFamilies. com and Onelevel.com, began 'to roll snake eyes'. The costs were estimated at $1.5 million a month for its 65 staff – paying for 20 of them to attend Urban Fashion Week in Miami was probably the height of the madness, though that was a modest oversight in the internet gold rush era of jam today, tomorrow, forever. There was also time for a charity basketball game, Simmons' 360.com staff against Puff Daddy's Hookt.com team. Soon some of those involved would be charity cases themselves.

He contacted fellow black entrepreneur Robert Johnson of the BET cable network, under the smokescreen of 'sharing technical and marketing efforts'. But the truth was that 360 was a visually impressive but content-weak website whose chat rooms were like morgues, while the sell-through levels of associated advertised brands was laughable. What Johnson got in return was some of Simmons' street credibility with younger African-Americans that the hip hop market represented. Simmons had already cut around 30 per cent of his staff by the time the deal was concluded, but more went as the two sites sought to use 'integrated teams'. Both sites were maintained as separate editorial entities. 360 Hip Hop.com may yet become the great entity that Simmons envisaged. But that's unlikely, and even if it does, Simmons no longer controls it. 360 Hip Hop.com is now solely owned by BET, though the original investors received an undisclosed equity stake in the company as compensation.

Which was a lot more than those thrown out of their jobs got. Simmons started 'talking down' the website just as quickly as he'd talked it up. Disgruntled former employees told *Urban Exposé* what was happening. "Many of the high salaried individuals at the company will not be receiving severance packages because BET.com felt they were overpaid. The good news is that the company is allowing them to keep their company-bought cell phones if they just sign the waiver to pay their own bill. The bad news, all two-way pagers from fired employees will be confiscated. Evidently, 360 Hip Hop feels letting them have those would be, 'too much flossing'." Other critics attacked the Castling Group, which helped out with initial management of the site, for failing to set any checks and balances on the group's spending. "Urban content can be profitable and will work in the internet space," *Urban Exposé* reasoned. "It just won't be 360 Hip Hop."

However, the experience was not an unqualified disaster. In 2001 360 Hip Hop.com announced its expansion into marketing campaigns in collaboration with urban music labels, offering access to both its cable and internet media outlets. The gist was that breaking artists could premiere both audio and video on the site prior to store releases. The programme was developed by BET's vice president of music development – none other than old Def Jam press officer Leyla Turkkan. Simmons' enthusiasm about the digital age did not dissipate totally, and he recently founded a new joint venture with Vtech Connect Ltd and Shared Technologies Cellular to launch Rush Communicator – a program that combines paging, internet access, local telephone services and other personal computer services. He was back on the promotional bandwagon straight away. "No one should be denied access to the latest information and technology," he said in a statement. "Information is power in this society – no matter who you are or what you do."

There was a further related, albeit more minor setback, when in June 2000 Simmons lost control of his *One World Music Beat* TV show. The name was changed to *Source: All Access*, with input from Mays' magazine, after ructions between Simmons and the African Heritage Network, who syndicated and owned the rights to the format. AHN executives were unhappy at Simmons' ceaseless cross-promotion of his website, to the point where some claimed it had become an 'info-commercial'. Simmons apparently attempted to have the show's name changed to 360 Hip Hop.com. They weren't overly impressed at the prospect of having Simmons' wife Kimora return as the anchor after her pregnancy either, citing diminishing ratings under her stewardship of the programme.

Simmons argued that AHN breached a good faith agreement and consulted his lawyers, but to no great effect.

Simmons' latest initiative is in an area that few could have predicted. His new idea is to do for black poetry what he's already done for black music and comedy. In the autumn of 2000, he invited a cast of celebrities and aspirant poets to a showcase at the Brooklyn Museum of Art to launch Def Poetry Jam, featuring Nuyorican Rule, a mixed comedy/poetry group who grew out of the Nuyorican Poet's Café, established in 1974, and Sonia Sanchez, author of 1985's *Homegirls and Hand Grenades*. "Def Poetry Jam is the Cartier of poets," boasted Bruce George, who executive-produced the show alongside Deborah Pointer and Russell's elder brother, Daniel. It led to a multi-media franchise including books, TV, CDs as well as, inevitably, a new clothes line. The latter, Bone Bristle, included pouches and 'pen-shaped zipper pulls' in its catalogue. In one of his most radical, not to mention impractical plans, Simmons seemingly intended to turn poets, known neither for there economic muscle nor contemplation of their wardrobes, into rabid consumers. There was also talk of a Def Poetry Jam management company.

An anthology was signed to Crown Publishers (who would also publish Simmons' autobiography), with the first volume edited by Sanchez, alongside fellow poets Tony Medina and Louis Reyes Rivera. The introduction was written by Abiodun Oyewole of the Last Poets, the Harlem 'urban griots' of the early Seventies whose combination of music and spoken word insurrection, most notably on 'Niggers Are Scared of Revolution', was a weighty influence on the hip hop generation. The authors were able to boast that the book received "the biggest advance ever for a poetry anthology," though we're probably not talking about the levels of finance that would keep Jay-Z in Swiss watches.

One could only smile at the title, however – *Bum Rush The Page: A Def Poetry Jam* echoed Simmons' hip hop legacy nicely. Each of the many contributors, some high profile, others unknown, were allocated equivalent space. The recurrent themes were, unsurprisingly, identity, injustice and oppression – subject matter that fits snugly into the hip hop tradition. The book was released in February 2001. In October *Def Comedy Jam* débuted on HBO, with Mos Def as compere, drawing on a talent showcase staged at the Aspen Comedy Festival in Colorado. Performers included the Last Poets, Amiri Baraka, Nikki Giovanni and Sonia Sanchez. "The poetry show was unbelievable," enthused Simmons. "The amount of response from people who ordinarily would not care; and what rappers are saying now is a lot more profound and important. But artists feel their voices are powerful and they're going to use them more, I think, in promoting social change in political climates that affect their ideas."

The *Def Poetry Jam* began its four-week run on HBO on 14 December 2001. "Poetry has been developing in the streets for so long, without Hollywood or anyone beyond the hardcore poetry audience really recognizing it," Simmons observed. One of the poets featured, Amira Barak, acknowledged the connection with hip hop. "Poetry has become popular today, thanks in large part to rap. So Def Poetry is itself a part of the continuum." If Simmons really can do something to revitalise a medium that has been dying on its feet for at least a century, then he can truly claim the mantle of miracle worker.

Simmons the businessman has managed to back a few losers; but he's also got a pretty impressive strike rate. While he once measured himself against the likes of Berry Gordy and Quincy Jones, he now sees Donald Trump as his real benchmark. And that puts us in the field of commodities and goods, products and services, rather than the human exchanges which forged hip hop. And that's a great shame, however damned rich you got in the process.

10

Can't Knock The Hustle

"The entire essence of America is the hope to first make money – then make money with money – then make lots of money with lots of money."

— Paul Erdman

By the mid-Nineties, Def Jam's reputation was assured. It could easily have become a venerated back catalogue, a flippantly quoted concession to rap in the rock'n'roll hall of back-slapping. But it was set to expand and prosper beyond even Simmons' panoramic imagination. A succession of acts not only re-established the Def Jam quality hallmark, they ensured the label was at the forefront of the next cycle of rap 'big willies' who would achieve, at least in pure sales terms, more than any of their forerunners. While many predicted that the label had peaked in 1994, Def Jam would astound industry watchers by becoming the pre-eminent marque of late-Nineties rap, attracting a vast body of loyal consumers to whom LL Cool J, The Beastie Boys and Public Enemy were irrelevant relics of a bygone era.

Vultures were hardly circling in the mid-Nineties, but some of Def Jam's lustre had faded. Gangsta rap sucked in those who desired the vicarious thrills of musical lemmings over cerebral artistry. Much of the resultant slew of murky, shockingly produced records bring to mind Ira Robbins' truism that, "The lowest of the low wear their recklessness as a badge to jack up music that has no guts of its own." After Nirvana's Kurt Cobain took his own life, the front covers of music periodicals began to offer odds on who the next alt-rock suicide might be. In the meantime, rappers were inflicting death by drive-by shooting on enemies and former friends. Which sums up the schism between the two genres' culture of complaint, and culture of retribution.

While gangsta rap resulted in several excellent records, most notably those associated with linchpin G-funk producer Dr Dre, Suge Knight's

Death Row was midwife to an era where the settling of scores was conducted with semi-automatics rather than lawyers or newsprint. And much of what followed in its wake was unremittingly tedious and as reprehensible as some of the outraged moral guardians on the sidelines suggested.

But, as former Def Jam staffer Andre Harrell reminds us, there was a genuine climate of resentment and fatalism that engendered what was essentially protest music. "We [Dr Jeckyll & Mr Hyde] felt like there was an opportunity for us being successful. I made a record called 'Gettin' Money'. I felt that there was an opportunity to get money. Now rappers are making smash hits, like 'Bring The Pain' [a hit single for Method Man, and also the title of Chris Rock's HBO comedy special]. People feel like they're growing up in a time when there's no system to figure out how to get money. I was born in 1960, so I might have been the last generation of the affirmative action rap movement. Now you've got Reaganomic rap groups. And Reaganomics took away after-school programmes, took away summer jobs, took away student loans. So you've got a whole generation of rappers who have grown up under the auspices of generation X, who grew up with no hope, and all they see is pain." Or, as Ice Cube postulated on 'The Nigga Ya Love To Hate', the urban existence had ceased to be about "how right or wrong you live", but about "how long you live".

But such insight was a rarity. Where once rap had been the most expansive of mediums, lyrics were now reduced to a handful of calibrated metaphors and clichés which revelled in ghetto's problems rather than attempted to ameliorate them. If anything, the music and the sources it drew on became just as formulaic and regimented. Simmons himself had yielded to some extent to this straitjacketing of the idiom by signing groups such as South Central Cartel. But no one was going to go to Def Jam for their gangsta rap. The label wasn't headed up by a 300lb former American footballer with a fetish for piranha fish, for a start.

Simmons was careful not to incur the wrath of these west coast upstarts, a situation his friend Puff Daddy found himself in with dire consequences. At the height of the internecine warfare, Simmons was diplomacy itself. "It's not like I got a problem with gangsta rappers, because sometimes they're telling their life, the way they see it. It's informative, it's helpful. But other people come along and they just do it because they think that's their ticket." And, possibly with self-preservation rather than true munificence governing his words, he offered this eulogy to his chief competitor. "I can't say much about Death Row Records, Dre and Suge Knight – I'm on they dick!" Knight, for his part, was happy to have an ally on the east coast. "You hear a lot of stuff about Russell, you hear it from every direction. Russell comes to me, I look at Russell as – whoever wants to deny, doesn't want to give him his props, they got to give it to him. Russell Simmons made the way for Suge, Dre, anyone in the hip hop business, because he started it."

Leaving the love-in to one side, the power base of rap had shifted from east to west coast. Knight was suddenly the label boss everyone wanted to profile – if not interview, stories of those piranhas having spread rapidly – leaving Simmons looking staid and, most insufferably for him, edged out of the limelight. While he didn't start throwing counter punches, as was Puff Daddy's instinctive reaction, he didn't entirely take it lying down either.

He was able to recruit Warren G without too much friction, which gave him some sort of gangsta rap collateral. He also set up Def Jam West to establish a presence in the booming Californian rap market. On the east coast, he befriended Notorious B.I.G., the Brooklyn behemoth whose enmity with Tupac Shakur inspired the east-west feud and eventually led to double murder. "I know he [Simmons] was dropping a lot of knowledge to his artists," Biggie reflected on *The Show*, "because he had a lot of artists. And Russell definitely knows how to make money. That's all I want to do, is sit there and ask some questions about how I can make money." Sadly Biggie would not make that money for Simmons, having already been tied up to manager Lance 'Un' Rivera and Puff Daddy. But waiting in the wings was an old high school friend of Biggie's, Shawn 'Jay-Z' Carter.

When Tupac was killed in 1996 and Biggie in 1997, the rap world, whether respectfully or not, paused for breath. Suddenly self-glorifying tales of gang life and territorial dissings seemed beyond the pale. The fascination with hardcore subject matter didn't disappear, but there was an appetite for someone with a lighter touch. And Jay-Z fit the bill as snugly as if he'd been drawn up on a Def Jam A&R executive's pie chart for that purpose.

His skilful, intuitive grasp of ghetto vernacular was rare but not unique among his contemporaries, but he also brought back rap's reverence for the high roller and the party jam. In the process he helped restart the hip hop party, and also reasserted Def Jam's claims as the definitive rap label – banishing at last the lamentable east-west fraternicide. Statistics bear this out. Since 1994, Def Jam's annual gross sales have grown by 300 per cent, grossing $200 million by 1999. While both Redman and Method Man were major draws and bridged the Def Jam of old and new, the label needed fresh blood. Indeed, there were strong industry rumours circulating in 1997 that the plug might be pulled if Def Jam couldn't find another hit artist.

However, the reasons were not entirely performance related. Simmons' friendship with PolyGram head Alain Levy became strained almost immediately after they started working together. The trouble started when Def Jam's marketing was moved under the auspices of Island, which proved totally unsatisfactory as a succession of artists were shunted to the bottom of the promotional pile. Simmons protested, which earned a move to Danny Goldberg's Mercury. But, again, Def Jam product was not considered a priority. Their frustration escalating, by 1998 Cohen and Simmons had begun to extricate Def Jam from the major, again putting the label on the open market for a rumoured $50 million. But Simmons wasn't prepared to cash in what he saw as Def Jam's prime future assets, DMX and Jay-Z, as part of any deal. Which was arguably the best decision he made in his entire life, as both embarked on careers that saw them top the album charts at will, with a frequency that was unheard of in popular music.

Shawn Carter, aka Jay-Z, aka the Jigga, aka Jayhovah, the man for whom a singular nickname is never nearly enough, divested rap of its gang affiliations as he steered jigginess, his particular take on ostentatious materialism, to the top of sundry charts as the Nineties progressed. Everything this hugely prolific artist touched turned platinum, making him the most marketable commodity in rap, arguably in all of contemporary music. "Jay-Z raps about Iceberg, it catches fire," purred Simmons. "That's a fact. The minute he said it, Fifth Avenue blows out Iceberg sweaters at what, $600 apiece? Instantly." But the perception of Jay-Z as a showroom dummy on which you can hang any old commodity as long as it's designer-labelled and hideously expensive irritates Jay-Z. "I don't like it when people just talk about jewellery or cars – it's much deeper than that. There's different layers and levels – when you hear that it means that they just skim through it and didn't really listen. When people say it's one dimensional – that bothers me."

Jay-Z had all the right credentials to take up the mantle for post-gangsta rap and lead it, if not towards the sunlight, then at least away from the funeral pyres. He was born in the Marcy Projects of Brooklyn, to parents who loved music so much, they individually stickered each of their jealously guarded albums. His truck and cab-driving father left the family home when he was 12, which devastated his youngest son, who was already getting himself into trouble – three years earlier he'd shot his brother Eric in the shoulder for trying to take a ring from him. Facing the same limited choices afforded his peer group, he took to selling cocaine and hustling, though for a short period he also staffed a local Kentucky Fried Chicken franchise. While there he was taunted by both his boss and some bored local troublemakers, before having his borrowed car hauled away for illegal parking. That fateful day he noticed future collaborator Memphis Bleek, quietly mulling over his book of rhymes. It prompted him to vow to take his rapping seriously.

The neighbourhood which christened him 'Jazzy', because he was a snappy dresser, was tough, but not as utterly bleak as some would have it portrayed. "It was cool, you know; we had our sunny days, and they'd be playing the Johnny Pump, and things like that. But it was low–income housing. And everyone's on top of each other. You got people to the left of you, right of you, under you, on top of you. You gotta deal with so many different personalities on a day-to-day basis, and you just gotta really know how to manage that. It's like you walk on eggshells every day. You say the wrong thing to the wrong person, and they feeling the wrong way, then . . . tragedy can happen – and it won't be in the paper. It's not going to be in the paper. Nobody saw nobody. It's just OK. Life goes on. It's tough. Real tough." Which is why he later quantified his output as "life imitating art imitating life imitating art".

While living from hand to mouth via a variety of nefarious means, he began perfecting his rap skills – a natural vocation having attended the same high school as Notorious B.I.G. and Busta Rhymes. He was friendly with local rapper Big Jaz, who secured a contract with EMI in 1988 and released a couple of albums, bringing the young Shawn Carter along for the ride. "I did a verse on this song, 'Hawaiian Sophie' [from 1990's *The Originators*], and that's how I got my start. [Jaz] introduces me to the entertainment business, and looking back, I was pretty much grateful for the opportunity to be put on. Too bad, things didn't pick up like they should have after that, so I kept hustlin'." In 1993 he cut his first single, 'Can't Get With That'/'In My Lifetime', with the help of long-standing friend Damon Dash. "I had a demo tape and I shopped it to all the major labels by myself. When I'd get down on myself, I'd think they just don't get it. So I started printing my own CDs and put them into the trunk of my car and sell them. It was real grass roots. Spending $200 dollars and making

$150 back." The single was eventually picked up for distribution by Payday.

But that deal soured, especially when Payday booked him for store appearances at outlets that didn't stock his record. Those experiences, and similar ones recounted to him by friend Big Daddy Kane, convinced Carter that rap labels were sharks, and he elected to set up his own imprint. Hence Roc-A-Fella Records, founded with friends Kareem 'Biggs' Burke and Dash. They took office space in the financial district of Manhattan, albeit a run-down spot on John Street, and signed a distribution deal with Priority. Jay-Z, to this day, remains evasive over whether or not the rent was paid with the help of income from the cocaine trade.

By the time Jay-Z's solo début was readied he'd already made waves with a series of guest appearances, the time-honoured apprenticeship for aspirant rappers. Records by Big L and Mic Geronimo showcased his, at this stage rudimentary, rhyme skills, before he enjoyed a more substantial role on Original Flavor's 1994 album *Beyond Flavor*, where he outstripped his contemporaries on 'Can I Get Open'. His solo career finally took off when the double A-side 'Dead Presidents'/'Ain't No Nigga' went gold and introduced two of the most iconic tracks in Nineties hip hop.

'Dead Presidents' was an axiomatic moment for rap, combining Puff Daddy's 'ghetto fabulous' credo with a little more musicality and a lot less corn, while offering a retrenchment of EPMD's stoic business mantra about remuneration being the bottom line. 'Ain't No Nigga' was an update of the Four Tops' 1972 hit 'Ain't No Woman (Like The One I've Got)'. Its video defined the new era of jigginess, featuring Jay-Z draped in a Versace top exchanging haughty boasts with the as yet unsigned Foxy Brown, who qualifies her tolerance for the jigster's romantic indiscretions on the basis that he 'gives me a lot'. One such gift afforded by Jay-Z's patronage was a career jump-start as the record alerted a number of interested parties to her talents.

Jay-Z's lyrical prowess was ably demonstrated on his subsequent 1996 début album, *Reasonable Doubt*, whose assured, amplified braggadocio succeeded despite the samey subject matter (hustling, drugs, life on the street). Many still consider it his finest album, bereft of the commercial concessions that would overtake him later. Opening track 'Can't Knock The Hustle' introduced his self-professed "Godfather flow", with sublime accompaniment by R&B singer Mary J. Blige, was the latest in a long line of rap songs to buy into De Niro-inspired Mafia mythology. The references to Remy Martin and Cristal, meanwhile, were staples his audience would grow accustomed to, those boasting of a serve "like Pete Sampras" provided a metaphor for rackets which was not to be repeated. But arguably the most noteworthy track was 'Brooklyn's Finest', a riposte to 2Pac's licentious 'Hit 'Em Up' on which he was joined by Notorious B.I.G., shortly before his death.

Before he could truly become 'the Don' of hip hop, as prophesied in 'Can't Knock The Hustle', Jay-Z had to negotiate Roc-A-Fella out of its Priority deal. "With Priority, I had a messed-up contract. And everyone knew. But we didn't know. We was like, 'Why were we . . .?' But they was like, 'Why you so offended? It's just business.' To them, it's good business; to us it was deceit." By the advent of his second album, *In My Lifetime Vol. 1*, with production by DJ Premier of Gang Starr, he'd signed a new distribution deal with Def Jam. Irv Gotti, brought to Def Jam by Lyor Cohen and another alumnus of Hollis, Queens, brokered the deal (and later signed both DMX and Ja Rule). "I used to DJ for Jay-Z and I was a part of Roc-A-Fella in the early days," Gotti told *The Source*. "I helped nurture their vision. I've known both X and Jay since around '88. I always felt that [DMX, Jay-Z, Ja Rule] were the best at what they do. Those three are the best in the game. They are the pinnacle of what they do and no one out there can touch them."

In My Lifetime didn't enjoy the same effusive praise afforded his début album and lacked a breakthrough single, though the mood of the album was deeply affected by the loss of his friend, Biggie. "It was real difficult making that album," Jay-Z acknowledged. "I was so disgusted with the whole situation. He was such a good dude to everyone around him. Everybody loved him. If you believe in karma – that if you do good things and are a good person, then good things will happen – that will just crush your whole theory."

But some felt he'd lost the attack he'd displayed on *Reasonable Doubt*, charges he rejected. "It was still a platinum album, and it yielded songs like 'Streets Is Watching', 'Imaginary Player', 'Where I'm From' – some of the best songs. The thing about rap is, if he's telling a story about a fire, how close can he bring you? Can you feel the flames, can you smell the smoke? I just think I brought people closer to my story, and it seemed more real to them. And then I have this sort of a sarcastic wit that's entertaining. Those two things are the biggest attributes."

'Streets Is Watching', also the title of a short he wrote and directed, featured dialogue purloined from Barry Levinson's *Sleepers*. The semi-justified paranoia of lines like: "If I shoot you, I'm brainless/But if you shoot me, then you famous" were a revelation. However, the album itself is uneven and its cold, cynical edge is best expressed in 'Rap Game/Crack Game', which drew a self-explanatory comparison between the two industries Jay-Z knew best. Particularly unsettling is the misogyny of 'Who You Wit II' and 'Face Off'. Both succumb to the oldest gender libel in rap's book – gold-digging women. Foxy Brown returned alongside Babyface for '(Always Be My) Sunshine', while fellow Cristal-sipper Puff Daddy checked in on 'I Know What Girls Like', which featured the chorus to the old Waitresses AM radio staple ('I Know What Boys Like') but ditched all the original's irony ("Want to buy you real jewellery/ When it hits the light, bitches'll momentarily lose they sight"). Around half the songs were produced by members of Puffy's camp, resulting in material which conceded a little too much in trying to appeal to pop audiences, though the presence of Gang Starr's DJ Premier, a regular on Jay-Z's first four albums, added vital contrast.

Jay-Z made absolutely certain that a paucity of hit singles wouldn't afflict *Vol. 2: Hard Knock Life*. Populated with stellar guest stars including DMX, Too Short, Erick Sermon and Jermaine Dupri, as well as hot producers Timbaland, Kid Capri and Swizz Beats, it housed three massive hits in 'Money Ain't A Thang', 'Can I Get A . . .' and particularly 'Hard Knock Life (Ghetto Anthem)'. The latter, appropriating a Broadway favourite from *Annie* and reconfiguring it as a hymn to ghetto life, was a step too far for some, mainly due to its retention of the stage school kiddie chorus. But it was the sort of rap song that conservative pop radio stations could embrace, at least in its 'clean' incarnation.

The song also brought old school production legend Mark James, aka the 45 King, back into the limelight. He found a copy of the musical soundtrack "for a quarter in the Salvation Army in Inglewood. I was looking for the horns on a record. I couldn't find the horns so I found the kids singing 'It's a hard knock life for us'. So I put it to a beat and played a bass line and I put it on my demo tape and I gave it to maybe 100 people trying to get work." Eventually it reached Kid Capri, who'd just DJ'd Puff Daddy's tour, where he played it every night. When Jay-Z enquired about its availability, he was told Queen Latifah was also interested. The jigster got there first, writing a typically self-aggrandising lyric to accompany it and filming a video in which his $360,000 Bentley almost upstaged him. "Thanks, Jay," high-fives Mark James. "Put me back on the map."

Although the synergy between stage musicals and rap music thankfully lacked longevity, the album became a commercial juggernaught, débuting at number one in October 1998 and selling 353,000 copies in its first week of release alone. In the process Jay-Z became the first rapper since LL to connect with mainstream pop audiences without losing the respect of the hip hop community (in fact, he pulled off the trick a great deal better than LL had done). Jay-Z was immediately the hottest commercial property in rap, a position he has not relinquished since. That he'd done so by dint of James' digging in the vinyl crates for the odd and unusual, an old school hip hop fetish that the mainstream had largely abandoned, added extra kudos to the achievement.

The closing weeks of 1999 brought *Vol. 3: Life And Times Of S. Carter*. In keeping with the title, Carter had just fleshed out his life experience by taking a sharp detour along the much-travelled rap freeway to trouble city. On 1 December he attended the Kit Kat Club in Manhattan for the pre-release party of Q-Tip's *Amplified*. While there he got into an argument with Untertainment Music CEO Lance 'Un' Rivera. Rivera was stabbed twice, once in the back and once in the chest, by an 'unknown assailant'. He was taken to New York's St. Vincent Hospital, but eventually recovered. Early reports suggested Jay-Z had claimed he'd discovered evidence of Rivera making pirate copies of his upcoming album. Other rumours concerned a 'love triangle' between Rivera, Jay-Z and Notorious B.I.G.'s one-time girlfriend Charli Baltimore – which Jay-Z later acknowledged in his contribution to Memphis Bleek's 'Is That Your Chick? (Lost Verses)' ("She keep calling me Big and my name is Jay-Z/She was all on my dick").

Manhattan police immediately launched a search for Jay-Z. Two days later he gave himself up and posted $50,000 bail, denying all the allegations – despite corroborating evidence from witnesses. Def Jam rallied round, Lyor Cohen telling the *New York Daily News* that Jay-Z's lawyers possessed video tape footage of the party that showed "he wasn't near the scene". Just three days before he was scheduled to appear in court, Jay-Z was in trouble again. On 13 April 2001 his Chevrolet was pulled over outside New York's Club Exit, where he'd appeared alongside Ja Rule. A handgun was found on bodyguard Hamza Hewitt, leading the police to charge all four passengers with illegal possession of a handgun. Damon Dash of Roc-A-Fella waded into his defence. "Donald Trump walks around with security and you don't see [police] doing what they do to us. The entire [hip hop] culture is being treated this way, as if there's no other way a black person can be successful without being a drug dealer. It seems like the police are always profiling, and they base that on an assumption or a prejudice that any kid with money has got to be doing something illegal." He remonstrated against the repercussions that rap's image had on his personal life. "Not only does this prejudice mess us up on a corporate level, but when I try to put my son and daughter in certain types of schools, I get turned away once they find out what type of business we're in – rap music."

Facing various charges relating to these misdemeanours as well as a further incident at a New York nightclub, Jay-Z was looking at a potential 15-year jail term. However, a peace was quickly reached with Rivera – an indeterminate sum of money changing hands on the condition Rivera would quash his civil suit. Thereafter prosecutors' court documents revealed Rivera had insisted he "would either disappear at the time of the trial or testify in a way that would help his friend".

Vol. 3: Life And Times Of S. Carter delighted but also perplexed in equal measure. When it was good, as Jay-Z himself noted in 'Hova Song (Intro)', "Jigga is the shit, even when he rhyme in third person." He could be brutally eloquent, as on 'Come And Get Me' – "Ignorant bastard, I'm takin' it back to day one/No kids, but trust me, I know how to raise a gun." The collaboration with Mariah Carey, 'Things That U Do', confirmed that there was no way Jay-Z was going to give up on any of his potential markets. Which was good news for his accountants and Def Jam, but not that great for music fans.

The Dynasty: Roc La Familia, whose title deliberately pushed the mob theme up a notch, saw Jay-Z discuss his musical entourage in terms of the Ming dynasty, "rather than Blake Carrington". All too many rappers dissipate their talent and standing by introducing the world to their second cousin and his mate under the guise of ghetto fraternity. Most have never succeeded on their own terms for a single, very good, and very obvious reason. But Jay-Z's rationale was admirable, and unusually articulate. "Blacks, when we come up, we don't normally inherit businesses. That's not a common thing for us to have, old money, like three and four generations, inheriting our parents' businesses. That's what we workin' on right now. A legacy."

The album housed the huge cross-over single 'I Just Wanna Love U (Give It 2 Me)', but principally served as a showcase for Roc-A-Fella's emerging acts, including Beanie Sigel, Memphis Bleek (an old friend from Brooklyn and Jay-Z's KFC stint), Amil and DJ Clue. Although tied to a distribution deal with Def Jam, Roc-A-Fella was acting as an increasingly autonomous finishing school for rappers. "It's a Jay-Z album," the

Russell Simmons plots his latest blue-sky money-spinner. *(Guy Aroch/Retna)*

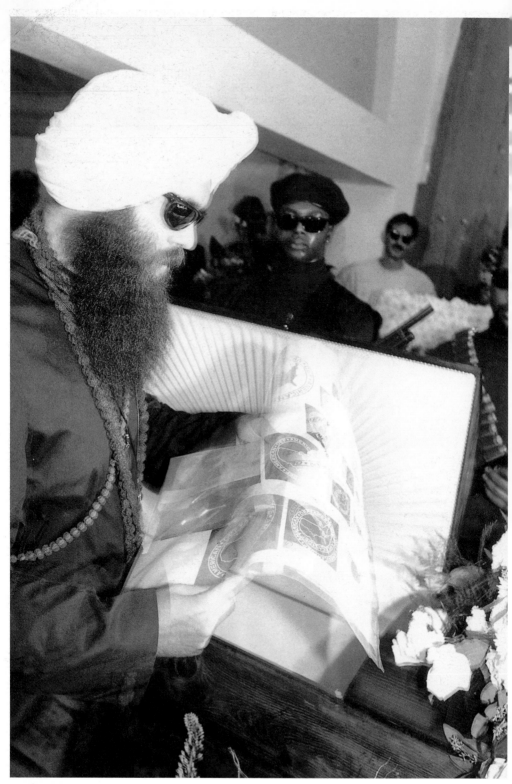

Rick Rubin presides over the ceremonial internment of the "Def" prefix on
August 27 1993. *(Steve Double/SIN)*

EPMD: Always open for business. *(LFI)*

Method Man: Def Jam's slice of the Wu-Tang franchise. *(Martyn Goodacre/SIN)*

Warren G: the producer/artist who brought west coast G-Funk to Def Jam. *(LFI)*

"Details man" Lyor Cohen ensures his product-placement is spot on again. *(John-Marshall/Mantel/Corbis)*

Russell Simmons demonstrates his credentials in cutting edge urban fashion. *(LFI)*

Someone really ought to tell Foxy Brown she'll get a chill going out dressed like that. *(LFI)*

Jay-Z: Def Jam's pivotal artist of the new millennium. *(LFI)*

Russell Simmons with the Rev Al Sharpton,
discussing hip hop's new mood of conscience. *(Rex Features)*

Ja Rule, Def Jam's latest multi-platinum
breakthrough artist. *(LFI)*

Ludacris; holding it down for Def Jam in the
Dirty South. *(LFI)*

Get at me, Dog. DMX and his pooch chill. *(LFI)*

Rick Rubin fails his ZZ Top audition at the City of Hope Spirit of Life dinner honouring Edgar Bronfman Jnr at Universal City, California in October, 2001. *(Steve Granitz/Wire Image.com)*

The Hitman and Her. Russell Simmons and wife Kimora Lee at the excite.com Awards, June 2, 1999. *(Rex Features)*

The three most important non-artists in hip hop? Cohen, Simmons and Rubin at the Def Jam reunion party at Manhattan's B-Bar & Grill in September 2001, just five days before the World Trade Center attacks. *(Theo Wargo/Wire Image.com)*

principal contended, "The family, they're on a lot of tracks, and they're dominating the tracks, and they're showcasing their talent. But that was my whole plan." *The Dynasty: Roc La Familia* débuted at number one on the charts and went gold in its first week of release – a reflection of Carter's personal standing rather than the quality of the contents. The last person to have two albums of original material top the US charts in the same year was Elton John. And Jay-Z had better dress sense.

In the aftermath of this success, Jay-Z became a one-man business empire, mirroring Russell Simmons' example. "My music is something people have to really sit down and listen to," he claimed. "So with the record company being the bridge to reach people, I was, like, 'Man, we gonna build our own bridge.'" He also shared Simmons' taste for celebrity friends, of whom the most noteworthy was Michael Jackson. "I was talkin' to him on the phone, and he was talkin' about 'Hard Knock Life'," Jay-Z recalled to *Rolling Stone*, "and he was like, 'You was just so in pocket on that record, landin' right on the beat. Incredible.' I'm like, 'Thanks.' But I'm lookin' at the phone like, 'What? Stop playin', man!' Mike was a superhero when I was a kid. Him wantin' to work with me, period, was bananas!" A Michael Jackson collaboration coming out on Def Jam therefore remains a possibility. Something that Russell Simmons could never have imagined when he first launched the label as an alternative to the black music mainstream.

In October 2001, Jay-Z changed his plea to guilty to misdemeanor assault over the Rivera stabbing, and was sentenced to three years' probation in December. Which must have shocked those who'd clocked his R. Kelly duet, 'Guilty Until Proven Innocent', on *Roc La Familia*. Perhaps he'd taken note of his new pal Michael Jackson, who sacrificed his reputation rather than contest allegations of child abuse because his lawyers could not guarantee he wouldn't do jail time. Jay-Z's attorney, Murray Richman, wasn't too chuffed at his change of mind either, claiming it was a "bullshit charge", and the district attorney's office were only pursuing it because they'd "lost the Puffy trial". But someone sure as hell slammed a five-inch blade into Rivera's stomach, and people don't generally admit under oath to such things without a very good reason.

The outcome meant Jay-Z could busy himself with promoting his latest release, *The Blueprint*. By now his compositional skills were second nature. He would simply pick a rhythm track he liked, and have the verses sketched out within minutes. These were memorised without the aid of pen or paper, and laid straight to tape. He claims to have up to half a dozen songs competing for room in his head at any given time, but occasionally you wish he'd let them fight it out for breathing space and impose some editorial discipline rather than simply spew them out, straight to CD. Despite this extraordinary work rate though, there is little evidence of his having exhausted his oeuvre.

What was especially commendable about *The Blueprint*, making it his best album since his début, was the fact that it offered straight-up Jay-Z, without the cast of thousands which normally populate his albums. The high-spot was 'Takeover', a battle rhyme which went after both Prodigy of Mobb Deep and Nas, who'd dared to diss him in their recent work. The put-downs felt like daddy bear cuffing errant cubs, such was Jay-Z's ease at arms. The vertically challenged Prodigy was informed Jay-Z had "money stacks bigger than you" while he poked fun at pictures that had surfaced of Prodigy in ballet school (which wasn't quite true, though his mother had run dance classes). The put-down of Nas, meanwhile, managed to condense what others in the hip hop community had been saying for years after the former boy wonder failed to deliver on the early promise of *Illmatic* – "Had a spark when ya started, but now you're just garbage." Where before he'd tried to perfect the R&B/rap torch song, this was Jay-Z in blowtorch mode, so much so that 'Takeover' utterly over-shadowed his collaboration with Eminem, 'Renegade'.

His work ethic spilt over into his business activities. He executive-produced the soundtrack to the director's cut of *Scarface*, while adding a rap to Michael Jackson's 'You Rock My World' remix. He also launched his own clothes line and sports agency. All of which helped pay for his expensive tastes in champagne, clothes and jewellery. His wardrobe included a Swiss-made Audemars Piguet diamond watch, a limited edition of one; Rolex was clearly fine for your common or garden platinum rapper, but not Jay-Z. But accuse him of crass commercialism and the jigsta comes over all aggrieved. "I don't give a fuck. I don't care about that shit. I'm not telling you to be me or do what I do. I'm not trying to rub people's faces in my success. What I'm doing is showing you: Look, I'm a ghetto nigga. I'm from Marcy Projects. And I made it to this point. When I'm talking about that shit, it ain't just me. I'm representing for everybody that came out the 'hood. Like: Yeah, we can do this. We can drive big Bentleys and own big homes. But that's not all I'm about. It's shallow people that just take those things out of the music and ignore all the other things I'm trying to tell them about – the struggle and everything going on in the ghetto." Jay-Z remains on course to be the biggest rap star of them all, but he wants his props to come on 'a serious tip', too. "Y'all take my words too lightly," he warned. "That's the problem. I keep telling y'all that: don't take my words lightly. I'm dead serious, man. I know what I'm doing here. I got an agenda."

The one thing that Def Jam lacked by the mid-Nineties was a successful female MC, previous experiments with Nikki D and Bo$$ unravelling for a variety of reasons. Foxy Brown, aka Inga Marchand, managed to turn the tide. Named after blaxploitation big sister Pam Grier's character, with whom she remains friends, Foxy became eternal tabloid fodder through speculated relationships with everyone from sports star Andre Rison (who doubtless has trouble getting fire insurance when he dates R&B stars, after Lisa 'Left Eye' Lopes of TLC torched his condo) to rappers Master P, Nas, and Def Jam stable-mates DMX and Jay-Z. She certainly had her own, distinctive take on feminism. "I tell a motherfucka, look: grow titties, get a pussy, get your heart broke before you talk to me about how I'm acting. Do that before you talk to me about shit." As Grier herself remonstrated with her detractors, "Foxy Brown represents the women in my family who taught me how to be independent. We fight for ourselves, for our family, and we fight for our man."

Foxy, whose mother Judith raised her and two brothers after their father fled at a young age, met Jay-Z through her cousin and producer Clark Kent when she was 13. She was signed, then dropped, by Capitol (under the names Big Shorty and AKA), when aged just 14. She and fellow Clinton Hill, Brooklyn resident Kimberley Jones, aka Lil' Kim, had already made a pact to record the definitive *Thelma and Louise* rap record once they'd got their start. But while Kim threw her hat in with Notorious B.I.G and Bad Boy, Puff Daddy turned Foxy down when she was brought to him by rapper Red Hot Lover Tone. Instead, she waited to take her chance with Jay-Z's camp.

First she befriended Steve Stoute of the Trackmasters, presently working on LL Cool J's *Mr Smith* album, who'd caught her at a Brooklyn freestyle event. Stoute and Tone used their connections with Chris Lighty, CEO of Violator, who managed acts including Busta Rhymes and Missy Elliott, as well as LL Cool, to sneak her into the studio. Lighty was persuaded to give her a shot at performing on the remix of LL's single 'I Shot Ya', though no one bothered to tell the featured artist. Not that he minded greatly. Her arrival was electrifying, if a little disturbing. "I'm sexing raw dog without protection/Disease-infested," she rapped, announcing her sexually provocative oeuvre, though she had to leave the studio sessions early because she had a school test the next day. Foxy was away, cementing her arrival with guest appearances on a series of mid-Nineties R&B hits by Total, Toni Braxton and Case.

But the crucial connection came when she appeared on Jay-Z's 'Ain't No Nigga', which also featured on the soundtrack to Russell Simmons' pet project *The Nutty Professor*. It saw her sketch her later image as the bolshy but assured foil to rap's big willies ("From Dolce & Gabbana to H. Bendel/I ring your bells/So who's the player?"). As she's fond of saying, while passing advice out to homegirls, "All his diamonds and ice will melt you, but you need to have your own."

A bidding war, genuine rather than the usual fabrication invented by the victorious label, ensued. Interested parties included Puffy Daddy, who'd changed his mind, Sylvia Rhone of Elektra, Andre Harrell at Motown and Russell Simmons at Def Jam. By now Foxy was the preferred pin-up girl of hip hop magazines, a situation encouraged by a dress code where the definition of scanty wasn't the only thing being stretched. "I just feel like I've never been someone to shy away from my sexuality," she protested. "To me, there's nothing wrong with what we're doing, nothin' different than what Madonna has done, nothing different from what Pam Grier has done in movies. It's just bananas. There's so much negative things out here, people are killing people, it's like – whatever! It's entertainment. I think when people understand that it's the music industry or the rap game, that's why it's called the rap game, 'cuz it's fun." She settled on Def Jam because "Russell had longevity". But it was Cohen who brokered the deal, waiting outside her home to persuade her that Def Jam were best placed to look after her interests. Signing with Def Jam also meant she stayed with Lighty, who'd shepherded her career thus far.

Her 1996 début album, *Ill Na Na*, named after her nickname for her private parts, lacked a consistent musical approach, veering, sometimes uneasily, between R&B and rap. The best accommodation came with 'Get Me Home', which featured male vocal backing from BLACKstreet (subverting traditional gender stereotypes by featuring female rapping supported by male backing vocals). But Foxy wanted to be perceived as a hardcore rapper, and was frustrated by some of the subsequent exposure, which concentrated on her visual appearance rather than her mic skills – a blight on her whole career. Lighty admitted in *Hip Hop Divas* that there were problems with the album. "I knew who I wanted her to be musically. Foxy was reluctant to do 'Get Me Home' at first. That was too pop. We had her on more mainstream records than she wanted to be on."

Others ragged on her for her defiant materialism – a facet of her lyrics that should be no surprise given that the album featured ghost-writing from Jay-Z. Despite these flaws *Ill Na Na* went platinum. So too did her next project: *The Firm*, a misfiring collaborative effort which linked her with Noreaga, Nas and AZ, with production from Dr Dre.

Thereafter Foxy elected to take time out before embarking on her second album proper, *Chyna Doll*. Eventually released at the end of 1999, she contended that she had "grown as a person . . . [On] my first album, you can tell, everything was successful, but knowing that it was rushed, and knowing that it was something that I always had to do what everybody else said, it was kinda hard and difficult. Now this time I have a lot more leverage, I have a lot more say, I have a lot more control." That new found control didn't necessarily extend to her temper, however, judging by her decision to physically attack the editor of *Vibe* on a sidewalk in New York late in 1999.

The album topped the charts after the hugely successful Irv Gotti production 'Hot Spot' opened up New York's dance-floors. For the rest of the album, however, the club grooves were replaced by more rugged production and harder themes, particularly on her no-nonsense duet with Noreaga, 'It's Hard Being Wifee'. Other issues tackled included single parenthood on 'My Life', while Jay-Z returned on 'Bonnie & Clyde Part II' and 'Dog & A Fox' teamed her with DMX. The album also included her remake of the Howard Johnson 1982 hit 'So Fine', with backing vocals from Next.

But it was not an unqualified success. In particular, she was still being attacked for her wardrobe, her demeanour and her language. Then there was her Calvin Klein billboard advert that distracted motorists and jaywalkers in Times Square, and endless speculation over her personal life – challenging even Puffy for stewardship of rap's rumour mill. "People harp on it more because she's a female," reasoned Lighty. "No one says anything when Q-Tip or Meth or DMX curses someone out or is late to a video shoot. It's just accepted. You be 15 and be chased by Puffy Combs and Russell Simmons and Chris Lighty – see how you handle it."

There was also the small matter of her running feud with Lil' Kim, which soured further when Foxy's collaboration with Noreaga, 'Bang Bang' upped the ante. Kim's *Notorious K.I.M.* included a series of counter-attacks that were as thinly veiled as Foxy's rear. In true gangsta style, the two parties exchanged gunshots in February 2001 in Manhattan after a date at Hot 97 FM. Which all made for a tantalising post-Biggie/

Tupac headline for the press corps, but was depressing for everyone else concerned. The dispute got so messy that Simmons, doubtless still feeling guilty at his anaemic reaction to the west coast/east coast rap wars, tried to mediate. "I really don't know how it started," Foxy told MTV News. "But Russell and I, we got together, and I said, 'Russell, I want to call a truce. I want to have a sit-down with Kim. I don't care what it is. Let's just end it. We can even do a collaboration.' We're bigger than this. If it has to start with me, let it start with me."

As news-friendly as the feud was, it caused Foxy to take her eye off the ball. Her momentum was stalling, judged by the top five entry of her 2001 album *Broken Silence*, which came in well below projections. Though it is ironically her finest album, it was also her least successful while the contents repeatedly pointed to personal turmoil. 'The Letter', which featured the unmistakable voice of Ron Isley, openly apologised to her family for some of her behaviour, specifically including her crotch-grabbing *Vibe* cover pose, which did so much to establish her wild child reputation. Jay-Z was this time conspicuous by his absence, as Foxy teamed up with old friend Noreaga as well as reggae producer Tony Kelly.

Stung by the disappointing sales figures, by the end of 2001 Foxy had returned to the studio. The first results were premiered on 'BK Made Me', which again alluded to soul-searching and personal doubt – "Got dreams of ending this bitch/My life is miserable/Make me end this shit." Having elsewhere claimed she was 'the female 'Pac', the song raised serious doubts as to her stability and wellbeing. She'd also fallen out with long-term supporter Chris Lighty and Violator, to that point her closest confidant. All of which leaves Foxy at a crossroads. Presumably, like her blaxploitation namesake, she'll come out lookin' fine and fighting, but it'll be a few years yet before it's prudent to assess the damage caused to her by being exposed to fame at such an early age in an industry where loco parentis usually translates as el loco parentis.

DMX, aka Earl Simmons, is not a stylistic virtuoso in the manner of Jay-Z. But his update on Tupac Shakur's 'thug life' aesthetic, his neo-gothic travelogues and propensity to lose himself in a fight between good and evil that seemingly endures daily replays in his head, are arguably more compelling attributes. His link with the gangsta rap generation is clear, yet there is a mix of melancholia and frustration at the core of his work that links the English metaphysical poets and Joseph Conrad with the Geto Boys' 'Mind Of A Lunatic'.

For that reason, but not for that reason alone, he readily appeals to white youths brought up on the fantasy images of extreme metal, but whose belated adolescence requires a little more authenticity. DMX (aka Dark Man X) provides one bloodcurdling trauma after the other, an abundance of vicarious thrills without straining credibility too far, or resorting to the easy clichés of gangsta rap. He also offered a timely riposte to Jay-Z's jigginess, a shadowy presence that spoke not only of the dark stuff of the ghetto, but the dark stuff of the soul.

As Russell Simmons explains, "DMX is kind of honest. You know, he's had a lifetime full of problems. And he always seems to be at odds with himself . . . he's a very confused person. And it's real true, it's real honest. And you can tell, that integrity comes through in his records. When you've finished listening to it, you really want to go right to God. You don't want to go nowhere else. Like, just take me somewhere and let me sit in church and stay away from him because he's not happy. Even though it's violent, even though it's sexist, even though it's a lot of things, his whole record is about wanting to change and the struggle he is going through."

Born in Baltimore, Earl Simmons was yet another child abandoned by his father at an early age. Unlike his contemporaries on Def Jam's roster, however, his mother was also frequently absent, leading to a youth spent in social housing and correction centres. The result was an aptitude for self-destructive behaviour and depression, and a seeming inability to feel safe and sheltered under even ideal circumstances.

Despite listening tastes that veer towards classic R&B and funk rather than hip hop, he started out as a human beat-boxer in Yonkers' School Street Projects, taking his name from the famed drum machine behind so many of rap's historic records (he would change the acronym intermittently to infer such properties as Divine Master of the Unknown). He grew his reputation via the mix tape underground, appearing alongside friends DJ Clue and later Bad Boy artists the L.O.X. (Shawn Jacobs, Jayson Phillips and David Styles). As his reputation grew, he earned *The Source*'s *Unsigned Hype* award for January 1991. That helped secure a deal with Columbia Records, but apart from a promotional single, 'Born Loser', released in 1992, nothing else materialised. "Columbia tried to put me behind other groups," DMX recalls. "They were like, 'Well, we're gonna put out Kriss Kross, then we're gonna put out Cypress Hill and then we're gonna put you out.' And I was like, 'Well I'm better than all of them niggas.' So I didn't wanna wait. I always knew there would be a point when someone would say, 'Somebody needs to make money off this nigga cus he's hot.' That's when Irv Gotti brought me to Lyor Cohen at Def Jam. I guess it's that point now. I guess the world wasn't ready for the gutter until now. Now they ready for the gutter shit, so now they get the fuckin' gutter."

Cameo appearances on songs by L.O.X., LL Cool J, Ma$e, Mic Geronimo and Cam'ron spread his reputation to such an extent that in a preview piece, *Vibe* magazine suggested he was "clearly about to pull a Foxy Brown" by leaping from collaborative notoriety to a hit solo career. If anything, DMX's timescale was much more compressed than that article implied. By the time he'd completed his début album, he'd already lined up a leading role in Hype William's feature film, *Belly*. Signed, alongside his record label Ruff Ryders, to Def Jam by Irv Gotti, DMX's brutal hip hop revolved around the deceptively simple, brittle keyboard stabs of producer Swizz Beats, a sort of skeletal, anti-funk sound with insidious, dirty hooks. It was introduced by his breakthrough single 'Get At Me Dog', whose ragged energy immediately connected with club audiences.

'Get At Me Dog' also announced DMX's enduring fixation with canines as a metaphor for male comradeship. But he loved the real thing, too. One of his many tattoos featured the legend 'One Love Boomer', dedicated to his late pit bull, his 'best friend'. *It's Dark And Hell Is Hot* followed, comprising similar raw-knuckled morality plays such as 'Stop Being Greedy' and 'Ruff Ryder's Anthem'. There was also the Yonkers posse cut 'Niggaz Done Started Something' and the Jay-Z collaboration 'Murdergram'. The album entered the charts at number one and quickly achieved quadruple-platinum status. With his innate, hurt-but-proud authority, this was self-evidently an artist struggling to reconcile personal demons. Which meant it didn't take long for critics to label DMX the new Tupac. He wasn't having any of it, grabbing at a sportsman's cliché in his defence. "I say they don't know what the fuck they are talking about. And when people say I'm the second 'Pac, I'm not, I'm the first X."

DMX set out on the *Survival Of The Illest* tour, alongside Def Squad, Onyx, Cormega and Method Man, an effort to revive the glory years of the *Fresh Fest* tours. But he then had to contend with unfounded allegations of rape, sodomy and unlawful imprisonment of a 21-year-old dancer. Two months later the case was dismissed after DMX submitted a sperm sample for a DNA test. The publicity did little to hamper his career, though his videos and songs were temporarily pulled from TV and radio. "There was a lot of downward pressure on playing his records and showing his video with this thing looming," reckoned Lyor Cohen.

"Now, since he's exonerated, I'm sure they are really going to go full speed to wrap their arms around him." His statement concluded with a forthright valediction. "He's most definitely the most important new poet of our time."

By December 1998 DMX had completed *Flesh Of My Flesh, Blood Of My Blood*, its cover picturing the artist standing erect in a bath (though it could just as easily be a coffin) of blood. The autobiographical 'Slippin'' expanded on the themes of his début, its Nietzschean spoken intro offering the observation that "To live is to suffer, but to survive, well, that's to find meaning in the suffering." 'Omen' was recorded alongside rock bad boy Marilyn Manson (though the two parties never met, and you wouldn't notice the frocked pipsqueak's presence if it wasn't pointed out to you). Yet the most extraordinary track was album closer 'Ready To Meet Him', a one-to-one Judgement Day confessional with God. DMX was never shy of big themes, but his approach was refreshingly sincere and impassioned. Released just six months after his début, the album again topped the charts – making DMX the first début artist to have two number one albums in the same year (and also, twice, removing Garth Brooks from the top of the poll as hip hop outpaced country as the dominant musical force in America. Hurrah). DMX's success turned his imprint, Ruff Ryders, into a family concern to rival Jay-Z's Roc-A-Fella. A spin-off album from his posse, *Ryde or Die Vol. 1*, went double platinum to prove his commercial prowess, while DMX prodigy and self-anointed 'pit bull in a skirt', Eve, sold more than a million copies of her début.

Within a year DMX had topped the charts for a third time with . . . *And Then There Was X*. This time the centrepiece was 'What's My Name?' ("I'm not a nice person/I mean I'd smack the shit out of you twice, dog/ And that's before I start cursin'.") But some were beginning to question his range. Peter Shapiro keyed into DMX's register when comparing him with Satan's own kennel-mate. "With his asthmatic growl, Doberman tenacity when he attacks a beat, his collection of attack dogs and tales of death and pain, DMX tried to be hip hop's Cerberus guarding the gates of hell. But where Cerberus had three heads (and presumably three different barks), DMX has only one voice, one flow and one gimmick."

The analogy may be beautifully wrought, but the conclusion isn't necessarily accurate. There's self-evident depth to DMX that you wouldn't readily associate with hardcore rappers, and while he mines a singular philosophical seam, the agonies of one man's God complex have rarely yielded such rich diversions. But . . . *And Then There Was X* is not his best album and suggests that no one can produce three albums within two years without running out of creative puff. And yet still there were highlights, particularly the matter-of-fact storytelling of a liquor store heist in 'One More Road To Cross'. "I love to express what real niggas feel, what street niggas feel," reckoned DMX. "They need to be heard. They need to know there is a voice that speaks for them, and I am that voice."

DMX remained hardcore hip hop's most visceral, vibrant presence. Rodd McCleod caught DMX promoting the album on tour in 1999 and published this testament to his raw power in *Rolling Stone*. "After all the rhymes about bloody street life and male sexual power ('I got the white bitches sayin' it's all a black thing/I leave that ho' with plenty of back pain') DMX pulled a 180 and got downright ecclesiastical. 'Let us pray,' he intoned. Preaching in rhyme with no beats for support, X worked the room like a born evangelist, pledging love to his wife, God and his fans, whom he loves 'like children'. He asked the Lord for forgiveness and noted that he always prays for his enemies, 'not because of what I'm gonna do to them, but because they haven't found God.' It was a truly masterful performance of virtuosic intensity, and the audience hung on his every word. 'Who know real?' he asked several times. 'How many ya'll niggas from the ghetto?' The implication was undeniable – Earl Simmons knows real, and his fans love him for it." The fuel behind DMX's epic journey, despite the satanic imagery that surrounds his image, remains a desperate attempt to reconcile himself with his God.

In the interim he was also having problems reconciling himself with his fellow man, especially those uniformed members of the species. He'd experienced a fraught separation from his Ruff Ryders crew and been forced to produce public service announcements telling children to stay away from guns and be kind to animals after he pleaded guilty to 13 counts of animal cruelty, and sundry counts of disorderly conduct and possession of drug paraphernalia. By this point his charge sheet included assault charges for attacking a New York motorist, a concert stabbing in Denver, weapon possession charges, and the illegal ownership of 14 pit bulls kept in violation of local laws, which were handed over to the American Society for the Prevention of Cruelty to Animals.

The Great Depression saw him move forward inexorably in 2001, routinely topping the American charts, though this time the gap between albums seemed almost perverse after his previous unearthly work schedule. 'Bloodline Anthem' (titled after his new imprint at Def Jam) subsumed previous affiliations to the Ruff Ryders. Swizz Beats was no longer overseeing the production, helming only two cuts, while 'I'm A Bang' and 'Who We Be' hinted at a fusion of hip hop and metal. But the production shake-up gave DMX a fresh canvas, and he responded with new verve. The best track was 'Shorty Was Da Bomb', a tale of the repercussions of lust and unwanted pregnancy (though DMX hardly came out of it the perfect gentleman, leaving the responsibilities of the unborn child to rest "on the next man's arm"). The biggest surprise was 'Trina Moe', an attack on rap materialism that came out of nowhere, but was all the more welcome for it – "We already know how much your watch is worth/Talk about helping the hurt, savin' a church." Just as 'Ready To Meet Him' had addressed DMX's spiritual quest, here 'A Minute For Your Son' was the rapper-talks-to-God track, which had actually become DMX's strongest suit.

DMX, not the most naturally gifted of MCs, nevertheless possesses the ability to instil even the most workmanlike recordings with messianic fervour and purpose, calling to mind David Bowie's bon's mots about an artist going through stages where he wonders if he is Christ, before concentrating on merely looking for him. *The Guardian* called him "the accessible, electrifying voice of a nihilistic underclass," though the reality is that Earl Simmons is a man driven by the search for meaning, like a modern day Othello guilty of loving not wisely but too well, with Nostradamus riding shotgun on his shoulder. Long may he continue to top the *Billboard* charts and hold the real devil, Garth Brooks, at bay, should further incarceration not intervene. It's about even-money both eventualities.

While the roll-call of platinum records continued, not all of Def Jam's signings were unmitigated successes. First, there was the frustrating case of Cormega, a talented MC and proficient lyricist who was tipped to be one of Def Jam's new stars, but fell victim to mishap and mis-management. He was due to record as part of the Firm after Nas befriended him while he was serving time in Rikers Island for murder, but it never happened. Then he signed to Def Jam, and that never happened either. An LP, *The Testament*, was recorded but never released, despite his single 'Angel Dust'/ 'Killaz Theme II' getting some good notices. "The industry is what it is," he shrugged. "It's a music business. They don't care about how nice you are or how dope you are. They care about how many records you could sell." He finally got to release his début, *The Realness*, on Landspeed Records, but by then most of the buzz surrounding him had dissipated.

There was also the tale of record company politicking that engulfed San

Diego's Jayo Felony. Felony, a veteran of California's penal colonies (his worst experience – being locked up on Superbowl Sunday), had been rhyming from the age of nine. His début single, the delightful 'I Piss On Your Tombstone', led to him signing with Jam Master Jay, who released his *Take A Ride* for JMJ in 1994. He also rhymed on South Central Cartel's 'Sowhatusayin'', which included a memorable put-down of Oliver Stone's *Colors* – "Gettin' paid off gangbangin'/I want my money, muthafucka." His Def Jam début proper, *Whatcha Gonna Do*, followed in 1998, with contributions from Ice Cube, Redman, Method Man and DMX – the latter two appearing on the title-track, also released as a single. Jayo's reputation seemed sufficient to ensure a longer stay. But it was his final release for the label, as he griped to the press about lack of promotion and representation.

An unreconstructed Crip, Jayo was angry at those who faked the gangsta lean while having no true affiliation to gang culture. He was particularly upset at Jay-Z's 'Streets Is Talkin'' and the lines "Is he a Blood, is he Crip", expressed in a manner that announced, categorically, that these things weren't important. As a result of Jay-Z's intervention, so Jayo claimed, he was shunted off Def Jam, leading to the non-release of his *Hotta Than Fish Grease* album. Instead Jayo took the tapes and independently released *Crip Hop*, which slammed Jay-Z on tracks such as 'Catch 'Em In The Mornin''. He was soon dissing the jigster wherever and whenever he could, including the pages of *XXL* magazine. "This morning we shot the video to 'Bullet Proof Love' in Marcy Projects . . . I'm out there with real niggas and they like, 'Fuck Jay-Z. This nigga ain't giving back to the community. We don't even see that nigga.'"

All of which got Jay-Z's back up. Jayo's 'True'd Up (The Crip Anthem)' was pulled from the Henchman Entertainment compilation *Bullet Proof Love Vol. 1*. Distributed by Motown, which became a sister company to Def Jam in the Universal Music Group reshuffle, Jayo insisted it happened as a result of Jay-Z's direct intervention. "Jay-Z snitched to Lyor Cohen and tried to keep the song from being put out," he complained. "We got calls from Lyor and everybody about not putting this record out. I feel like this: If we're on the streets, keep it on the streets. Don't go to the higher-ups."

Jimmy Henchman confirmed that he was 'pressured' into removing the track. "It's like [Jay-Z] called the police on me," he revealed. "I couldn't understand why he felt so strong about the record. Rap was built on diss records. He dissed niggas on records before, talking about [how] he's 'the one' and all this. He can't feel he's untouchable." Jayo may have a legitimate grievance about the music industry black-balling him, but it was going to take more than a disgruntled, displaced MC to knock either Jay-Z or Def Jam off their perches.

11

It Takes Russell Simmons To Hold Us Back

"There's no reason to be the richest man in the cemetery.
You can't do any business from there."
— Colonel Sanders

Def Jam prepared to enter the new millennium under new proprietors. For some time Simmons had been negotiating with Seagram's Universal Music Group over his remaining stake in Def Jam. The monolith wanted to consolidate its entertainment interests and was initially prepared to pay up to $70 million for the remaining 40% stake. Simmons pushed them up to the nice round figure of $100 million in a deal completed early in 1999. That showed the value of the brand and its continued growth – Simmons had sold the original 60% in 1993 for $33 million. Simmons was also keenly aware that Priority's Bryan Turner and Mark Cermai received $100 million from EMI in 1997 for 50% of Priority – then flush from the success of NWA, Ice Cube and Dr Dre – which set some sort of benchmark.

The consolidation allowed Universal to re-brand its Island-Mercury subsidiary the Island-Def Jam group. Industry commentators were impressed by the price tag, given that the deal was concluded at a time when Simmons was in conflict with Public Enemy, and the returns for Foxy Brown's *Chyna Doll* were deemed 'disappointing' (despite it débuting at number one, the album fell off the charts quickly). But after successful albums from Jay-Z and DMX, revenues were expected to touch $200 million for the year and there were clearly massive assets involved – not least DMX and Jay-Z (although the latter was signed to Roc-A-Fella Records, with whom Def Jam shares a distribution deal), meaning label sales had risen 200 per cent between 1997 and 1998. Simmons drove a hard bargain and got a good price. But Universal knew what they were buying. As the CEO of the Universal Music Group, Doug Morris, commented: "Def Jam keeps setting the standards and opening up new horizons for the genre." The statistics alone were impressive, without the brand identity and cachet that Def Jam brought.

Simmons remained as chairman of Def Jam, while Lyor Cohen, formerly Def Jam CEO, became the head of urban music at Universal and eventually president of Island/Def Jam. Kevin Liles, who'd started as a lowly intern, before progressing to head of radio promotion, became Def Jam's president. Most of the other key executives, such as music video head Margo Wainwright, were happy to follow Simmons and Cohen. As Simmons noted, "We keep people by paying them fairly and providing an environment that's supportive." That was something he would observe from the other side of the table now. For the first time since he'd been working in that Manhattan juice store, Simmons found himself in salaried employment collecting a monthly Universal pay cheque.

But he wasn't unduly inconvenienced. "Selling Def Jam was great. I did it for 20 years. I'm the chairman now. I do the same work I've been doing, I still work at Def Jam every day in some capacity, it hasn't changed at all . . . I manage the company from afar. Def Jam was always my baby, it still is. I sold it, but it's the same working environment." He also had a rationale for the decision to sell, though it didn't sound like he was about to let go of the baby completely. "When we sold the first half of the company, we did it to give the artists a better opportunity and we weren't able to do it as an independent company. With the power that we have in that building right now, we can do a lot more for the artists. It feels good now. I can market this thing. I can put my foot in it. Which is what many record companies do for their rock stars. Now Def Jam can do it for their rap stars."

As if anticipating claims that he'd passed Def Jam into the hands of the enemy, he pointed to his continued sovereignty in the hip hop marketplace. 'We still have Rush Media, which has Coca Cola, HBO and BET as clients . . . We have a clothing company which has gone from $35 million to over $100 million this year. We have a film company. *Nutty Professor II* is starting. We got a magazine and a TV show. That company [Def Jam] has had fluctuations for a long time. It's been our most profitable [company] for a long time, but it's OK to cash something in." What that statement neglects to mention is the fact that all those allied businesses were not built from scratch, but instead relied heavily on Def Jam's status before they in turn prospered.

By October 1998 Simmons' networking, which had already seen him court the rich and famous, brought him alliances with the politically powerful. Together with girlfriend Kimora Lee, he hosted a $1,000 a head fundraising dinner for Hillary Clinton, then the First Lady, running for Senate in New York City. The venue was his own SoHo apartment. Russell Simmons as political lobbyist? Well, it was certainly a new market. He also became the subject of a made for TV four-part mini-series, allegedly as the result of pressure being applied to TV networks by the NAACP to feature more biographies of minorities.

Simmons had changed his lifestyle drastically. He was now a committed vegan (among his favourite foods was 'Fib Ribs') and yoga student. His first yoga teacher was Steve Ross, dubbed the 'guru of LA' by *Vanity Fair* magazine – the fact that Ross was a quasi-celebrity must have been part of the attraction. They were introduced by Bobby Shriver in the mid-Nineties, when Simmons was living in LA. Back in New York, he joined the Jivamukti Yoga Center, run by Shannon Gannon and David Life. He claims that yoga opened him up so that "the teachings of all the great religions sound good to me." Indeed, while he talks with pride about brother Joey's rebirth as a Christian, he maintains strong links to Louis Farrakhan and the Nation Of Islam whilst also advocating the tenets of eastern spiritualism, shying away from any denominational commitment in favour of a religious pick and mix theology. "The whole yoga philosophy is about the wonders of God, and that all of these roads from all of these religious teachings and all of these prophets taught the one road to God," he explained. "No matter how people might perceive them as different today, they're all messages about the same God, and of how to get to the same God. God is in you and is a part of you. We are connected to each other, and we are connected to the same road to God. I believe that, and I believe that all these teachings are great, and I wish that these people understood that the prophet said the same."

That meant a revision of his business attitudes, too. "The things nowadays that make me happiest, besides from the things I can buy, and the other shit that comes along with people's conventional idea of what can make them happy – if I get a little paper and I can hire a nigger straight out of jail, who I grew up with, which we do all the time, friends we help, and they become successful, and they get their shit on, I see that. Or if I find an artist who just came out and the nigger's really hard working and really has a vision and believes in himself, and he's trying and trying, suddenly I give this man a contract and he blows up, and he's on the cover of *Rolling Stone*. He's going to have little rich black babies, that kind of thing means a lot to me, now. I didn't realise how much I appreciate seeing those things happen."

That happiness spilled over into his personal life. On 15 December 1998 he married Kimora Lee, known throughout Simmons' businesses as a feisty, no-nonsense companion. Concurrently studying for a degree in psychology at New York University, Lee was the daughter of a district manager for the social security administration unit in St Louis. The couple met in 1994 when Lee was modelling at Fashion Week shows in Manhattan. A civil ceremony was presided over by Sherry Klein Heitler at the State Supreme Court in Manhattan, before younger brother Joey (now the Rev. Joseph Simmons of the Zoe Ministries, of course) conducted a non-denominational service at St Barthelemy the following Sunday – which Simmons nearly missed after his plane was stranded in Puerto Rico.

Some brief fashion notes: the bride wore a white gown by Susan Lazar, while the bridesmaids included models Tyra Banks and Veronica Webb, both clad in lavender chiffon. Simmons, naturally, made sure his grooms-men were decked out in Phat Farm apparel – specifically khaki slacks and golf sweaters. A wedding was no excuse to miss out on such a heaven-sent cross-promotional opportunity, after all. However Simmons' Adidas sneakers, worn in the hip hop fashion without shoelaces, was a nice touch. The male guests included Danny, his other brother, Andre Harrell and Lyor Cohen.

By April 1999 Simmons had sold his Beverly Hills home for $2.2 million and moved back to New York full time, paying $2 million for a 4,000 square foot apartment formerly owned by Rolling Stones' guitarist Keith Richard (he'd also previously rented a penthouse once owned by Cher in the East Village). In it he installed a 'meditation room', which is something Richard wouldn't have had much use for, though it is currently all the rage with celebrities like Madonna. His 'new age' beliefs were con-firmed in an online interview with ABC News, though, typically, these epithets were closely tied to business objectives. "In yoga, all we talk about is focus and staying focused. Everybody has a great idea, but very few are successful without true focus. There's going to be a time in any business when you have some doubts. Certainly people around you are going to doubt you. But you have to stay focused and not start over in some other field. You have to stick with what you start. That's the most basic thing: stick with your vision. Don't let other people dissuade you because you don't have instant success. Every business I've started including clothing, advertising, film, television and records took years to develop."

197

While still enjoying the credibility afforded him by his status as rap's great playmaker, Simmons wanted to stress his caring side. When ABC's current affairs TV programme *Nightline* profiled him in terms of the workaholic deal-maker he'd always aspired to be, somehow that was no longer enough. "I think that the piece on *Nightline* was very flattering and it was very good for selling T-shirts, but it left out all my philanthropic work, which takes up about a third of my time and all of my spirit. When I'm running my advertising company, which I guess they failed to mention as well, the interest in Robb Report (an Argos catalogue for the impossibly rich) and 'things' was important as part of my study of the culture, but it didn't change my life. And the money hasn't changed my life a single bit." The funniest moment, though, came from his wife's stoic, mid-conference interjection. "Russell? Is this a dictatorship?"

Not everything was kisses and flowers. Public Enemy, for a start, had beef with Simmons. Their resentment boiled over when two projects slated for 1998 were delayed. The first was the soundtrack for Spike Lee's movie *He's Got Game*, the second had the working title *Bring The Noise 2000*. Chuck D complained bitterly of the lack of promotion the former received, and delays affecting the latter (its release date was pushed back twice). He eventually went public over the rift in his bi-monthly online column *The Terrordome*, referring to Simmons as 'Hustler Scrimmons' and Cohen as 'Liar Conman'. Def Jam had become 'Def Scam' before Chuck's jaundiced eyes.

Disagreements that had originally been put down to "growing philosophical problems with Russell Simmons and Lyor Cohen" became much more rancorous and entrenched, particularly when Public Enemy made clear their intentions to release their next studio album as an internet download before it reached the shops. Def Jam threatened a retaliatory lawsuit. Public Enemy's line was that they were trying to create a 'street buzz' for the album's official release. But this clearly gave the jitters to Def Jam's corporate handlers who, like many in the music industry, were anxious about the new technology taking power out of their hands. Chuck D railed against the intrusion. "The execs, lawyers and accountants who lately have made most of the money in the music biz, are now running scared from the technology that evens out the creative field and makes artists harder to pimp."

It is a subject that Chuck D has registered several pertinent points about, highlighting the unequal relationship that exists between artist and label. Those arguments were crystallised in an article headlined *'Free' Music Can*

Free The Artist, a specific defence of Napster, the internet application that allowed users to share MP3s, digitised versions of an artist's music, through the internet. At the time it was written the music industry was searching for legal remedies in order to shut it down, though eventually they managed the next best thing and essentially bought it out. Among those who attacked this 'exchange' were Metallica's drummer Lars Ulrich, and, from the rap community, Dr Dre. Chuck's piece criticised the economic premise of the label-artist relationship – that artists only earn a few cents on each record sold, but if it's not a hit and the label decide to pull support, they still own the rights to that material in near enough perpetuity. He also pointed out that record labels' reaction to technological advance has been selective, embracing it only when it maximised their advantage. "The last straw was the CD period, when labels increased their mark-up without raising artists' royalties in kind."

He went on to critique the music industry's success in 'squeezing out' the independent entrepreneur from the distribution of music – exactly the sort of figure, like Russell Simmons, who had been so important in exporting hip hop to its current worldwide audience. "Well, Napster has been a thorn in that bull's side. By exposing people to music, companies like Napster are creating new fan interest and establishing a new infrastructure for unknown artists to attract an audience – a new radio for the new millennium." The piece concluded: "The internet has created a new planet for musicians to explore, and I'm with that."

Def Jam, and the wider music industry, clearly were not. Public Enemy severed their ties. *There's A Poison Goin' On*, which *Bring The Noise 2000* had become, was eventually released on the internet and through independent label Atomic Pop Records in 1999. Cohen hit back, stating their departure was nothing to do with "this computer stuff". He was also quoted in *Vibe* magazine, stating: "We were negotiating their departure a long time before the MP3 incident." The ruckus was arguably to the veteran group's advantage – Public Enemy without controversy was hardly Public Enemy, and it did produce significant media exposure at a time when the group's status had slipped. But Chuck clearly believed wholeheartedly in what he was saying. Further column inches were filled by the inclusion of 'Swindler's Lust', which again brought accusations of anti-Semitism. In truth, the track was simply anti-record company ("A dollar a rhyme, but we barely get a dime" ran one of the lyrics). Although Public Enemy weren't the fire-starters that once fused the media radar that they once were, in many ways the album was an overlooked return to

form, featuring some of Chuck's most incisive attacks on hip hop con-
formity, media ignorance and record industry politicking.

Simmons' newfound wealth hadn't escaped the attention of Chuck and
the rest of the hip hop community. The Bronx founding fathers had suffered mixed fortunes, and some had been left out of the loop completely.
When S.H. Fernandez tried to get an interview with Kool Herc for his
book *The New Beats*, Herc asked for $500, which Fernandez couldn't run
to. But, as he admitted in an interview with *HHC*, "I can understand why.
He started this whole thing and he hasn't received a penny from it. And he
sees artists now signing million-dollar contracts." Even now, Herc com-
plains that no one will offer him a ticket to a rap show, despite being the
godfather of the entire shebang. Chuck had similar reservations about the
way the great rap dividend had been shared. "I'm a supporter of both
Russell Simmons and Andre Harrell to a degree. They've done some
remarkable things in this industry. At the same time when you rub your
nose with the white boys, and you're in a position to make things happen,
especially if you're the figurehead of an industry, you should do whatever
it takes to make waves and force changes. I don't believe they've done
enough of that."

Although Simmons rarely responded directly to such remarks, he never
fought shy of journalist's microphones when they were proffered. He'd
even started to call himself the 'grandfather of hip hop', which may have
upset Herc and his peer group. He stressed, instead, the importance of hip
hop in educating whites about the black inner-city condition. "Seventy-
five per cent of [the hip hop] audience is non-black. Now you have kids in
Beverly Hills who are sensitive to situations in Compton," Simmons told
Jet magazine. "Rap has taken a lot of back culture and put it in the forefront, in the mainstream. It's a globalization of the black culture. [The
artists] are showing an honest representation of their feelings. So as long as
the mainstream doesn't accept that, then it makes it more appealing to the
youth."

He also shrugged off charges that his pursuit of money had in any way
cheapened the art form. "They always talked about getting money, from
the beginning. Jazz and blues and rock and roll . . . always talked about
getting money or the American dream; and then some affluent group of
people got into it for the hell of it. And they brought holey jeans and shit.
Chuck Berry had a Cadillac, and fucking shiny suits, and all the blues
singers and the jazz singers sang about how the fuck can they get their
piece of the American dream? That's what they sang about. They didn't

sing about abandoning all hope, and all that shit like dropping out. That's when the next generation of jazz, blues and rock and roll singers came. In rap, we didn't get that next generation. We got on MTV ourselves without having some group of more affluent, upper middle class or successful people making music, and trying to rebel by making their music. These people made their music from the heart, they still do. They still talk about the suffering in our communities, they're the same as the other early artists. And all of them want to get some money." Criticising commercial artists for making money is like telling pigs not to roll in the dirt, in other words.

For now, Russell Simmons had other matters on his mind, not least his impending fatherhood and a little back-slapping gong acquisition. Established 'to honor those artists, producers and industry leaders who have made lifelong contributions to hip hop culture', he picked up the 1999 *Source* Lifetime Achievement Award. The mantelpiece groaned further when he and Kimora, now eight months pregnant, collected the United Jewish Appeal Federation's Spirit of Music Award, recognising those who make major contributions to its work of music education in public schools, a notable benediction given Def Jam's previous clashes with the Jewish community.

Simmons told *People* magazine that he and Kimora were well prepared for parenthood. "It's all done. We have enough clothes for another country." His wife featured in the celebrity columns at the end of 1999 when she allegedly toured the hall of a gala event and asked for money for her baby shower. She raised $6,000, and anyone who didn't contribute was declared 'cheap'. It looked like some of the Simmons hustle had rubbed off. You can't keep a good spendthrift down for long. "Since we got married she shops even more," Simmons complained to *People* magazine, who cornered him at the launch of watchmaker Cartier's new range. "They have to keep coming up with new collections. If they didn't, she wouldn't have anything else to buy."

Russell Simmons entered the new millennium as a father, after Kimora gave birth to their first child, daughter Ming Lee, in January 2000. One can only imagine the emotional turmoil Simmons faced at the maternity unit – facilities notoriously inflexible over the use of cell-phones. The Reverend Jesse Jackson graced the christening. While Kimora attended to the new arrival, T-Boz of TLC took her place as host of Simmons' ill-fated TV series *One World Beat*.

Though he didn't abuse his parental leave and returned to business in short order, from the birth of his daughter onwards, Simmons spent an increasing proportion of his time campaigning on social issues. While his thirst for business expansion wasn't entirely quenched, the arrival of Simmons Jnr helped accelerate the shifting of priorities. Before he had little time for such issues. When C. Delores Tucker and *Soul Train* founder Don Cornelius attacked hip hop at the February 1994 Committee on Energy and Commerce's subcommittee on Commerce, Competitiveness and Consumer Protection, Nelson George was despatched along with then Def Jam president David Hareleston to argue their case. From now on Simmons would give such matters his personal attention.

Fatherhood and his yoga-inspired spiritual reawakening resulted in a radical overhaul of his life goals. "When I pass, I want it to say, "Russell Simmons: Philanthropist" on my tombstone. At 43, I'm married, I have a child. It's a dramatic difference in my life in terms of my focus. I don't want to die and they say, "Russell Simmons, here he lies: Greedy entrepreneur." I want to have made a difference." It's strange how the attraction of that word entrepreneur, which once Simmons cherished as a cover-all means of self-definition, has faded over time.

The reborn Russell Simmons started to address issues facing the black community in general and the hip hop generation in particular. He began by registering his unease at the alarming case of Amadou Diallo, New York's very own take on Rodney King-like police savagery. Savagery which, just as in the Rodney King example, they were never held to true account for. In searching for a rape suspect in the Bronx on 4 February 1999, four white policemen fired 41 bullets at the unarmed Guinean immigrant, hitting him 19 times and killing him instantly. They claimed he had reached for a gun, when in fact he was attempting to pull out his wallet to confirm his identity. In their trial on 25 February 2000 they were acquitted by a New York State Supreme Court, the jury finding their actions to have been 'reasonable'. The same day Simmons issued the following statement. "I am horrified by the outcome of the Diallo case. This verdict stands as another reason for the community to stand together for change. The hip hop community moves as an army that has the power to elect government that puts the people first versus the officially sanctioned and promoted police state mentality of [New York] Mayor Rudolph Giuliani. This verdict will continue to motivate me to be part of the aggressive effort that galvanizes our youth to register, vote and make changes in the current system."

Giuliani had been discredited among the hip hop community for his pursuit of what they believed was 'racial profiling' in an effort to reduce New York crime statistics, which he'd achieved via the closing of clip joints and strip clubs around 42nd Street. However, his efforts to sanitise the city, cleaning up the subways (which was always going to bring him into conflict with hip hop's graffiti community) and clearing the streets of petty crooks and prostitutes, made New York a safer, though potentially less colourful place to live. His refusal "to reach out, to work with a community that is in pain" was publicly criticised by both the First Lady and President Clinton. Resentment in the hip hop community of the NYPD hardened when New York magazine uncovered a spreadsheet containing the car make and licence plate of vehicles belonging to nine different rappers.

The Diallo case saw Simmons step up to the plate and embrace political dialogue. Others to join the protest included Bruce Springsteen, whose song 'American Skin' didn't mention Diallo by name but began with a reference to the '41 shots' used by police, as well as the line, "Is this your wallet?/Is this your life?" It brought the following, scarcely credible response from Bob Lucente, president of the New York chapter of Fraternal Order of Police. "He goes on the boycott list. He has all these good songs and everything, American flag songs and all that stuff, and now he's a floating fag. You can quote me on that." The Patrolmen's Benevolent Association launched a boycott of Springsteen's Madison Square Garden concerts if he wasn't willing to withdraw 'American Skin' from the set, and asked its members to refuse to work security overtime at the events. The boss wouldn't back down, though the concerts eventually proceeded without incident.

Simmons stepped up the pressure, joining Mos Def, Mary J. Blige, Martin Luther King III and Reverend Al Sharpton on a march to publicise Rap The Vote 2000, scheduled to start at Manhattan's City Hall on the 31 March. Among the issues Simmons wanted to raise were police brutality, the penal system and racial profiling. He also launched a series of attacks on Giuliani, lampooning him with the epigram, "I'm not hip hop" across a photo printed on flyers and prominently displayed on 360 Hip Hop. But Giuliani prevented the rally, claiming that Simmons had deliberately left his application for a permit to hold the rally too late so that he could claim political censorship, and that he was exploiting the event to promote his website (360 Hip Hop was one of the event's major sponsors).

Despite his attempts to raise suffrage among young black citizens, Simmons hadn't actually taken part in the voting which resulted in the re-election of Giuliani (whom polls revealed has as little as 3 per cent support among the black citizens of New York). In July both Simmons and co-Rap the Vote promoter Puff Daddy were taken to task when their voting records came to light in the *New York Post*. The New York Board of Elections revealed that Simmons had registered twice, but hadn't actually cast his vote since 1992. But Simmons wasn't offering any apologies. "I, like many others in the hip hop community, have felt alienated, disenfranchised and misrepresented by this nation's politicians and the political process in general. Unfortunately, millions of people continue to be mistrustful and disillusioned by the candidates for public office, and a judicial and governmental process that systematically erodes any faith of representation, justice and equality for minorities in our nation. Yes, there have been times when I haven't voted, but what I have come to realise in the past several years, especially under the Giuliani administration, is that not voting contributes to our problems. That is why, through "Rap The Vote" and "Redeem the Dream" [a march honouring Martin Luther King's 'I have a dream' speech] I have committed myself to aggressively registering one million young voters by next November."

Simmons was clear on his own present voting intentions, making public his distaste for George 'Dubya' Bush's Republican campaign. "I'm in a position where I could take full advantage of his tax cuts, but at the same time with all the money I have been fortunate enough to make, why would the Republican Party want to give me even more money while poor and young people suffer? The only politics I'm interested in are those that effect poor people and George W Bush is not looking out for them." An interesting observation from a man previously noted for his embarrassment *of*, rather than embarrassment *at*, riches. He was particularly sore at Bush for the series of adverts he produced comparing civil rights campaigner Reverend Al Sharpton with Adolf Hitler. But he failed to go so far as to give environmental campaigner Ralph Nader his vote. "I love Ralph Nader. I think his policies are sound and I admire the fact that he is willing to take on all the big corporations. He probably has more integrity than any of the two candidates combined. However, the race is too close to mess with Nader. We cannot afford to play around and risk Bush getting into office. It's not that I'm so pro-Gore. I am just very anti-Bush."

There were further controversies surrounding the Rap The Vote campaign, including a $20 million lawsuit brought by James Thompson, who founded the Hip Hop Hall Of Fame in 1992. Thompson, one of the peacemakers in the gang truces that followed the LA riots in 1992, claimed that at that time his institution organised a Rap The Vote chapter, and that he was recruited by Rock The Vote in 1992 and 1996 to work on their campaigns. As well as Simmons, his other targets for litigation included the manufacturers of a board game, also entitled Hip Hop Hall Of Fame. Which made it sound like he was chancing his arm somewhat.

On 16 October 2000, through Phat Farm and 360 Hip Hop, Simmons sponsored the Million Family March in Washington, an extension of the Million Men March of the same date five years previously which had caused a storm of protest, much of it ill-founded, by inviting only black males to participate. The event, whose stated aims were to 'focus on strengthening the family through the principles of atonement, reconcilia-tion and responsibility', again culminated in a speech by Minister Farrakhan – one that was far more inclusive of different races and denomi-nations than had previously been the case, with priests, rabbis and preach-ers sharing the dais with him. His speech, in which he thanked Simmons for his efforts, also included a brief section on the responsibilities of rap lyricists.

While some weren't prepared to accept the olive branch, Simmons stepped up to defend the minister. "While there's been controversy around Farrakhan, he's done a lot of good for the black community. I reject any kind of statements about hate, or anything that is divisive in any way. I've had relationships with Jewish people since childhood. But I can look beyond that, to look at the struggle in the black community and how difficult it is sometimes, and how difficult it was. And I'm encouraged by the fact that the Nation Of Islam has done so well in giving discipline to so many people who need it and hope for so many people who needed it and now is reaching out to the whole human family. I think it's a big sign of the times that — the fact that the Nation Of Islam is making the march not for black families, but for everyone. I think that's good that Farrakhan's message is for everyone, and I think that it's good that this march is inclu-sive, even if it's only a statement."

Hip hop was still problematic for leaders of the black community, though they'd begun to recognise its demographic importance as a means of reaching young audiences. Rap, for its part, hadn't yet put its own house in order, despite some world famous casualties. Tensions between the east and west coast were replaced by internecine quarrels between former friends and allies. The conflicts boiled over again at the 2000 *Source* Awards, held at the Pasadena Civic Center. The show had to be cut short when fights broke out. And it wasn't just one incident. DJ Quik was taken into custody after trying to break up a tussle, though he was the innocent party. Bad Boy's crew lived up to their reputation by getting into a fight that was broken up by, of all people, boxing promoter Don King. There were scuffles between E-40 and his former friend Mack Minister. Doug E. Fresh tried to calm the crowd, but the most sinister moment came when hoodlums associated with the Death Row label paraded in red T-shirts with a picture of Snoop Dogg and the legend 'Dead Man Walking' scrawled over them (reflecting rumours that Suge Knight was less than enamoured of Snoop's decision to badmouth his former label).

It was the last straw for Chuck D, who was distraught at what he saw. "What more is there to say? I ain't just talking about the 'fight' at *The Source* Awards. That was just the aftermath of a condition that has been festering for the past ten years, ever since the corporate takeover of the culture. Yeah the survey might say Chuck D is a madman who might be bitter . . . yeah, whatever, but the facts are glaringly obvious. Coon-ism is dominant when it comes to the representation of black people in the new millennium . . . I'm tired of hearing how successful this black person is or labelling him/her a 'genius' just because they're continuously hilarious or 'triple-doubled' themselves to represent black people in predominately white-walled boardrooms. Yes Amerikkka has finally frankensteined a morphing of what/who were previously categorized as black folk into a new race; the NIGGRO . . ."

It was pretty obvious who and what Chuck was talking about. And even by his standards, he came across angry. "The NIGGRO accepts almost anything that is approved by white society. Anything that thrusts itself into 'bling-bling' millionaire status, even if the credibility of black folk is flushed down the token toilet. The NIGGRO is lauded in *Vibe* and *The Source* for its thug spirit, thus confusing it with rebellion and accepting illogic as an oath amongst young cats just to 'stay in touch' or appear to be down."

One of the issues that resonates across America's black community is the move towards slavery reparations, a contentious, politically charged debate about whether America should compensate the descendants of slaves for forced labour. Randall Robinson, head of TransAfrica, a lobbying organisation, wrote a book on the subject in 2000 which helped galvanise the movement. "Whether the monetary obligation is legally enforceable or not, a large debt is owed by America to the descendants of America's slaves . . . This demand is not for charity. It is simply for what [African-

Americans] are owed on a debt that is old but compellingly obvious and valid still," he told *The Guardian*'s Tara Mack.

Although slavery had been officially abolished in 1865, the reparations movement encouraged black communities to look at the ownership of their efforts – exactly at the time Simmons, one of the two or three most celebrated black businessmen of the last 20 years, was signing off on the sale of his work to a multinational. Others in the hip hop industry were concerned about the loss of sovereignty. "I don't completely understand it," remarked *Source* editor Selwyn Seyfu Hinds. "There are deep, deep questions in black culture in terms of ownership, in the sight of somebody who is the very paragon of success selling his share off to the Man. People wonder, 'Is this Berry Gordy Part Two?'"

$100 million was not a bad return on his '40 acres and a mule' (the 'starter pack' for freed slaves). But some, like Chuck, felt history was repeating itself. Others shared his opinion. As an editorial in the Nation Of Islam's *Final Call* noted, "No doubt, hip hop is everywhere . . . music, fashion, language, culture and even in hairstyles. The other reality is while hip hop, or rap music, and its offshoots have become a billion-dollar industry worldwide, many of those sculpting the culture of modern youth complain of feeling like 'slaves on the plantation'."

Chuck D's anger at hip hop's descent into rampant consumerism (bling-bling denoting the modern rapper's devotion to the acquisition of precious metals) signalled a distaste for hip hop's current agenda and priorities. Somewhere along the line the music had become a secondary issue to the image. An illustration of the way in which hip hop had been product-matched came early in 2001 when FUBU, one of the biggest names in hip hop designer chic, announced they were joining forces with Universal Music – now the proprietors of Def Jam – to launch a music label. Jean Riggins, executive VP at Universal, cooed: "FUBU is a lifestyle and I think music is important to that lifestyle." Truly the cart before the horse.

One particular affront to hip hop's dignity, which Chuck's tirade touched on, resided in a single, but ultra-powerful word – nigger. NWA (Niggers With Attitude) had given the term a fraternal makeover in the early Nineties, subverting its context by turning it into a term of affection. As Nelson George wrote in *Hip Hop America*, "Whether anointing oneself royalty or basking in words originally designed to demean, African-American males are restless in the desire for self-definition." Others, like Tupac Shakur, who came from a Black Panther background, offered the following definition. "When I say nigga, I mean NIGGA: Never Ignorant Getting Goals Accomplished. Not Nigger. NIGGA."

But that was semantics and lazy thinking at best, as hip hop writer Davey D countered. "What hurts even more is you have this ridiculous assertion being spouted by some brothers who will point out that there's a big difference between the word 'Nigger' and 'Nigga'. Hence when I was growing up I was being called 'Nigger' which is offensive . . . but when some white or Asian kid comes rolling up to me today talking about 'What's up, my Nigga?' I should embrace him because this kid is down with hip hop culture? Even sadder is you have some brothers who take this word and flip it so that it empowers them. So now nigga is a good thing. We've internalized so much negativity it's ridiculous . . ." He was particularly disgusted after watching Jay-Z's appearance on Chris Rock's show, where Def Jam's number one act performed a 'clean' version of 'Hard Knock Life', yet repeatedly used the term nigga while black children swayed to the music behind him. Chuck D, too, was unimpressed with the term's proliferation. "I don't agree with the word 'nigger' in mainstream language. I don't think Jewish [people] would go for whatever derogatory term for them being part of mainstream language, and I don't think other nationalities would go for that either. It's just that we're easiest to pick on, we're the most powerless people, so that you can say anything about us."

Members of the hip hop community wanted action over this self-defeating double-speak. Adisa Banjoko's 'Anti-Nigga Machine Petition' was the most visible outpouring of concern. "[The petition] will be delivered to the record companies of America and the world telling them to no longer release music with the words nigga/nigger and bitch in them. This is not a witch hunt. It is a voluntary effort to better the hip hop community from within. By signing this document you promise to remove the word nigga/nigger, and bitch (basically a feminine version of nigger) out of your vocabulary. As well, you are saying that starting in the year 2000, you will not support record labels or radio stations or print media that celebrates artists who speak like that to our children." But his was a simplistic response that would have resulted in everything from the Last Poets' 'Niggers Are Scared Of Revolution' to the Public Enemy song that lent its name to the partition being banned, which, we hope, is hardly what Adisa Banjoko intended.

The reverberations grow more complicated when the term is deployed by whites. In Boston, a local general interest magazine found itself in the firing line after referring to Harvard black studies director Henry Louis Gates Jr as 'Head Negro in charge'. As journalist Amy Alexander reported, "That flap led to a wider discussion among black academics, clergymen, and politicos about use of the words 'nigger' and 'niggas' by blacks and whites, as in, 'How can we criticize white folks for using the hurtful word "Nigger" or any variation if black people continue using that word?'"

That's the eternal problem with hate-speak, and while those on the receiving end have every right to subvert their debasing power by taking ownership and forging new meanings (see *Queer As Folk*, etc), the word nigga retains a toxicity that everyday usage cannot assuage. Rap music has helped no one, least of all itself, with its continued espousal of the term. Russell Simmons has been one of those senior players in rap culture to employ the term as an acceptable form of address, and that is to his eternal discredit. He also discusses the culture in terms of rap rather than hip hop, and those two facts are not unconnected.

Language was one aspect of the groundswell of concern over rap music at the turn of the century. Others included the glorification of violence, rampant materialism and vicious misogyny. And these problems were no longer limited to the West Coast. All of Def Jam's major rap stars have found themselves in conflict with the authorities at some stage. And while you could ascribe some of their tribulations to racist profiling, as Simmons suggests, the mast majority of these acts were self-induced, self-ordained acts of wanton criminality. Senior figures in the black community were starting to point fingers, as was Capitol Hill. Where once Simmons would have dismissed such objections as irrelevant, his new campaigning role didn't afford him that option.

But he too was concerned with the way things were going. Some sort of showdown with authority was definitely in the air, with the hum of discontent over rap music's more extreme manifestations rising in volume over Washington. Several politicians were again talking about the need to censor the art form, objections that seem to rise every five-year cycle and are often incited by the representative's public standing in election season. Simmons was especially perturbed by a fine of $7,000 imposed on a Pueblo, Colorado FM radio station for playing (the clean version of) Eminem's 'The Real Slim Shady' – the ramifications of which escaped no one in the hip hop community.

In an attempt to reconcile defendant and plaintiff, Simmons put together the hip hop summit of June 2001. Given huge advance publicity and hosted by the New York Hilton, the cast list was the greatest who's who of rap music ever assembled, including Chuck D, Queen Latifah, DJ Red Alert, Jermaine Dupri, Luther Campbell, Wyclef Jean, Sean 'Puffy' Combs, KRS-1, Naughty by Nature, Kurtis Blow, Eric B, Will Smith, LL Cool J, Afrika Bambaataa and the Zulu Nation, Crazy Legs, Redman, Fat Joe, Sister Souljah, Grandmaster Flash and the guy who started it all, Kool Herc. Other delegates included academics Cornel West and Michael Eric Dyson, Hillary Rosen of the Recording Industry of America Association, NAACP head Kweisi Mfume, Hugh Price of the Urban League and Martin Luther King III, as well as Congress members Earl Hilliard, Cynthia McKinney and Benny Thompson.

The keynote address again came from Minister Louis Farrakhan, his speech a rejoinder to senior figures in hip hop about the importance of accepting responsibility – "You've become fat and wealthy off the people as leaders, now what are you going to do to feed back the people who've fed you?" His two-hour address saw him grandstand impressively on a number of issues, before laying down the gauntlet to his audience. "The mind is as sacred as the womb and whatever it feeds helps the growth or deterioration of the person. So the question is, will you accept your responsibility as a leader, and as a teacher, and lead and guide the youth of the world so that the elites, the governments of the world, will never make merchandise of young people again and use you to fight unjust wars that enrich the rich and aid in the destruction of the weak and the poor?"

Any event featuring Farrakhan was going to be problematic for the liberal media, with whom the minister has clashed on numerous occasions over charges of anti-semitism and inverse racism. But Simmons was un-repentant. "Rap has done more to break down the barriers of racism and there are those who don't want to see the youth united. That is why Minister Farrakhan's address at the summit is important. Minister Farrakhan will inspire the youth of America to a higher level of understanding."

The Nation Of Islam certainly enjoyed the warm glow of publicity generated by their connections to hip hop. But Farrakhan, in a past life a calypso singer himself, was clever in appealing to the assembled egos. "You may have only wanted to make a good song and make a great impact, but maybe you are not aware that you have been chosen to lead," he cajoled. "I am very excited about this summit," Simmons told Farrakhan's house publication *The Final Call*, stressing his gratitude for the NAACP (the National Association for the Advancement of Colored People) signing on as co-sponsor of the event. "That shows the interest in the hip hop industry from the outside world," he concluded.

The ever eloquent KRS-1 gave *The Final Call* this rationale for the involvement of so many rappers. "We are coming to the National Hip Hop Summit to document our genre in a positive light. Too many times we see hip hop on trial – this one shooting at that one – some scandal, some gossip, but those are strange, bizarre stories and we want to make that clear." Sean Combs augmented Simmons comments by advancing the summit as an effort to "emphasize truth, we're not telling any artist to censor themselves or to not tell the truth. A lot of the dark things you hear are simply the truth." He even suggested talking down young, impressionable rappers from waxing lyrical about gang-banging and drug-dealing if these were merely exaggerated flights of fancy. Treach, of Naught By Nature, bemoaned a situation where hip hop used to be about harmless freestyle battles, rather than the savage cult of retribution that marked the Biggie-Tupac episode. "I think Russell feels responsible for the state that rap and hip hop are in, and took it upon himself to do something about it," surmised Chuck D.

Simmons wanted to demonstrate some practical progress, and told MTV he was "preparing a list of things, of how we plan to police ourselves in terms of how we market the music." He also acknowledged the discomfort some felt over the 'nigga' issue. "There are people who say that they are concerned about the language used in rap music and in time we will work that out, but right now I am more concerned about ideas. I want these young people to vote – to choose the next president.

"Our intention is to bring everybody together first, to feel how powerful we are and to celebrate the success," Simmons continued. "But to make clear to everyone what responsibilities come with that power. I want to say this because a lot of people have been [asking] am I intending to clean up rap? I absolutely am not looking to clean up anything. I think that we've built an amazing and probably the most powerful cultural influence in America and probably in the entire history of the music culture . . . it has become lifestyle. We've brought all these races together in dialogue. The CNN of the hip hop generation, as Chuck D referred to it years ago, was at that point the CNN of the young black community . . . but now its [audience is] 80 per cent non-black, so now it's the underground dialogue amongst all young people. Not many people in hip hop realize that they are more powerful than the politicians, and they're more powerful than any other cultural influence and that they have the power to change the world in any way they decide."

There had been a history of rap summits dating back to the Jack The

Rapper convention in 1979, at which Minister Farrakhan also spoke, and accurately predicted the co-opting of black radio, black labels and artists. Public Enemy later used samples from that speech on 'Terminator X To The Edge Of Panic' (*It Takes A Nation Of Millions To Hold Us Back*). Afrika Bambaataa convened the Unity Summit in 1987 at the Latin Quarter nightclub, where the Stop The Violence Coalition was inaugurated (leading to the 1988 recording of 'Self-Destruction' to raise awareness about black on black crime). The song made $600,000, which was then donated to the National Urban League. Then in 1996, in an effort to quell the east-west conflict, a National Hip Hop and Rap Summit was spearheaded by the National African American Leadership Summit, headed by Dr Benjamin Chavis, which brought together label heads including Suge Knight, artists, including Chuck D, and activists. So, again, this was not a new idea, but Simmons had the connections and the profile to make sure his summit was better publicised and organised than any that had preceded it.

However, there was disappointment at the reception afforded the Hip Hop Summit in the mainstream media, particularly those sections of it which had made capital out of rap sensationalism. While MTV, VH1 and BET News provided coverage and a couple of newspapers printed articles (including Britain's *Guardian*), the Big Apple's media corps reporting of the conference was thin. In the end, black-owned media outlets, like *The Final Call*, the New York-based *Daily Challenge*, *The Black World Today* and the daily *Chicago Defender* led the coverage.

Not everyone at the summit was convinced by Simmons' latest makeover. Chuck D had some predictably tough love for his former label boss. "I give Russell Simmons props for using his star power to get everybody to the same city, and even the same room. It was pivotal and essential. In talking with Russell I evidently saw a concern in protecting, and yet bettering, a situation needing his leadership. After all, Russell's involvement harks all the way back to 1979, as far back as hip hop recorded music as Kurtis Blow's manager, thus I've always deferred that power to him because of his seniority. The hundred or so million that he sold Def Jam to Universal [for] was deserved to him because of his contributions. However, as far as the culture is concerned, it is rather limited to think that because five corporations opened their wallets to a few, that they should think that they own what has come out of the people. They own record masters, NOT the culture." Chuck also took offence at Simmons' gate policy for the event, when he allegedly refused to allow entrance to community agitants Conrad Muhammad and Rosa Clemente, as well as a heap of label heads and promoters from the smaller hip hop record companies.

Chuck D wasn't Simmons' only critic. There was a war of words with minister and activist Conrad Muhammad over the direction of hip hop, reported in the *Village Voice* as 'The Minister versus the Mogul'. Simmons attacked Conrad Muhammad as an "open and aggressive critic" of the hip hop community. Conrad lashed back that, "Whites have accepted Russell Simmons as the guru of urban black youth culture. He has sold them a bill of goods – that we are penny-chasing, champagne-drinking, gold-teeth-wearing, modern-day Sambos, pimps, and playas."

A former Nation Of Islam minister, Muhammad had presided over Harlem's Mosque No. 7, 'the house that Malcolm X built', and was once specifically employed by Farrakhan as an 'emissary to hip hop'. So Simmons' suggestion that he was merely a critical outsider does not tally with the facts. He'd also founded A Movement for CHHANGE (Conscious Hip Hop Activism Necessary for Global Empowerment), which proved he shared the body culture's taste for ludicrous acronyms if nothing else. At the mosque he'd summoned groups, including Afrika Bambaataa's Zulu Nation and A Tribe Called Quest, to help heal differences between warring factions. He also intervened in the 'diss wars' between Suge Knight and Death Row and Sean 'Puffy' Combs and Bad Boy before Farrakhan replaced him at Mosque No. 7 with Benjamin Muhammad.

Formerly known as Dr Benjamin Chavis, Muhammad was a member of the Wilmington 10, the first group to be classified as political prisoners by Amnesty International in 1978 after their efforts to end school segregation in North Carolina resulted in illegal incarceration. He became the youngest leader in the history of the NAACP, before he was ejected for diverting funds to fight a sexual harassment case. He'd already set up his own hip hop summit in 1996 and converted to Islam, organising Farrakhan's Million Men March. But while helping to prepare the Million Family March, he was again implicated in serious sexual harassment charges. Nevertheless, he was selected as moderator for Simmons' hip hop summit.

Conrad Muhammad, at one time considered a possible heir to Farrakhan, had a proven record in trying to reduce rap's reliance on derogatory terms such as 'nigger' and 'bitch'. His original intervention came in April, when he attacked hip hop executives like Simmons (though he was not mentioned specifically) for failing to mentor aspiring rappers and encouraging them to live the gangsta lifestyle portrayed in their lyrics. That speech followed the sentencing of Jamaal 'Shyne' Barrow, a 21-year-old rapper. He was convicted of assault at the 1999 Club New York shooting, where fellow defendant Sean 'Puffy' Combs was eventually acquitted of gun possession and bribery charges.

Contradicting Muhammad's statements, Russell Simmons went out to bat for Shyne, claiming to *NME* that he was "a great writer and he could've written anything. He admitted he had a gun and that he carried a gun because of the songs he wrote. I think he didn't have to write those songs, because he had kind of different options in life and I think to some degree he is a victim of his own lyrics." More astutely, Simmons noted of Puffy's court time that it was "an experience he had to have". Muhammad, for his part, levelled the accusation that Puffy had conveniently ditched his protégé, to whom he was now 'spiritual advisor', as soon as his own neck was on the line. Before sentencing, he loaned Shyne a copy of Marvin Gaye's *What's Going On* as an example of what rappers should be projecting back to the world.

The disagreements with Muhammad had also been precipitated by a CHHANGE meeting with black record executives, which took place in May, just before Simmons' summit. At it, he announced his 'Campaign For Decency' to combat negative images and lyrics in rap music. Simmons contacted fellow hip hop industry members by e-mail on the day after Muhammad's statement was issued, attacking the activist and placing him in the same category as belligerent but misinformed hip hop critic C. DeLores Tucker and Bob Dole. But Muhammad, tipped off by one of the e-mailed executives, wasn't taking that lying down. He hit back in the *Village Voice*. And this time he wasn't merely targeting Simmons by implication. "This [Simmons] is an entertainment figure who really has contributed mightily to the degradation of the African American community by corrupting the morals of young people. Instead of him being in a spirit of repentance and offering to use his power to right some of his wrongs, he engages in a divisive campaign to stop a minister whom he has called on many times in the past for help when he was in trouble."

He also poured scorn on the appearance of Farrakhan at the hip hop summit. "Russell really thinks he's clever. In his attempt to stop me, he goes to Minister Farrakhan so that when I hear Minister Farrakhan's name, I'll back up and stop doing what I'm doing." In a separate interview he offered an unflattering comparison between Berry Gordy and Russell Simmons. "Motown under Berry Gordy was a great example of how a black businessman spent money and took the time to teach young artists how to handle themselves in public, how to interact with their fans, and how to be an ambassador for their community. We are tired of seeing young artists have one hit, and then [are] thrown away to the wolves, never to be heard from again, with their life ruined." Simmons remained unapologetic, claiming rappers and hip hop executives had "closed ranks against Muhammad". "We have a much bigger army than he could ever put together. He can't hurt us."

Among those who spoke at Simmons' summit was Master P, whose empire had expanded on an almost exclusive diet of pimpin' and hustlin' narratives. Predictably, he defended his artists' lyrics as a reflection of the neighbourhoods where they grew up. Simmons agreed, suggesting that rappers "will get back to writing from their hearts". That resonates with a later statement that seemed to reflect his own boredom with negativity in rap. "What's selling is Will Smith. What's selling is Lauryn Hill. I think that people ain't making the records. There's no normal people that looks like you, that are making the positive records. All you got is Common, Mos Def, Dead Prez, Talib Kweli. Everybody got a funny name or a headwrap or an incense. Where are the real niggas making the true stories? You can't always be thinking about dying. People are bored. They are saying I don't want to hear none of this death shit no more." The summit was intended to "celebrate, defend, and fix rap music," Simmons argued, "but I want rappers to continue to stick with the truth. I can't force my religion or anything else on them."

To that end the summit discussed the daily racism encountered by rappers. Fresh in everyone's minds was the 13 April incident when Jay-Z and members of Roc-A-Fella family were arrested outside a Manhattan nightclub, prompting Giuliani to issue a statement stating: "Here's a way not to get into trouble with NYPD: Don't shoot anybody, don't rob anybody, don't rape anybody, and don't carry guns illegally." But others, particularly Simmons, saw the incident as part of a pattern of 'racial profiling' of young black men. On this point Simmons and Muhammad clashed again – the minister suggesting there was no singling out of rappers for police attention, and that the behaviour of the artists concerned was the problem. He was 'suspicious' of Simmons' behaviour in the wake of Jay-Z's arrest. "Jay-Z, one of Russell's main artists who advocates gangsta, pimp, and thug images, is in trouble with the law again," was his muted response.

There then followed a robust 'open letter' from activist Rosa

Clemente, the youth organiser for the F.R.E.E. Youth Empowerment Program, a senior figure in the Malcolm X Grassroots Movement and co-host of *Where We Live* on WBAI. It was squarely aimed at Simmons. "Here is a news flash. As quiet as it's kept YOU ARE NOT HIP HOP! You didn't know? Many of us have this conversation about you and other music industry people like you every day. Yours is the industry that has pimped hip hop culture so the chosen few can live in MTV cribs, wear Iceberg jeans, Phat Farm sweaters and Sean John fur coats. And we cannot forget about the bling-bling of diamonds mined by exploited South African laborers. Russell, as quiet as it's kept YOU ARE NOT HIP HOP!"

Her position is not as isolated as Simmons would have you believe. Many have long harboured suspicions about Simmons' motives, including the *Washington Post* reviewer of his autobiography who castigated him as "an individual who has, better than anyone else, exploited the desires of mainstream consumers to experience vicariously the trappings of an authentic 'ghetto' lifestyle. Just as he once pushed fake cocaine, Simmons has essentially gone on to sell a fake cultural bill of goods: The commodified image of 'blackness' so central to the market is anything but authentic." That may be the case, but without Simmons, hip hop would not have touched just about every young person in the developed world. And while he was a late developer when it came to acts of conscience, he at least got there in the end.

Another criticism concerned the event's stage-management. Yvonne Bynoe, co-founder of Urban Think Tank, Inc., had a list of complaints. "First there was no agenda. While the organizers thought that it was a sign of flexibility not to have an outline of subjects to be addressed, in truth it was a sign of chaos." She continued, "At this summit as well as prior ones, most of the artists and the few industry leaders who participated said a few words about the importance of artists speaking about what they see and know and then they bounced. In shorthand this means 'business as usual' because the corporate entities and the artists know that there will be no repercussions from the hip hop public if they do not change their behavior. If anything is ever going to change in hip hop, in connection with social responsibility, it will not come out of any closed-door summit. Change will come when the hip hop public around the country wakes up, organizes in their communities and tells the artists and the corporation entities (radio, video shows and record companies) what they want and what they will no longer tolerate."

One of the ideas aired at the summit was the model of a hip hop union to protect artists' rights – a concept spearheaded by Courtney Love in the rock world, although she too was sniggered at by those ignorant of the true casualty list across both forms of music. According to KRS-One, rappers had "been talking about forming the union and taking control of production and distribution since 1987, when about 25 of us met one night at the Latin Quarter, in Manhattan," a meeting chaired by Afrika Bambaataa. KRS-One's suggestion was supported by others including Chuck D and Master P, as well as comments in *The Final Call* by Drayton Muhammad, chief executive of Brooklyn-based Quiet Man Entertainment. "Like any child there comes a time when you must become independent. That is why Master P, Chuck D and KRS-One are calling for control. To be real with it, we do need a union."

By July 2001 Simmons had instigated the formation of the Hip Hop Summit Action Network, dedicated to delivering on some of these goals and initiatives, drawing on a report entitled Hip Hop Summit Results and Resolves, that stated, "Now is the time to assume a strong political stance." Summit moderator Benjamin Muhammad of the Nation Of Islam spelt out the action to be taken. "We are establishing a national Political Action Committee (PAC) that will work to educate our constituency on the issues. Our PAC will also choose candidates that we are going to work to put in office, and we are going to oppose candidates that oppose us and put them out of office."

There was an immediate commitment to the New York mayoral race. "Many in hip hop are interested in unity and bringing the races, black and white, together. To that end, we are endorsing mayor Mark Green," Simmons told a press conference. Alongside him sat Sean Combs, who emphasised the power a unified 'hip hop nation' could wield. "Whoever is chosen – because we might change our minds – that person will stand up to their responsibility to us. You are going to see the difference in the numbers that we turn out to the polls. Beyond that, though, you will see the power and strength that we have in the marketing arena. This is not just about political enlightenment. These candidates must come to the hip hop community to listen to our concerns and the concerns of the poor people all over this city." Or, as Simmons told *Rolling Stone* magazine, "The hip hop community is more tightly knit than any other music community. The hip hop community moves as an army – on issues, on politics, on social conditions, on subject matter. They choose a car, that car is hot. They choose a watch, that watch is hot. They choose a clothing company, that company is hot. And when they choose a potential president, it's the same thing."

The Hip Hop Summit Action Network promised to provide, through its Hip Hop Political Action Committee (Nu America PAC) 'political contributions' to election candidates who were pro-freedom of speech and supportive of the hip hop community. But it's debatable how much real influence they were able to exert – as evidenced by Republican candidate Michael Bloomberg storming home from 22 points behind in the polls to take the New York mayoral race in November 2001 after Nu America PAC had pledged to support Mark Green. Bloomberg's receipt was 25 per cent of the black vote, the highest figure in the city ever and twice as high as the national average for a Republican. As if to dismiss the thought that there was unanimity in the black community, among his most prominent supporters was Earl Graves, publisher of Black Enterprise magazine.

Outside of direct political lobbying, some of the other key initiatives included extending 'Parental Advisory' labelling to marketing campaigns and a mentoring programme for young rappers. The organisation took up offices with *The Source* magazine (whose editor David Mays had helped instigate the summit) while Benjamin Muhammad was appointed executive director – thereby cementing hip hop's new mood of conscience and reflection with the Nation Of Islam. Other members of the HHSAN board included the all-male team of Simmons, Rev. Al Sharpton, Sean Combs, Dave Mays, Kevin Liles, Motown president Kedar Massenburg, Loud Records CEO Steve Rifkind and Interscope/Geffen A&R vice-president Steve Stoute. Combs, incidentally, had previously faced criminal charges over an assault on Stoute, so smoking of the peace pipe was evidently the order of the day. "Realizing the goals that came out of the Hip Hop Summit is something we're all very serious about," responded Mays, "so we are very happy to extend the use of our offices as the headquarters for the Hip Hop Summit Action Network. We look forward now to working with Russell, Minister Ben and the other members of the board to help our community realize the power it holds to create positive and proactive change and to also celebrate and inform the world about the good works this community already has accomplished."

For his part, Minister Benjamin Muhammad was now sounding as if he'd bonded with his new hip hop pals to the extent that he spoke like he'd come from the same 'hood, though his elocution was better. "Some are concerned with the profanity and vulgarity in hip hop, but that is just reflective of the profane and vulgar world we live in. If you want to change the lyrics, you must first change the social condition the lyrics come from." It echoed a previous assertion by fellow board member Puff Daddy almost exactly. "Hip hop has always been raw and is always going to reflect what's going on in the neighbourhood. So we say to the government, if you don't like what they're saying, change what they're seeing."

Simmons set out the new agenda in a press release. "The hip hop community has been incredibly receptive to our attempt to organize and mobilize their efforts toward making young peoples' concerns a priority in Washington and in U.S. government . . . We're very excited and we are sure their input will help to shape a better America." Not everyone was singing from the same hymn sheet, however, even those on Simmons' own label. Asked about 'conscience rap', Redman hit back: "Fuck all that, everybody know that peace-treaty rapping shit don't sell nothing. Everybody know that, even Chuck D."

Simmons' profile as a political lobbyist continued to grow, whether or not he had the backing of the hip hop community he sought to represent. In August 2001 members of the Senate Governmental Affairs Committee rounded on rap music. A Federal Trade Commission report on explicit content on records singled out 29 albums. "22 of those were from African-Americans," wrote Simmons, for a *New York Times* feature. He was especially angered by the fact that there was "no one to represent the black rap artists who were clearly being singled out." He believed those chairing the hearings had a vested interest in talking about young African-American artists rather than talking *to* them. He went on to defend hip hop as the "first new genre of music to emerge since rock and roll". Further, he upbraided the senators for their ignorance. "Only by listening carefully to what these young, urban African-Americans have to say can the senators – who are overwhelmingly white, middle-class and middle-aged – possibly understand what is at the heart of the music. There are many cultural and economic facts of life that drive hip hop and its themes, lyrics and language. The senators have to make an effort if they are to appreciate why this music exerts such a hold on American culture, how it unites and educates our youth, and why its popularity spans divides of race and class."

In September he gate-crashed the Senate hearings. Former vice presidential candidate Senator Joseph Lieberman refused his request to speak, as he tried to push his media accountability act through Senate – a piece of legislation which would penalise record labels and movie companies who marketed 'obscene material' to young people. His S-792 bill intended to put on the statute books the following ominous words: "Targeted marketing to minors of an adult-related motion picture, music recording or electronic games shall be treated as a deceptive act or practice." His position was straightforward, if simplistic. "If the entertainment industry continues to market degradation and death to our children, paying no heed to the bloodshed staining our communities, then the government will act."

Rap music was widely expected to be designated for 'special attention'. Liberman offered Simmons a private consultation, but still refused permission for him to address the hearings. Simmons stubbornly stationed himself in the audience and was eventually given leave to testify. He made the point that hip hop represents the same tradition of protest music as Bob Dylan and others, citing NWA's 'Fuck Tha Police' as an example – his favourite record – saying it brought attention to racial profiling by police.

Simmons was subsequently asked how he'd react to having his daughter hear such a record. "I feel . . . that [it is] for parents to govern what their kids' understanding [is] of what's in the world," he bumbled and stumbled to Ifé Oshun. "What part of it do they want them to hear at an early age is the parent's choice and the way they want to explain to them what they hear – if they hear it. Now if you don't have parents [who can do that] . . . then it's a hard world that you've fallen into . . . You can't stop sexist statements . . . There needs to be a real dialogue . . . When she's old enough, [my daughter] will hear what she hears and we'll have a dialogue about it.' As for those Senate meetings, he claimed the "effort to censure hip hop has deep-seated racial overtones".

Meanwhile, the wisdom of inviting senators Cynthia McKinney, Benny Thompson and Earl Hilliard to the summit was paying dividends. The three, all members of the Congressional Black Caucus, held a closed doors meeting before speaking to the press. While Thompson warned that, "Washington can regulate you out of business if you do not know how to react," McKinney issued a more optimistic statement: "We are not speaking for the CBC. We are here because these are our constituents and we believe that hip hop should be given the opportunity to police itself." We shall see.

12

If Black Is The New Black,
Lyor Cohen Is The New Russell Simmons

"The music business is a cruel and shallow money trench,
a long plastic hallway where thieves and pimps run free,
and good men die like dogs. There's also a negative side."
– Hunter S. Thompson

According to the Recording Industry Association of America, in the year 2000, hip hop accounted for 12.9 per cent of all domestic record sales, giving it a huge slice of the total $14.4 billion pie. Complementary surveys revealed that up to 80 per cent of hip hop purchases were made by whites – a demographic imbalance lampooned by the Offspring's 'Pretty Fly (For A White Guy)' – as the genre surpassed country music to become the third largest music category behind pop and R&B, with gross sales of well over $3 billion. As *Time* writer Christopher John Farley once noted, the till returns are fitting for "perhaps the only art form that celebrates capitalism openly."

Or, as Kevin Chappell writes: "For the first time in its 25-year history, rap music participants seem to be somewhat content – and the world seems content with it. The music is now being celebrated in museums, studied at universities, honored at awards shows, listened to in every suburb in America, and imitated by teenagers as far away as Germany, Japan and Africa." Suddenly everyone was 'getting' hip hop, from the grandmother offering an impromptu rendition of 'Rapper's Delight' in *The Wedding Singer* to Hollywood stalwarts like Warren Beatty, who directed a film, *Bulworth*, inspired by a fictional US president becoming infatuated with hip hop, which he considered America's new "voice of protest". Russell Simmons had a simple answer for what was taking place. "Rock is old. It's old people's shit. The creative people who are great, who are talking about youth culture in a way that makes sense, happen to be rappers."

Simmons himself was able to point to Rush Communications' best year

221

to date. While Def Jam grossed $300 million in 2000 his clothing company, Phat Farm, more than doubled its turnover from $60 million in 1999 to $150 million. His advertising agency dRush was also enjoying frenetic growth, representing blue chips including Coca-Cola and HBO among others. From a standing start in 1997 the company's revenues had reached the $100 million mark. "Everything feeds off everything else," Simmons shrugged. "We're coming off our best year ever."

Simmons also committed his memoirs to posterity, collaborating with Nelson George on *Life And Def*. Prior to *Hip Hop America*, the definitive travelogue of the rap generation, George had in 1984 penned *Where Did Our Love Go?*, a mould-breaking chronicle of the machinations of Motown which similarly defined an epoch in music. It also resulted in Berry Gordy freezing him out of any contact with his acts. Three years later George delivered *The Death Of Rhythm & Blues*, a provocative and critically acclaimed account of how black music had been systematically neutered by the white dominated record industry. This time round George refrained from biting the hand that fed him. As Simmons recounted in unwarranted depth his encounters with celebrities and models at the expense of any thoroughgoing analysis of his real achievements, it's easy to picture Nelson's pained expression. It's probable that he, as much as the rest of us, would have liked to have known what Simmons really thought of the Public Enemy fall-out or Jay-Z's foxtrot with the legal profession, instead of Simmons' supermodel tally.

Though Simmons' stewardship of it was becoming gradually more symbolic, Def Jam was expanding. In 1999 they moved into Germany, and by the end of 2000 Def Jam Japan was open for business. A subsidiary finally opened in London at the beginning of 2001, in a bid to provide an outlet for that much-discussed but poorly promoted entity, British hip hop. The Gucci-wardrobed, cigar-smoking Jaha Johnson, responsible for nurturing R&B singer Sisquó's career, relocated to England to take up his post as vice-president. The label, whose first signing was Aaron Soul, took office space in Mercury's headquarters. Mercury's MD Howard Berman told *Music Week*, "We want to use the experience that we have gained working the US repertoire from Def Jam and Def Soul and actually intensify what we are doing, while making ourselves the obvious home for any UK urban act." Def Jam UK's first success came with Tim Westwood's eponymous compilation series. Def Jam USA, meanwhile, announced a new, underground imprint, Spit, to try to make inroads on rap's flourishing grass roots scene.

After a sensational millennial year, Def Jam showed no signs of slackening its pace or running out of steam. Jay-Z successfully courted the mainstream to an extent where his saturation of rap, pop and R&B markets was enough to interest the Monopolies' Commission. And when he wasn't breaking sales records, he was fleecing his label head and associates as an accomplished poker player. DMX, the new thug prince, cemented the Tupac comparisons by making his cinematic début in *Exit Wounds*, also starring as a gang leader in a remake of the 1931 German cult classic, *M*.

Though unquestionably Def Jam's star lots, Jay-Z and DMX were backed by a supporting cast of immense quality and, within the rap idiom, no small variety. Chief among these were Redman and Method Man, who will always sell records, and who capitalised on their inimitable *Cheech & Chong* dynamic by putting together the film *How High*. That helped make the loss of the label's cornerstone acts over the previous decade and a half easier to bear. While Public Enemy's misgivings had been widely aired and debated, LL Cool J slipped away with less fanfare. Despite *G.O.A.T Featuring James T. Smith: The Greatest Of All Time* débuting at number one in the album charts in September 2000, the two parties were heading for an amicable split. "It's not any bad blood," he told a webcast. "We did what we did for a very long time . . . Def Jam is a great label and they'll continue to have success. I plan on having success, God willing."

But the shoes of the ancients were quickly filled by established pros like Capone 'N' Noreaga, aka CNN, Keith Murray and Funkmaster Flex. CNN, a Queens hardcore duo who'd met in prison, were responsible for 1997's corrosive *The War Report*, arguably the definitive post-Tupac thug rap album. Victor 'Noreaga' Santiago (aka N.O.R.E.) was delighted to move to Def Jam after frustrations with former label Tommy Boy. "It was crazy! When you first come into this game, you don't really care what label you're on because you just want to get signed. We weren't trying to look for the best deal, we just looked for a label and knew we could make it work. Our relationship with Tommy Boy was doomed. We had a CEO at Penalty Records who listened to us, but then Tommy Boy dropped Penalty and inherited our album. We had nobody working on our record. I can't really recall the year exactly 'cause I smoke the herb, but that relationship was doomed, pure hate. So, I was going out and meeting people, retying my relationships with Kevin Liles and Lyor Cohen. Then I got on Hot 97, and said CNN is not with nobody, we free agents. Within five minutes, Lyor hit me on the two-way and said he wanted us on his team.

So basically, we went from the Clippers to the Lakers." It was another example of Def Jam's reputation helping them to woo quality artists disaffected with less sympathetic handlers, while ensuring the new intake bought into the label's mythology.

Noreaga stepped out in February 2002 with *Grimey . . . God's Favorite*, by which time he'd already enjoyed success with the title-track, 'Nahmeanyaheard' and 'Live My Life'. It immediately re-established him as a major presence in east coast rap after the disappointment of his second album, *Melvin Flynt*, a confused effort that he subsequently disowned. His intention was to return to his core audience, though he wasn't in a hurry to return to the lifestyle that once informed it. "I wanted to stay grimy without going overboard. I went overboard on [the last CNN album *The Reunion*]. I started sleeping in the 'hood. I got roach bites, all types of crazy shit." And as hardcore rappers go, he's a sweetheart. In keeping with the contemporary obligation for a sentimental hymn to family values to counterpoint the hardest of hard men's agendas, Noreaga took the milk and cookies with the starry-eyed 'Love Ya Moms'. A new CNN project was slated to follow later in 2002.

Keith Murray, best known for his 1994 hit 'The Most Beautifullest Thing n This World', signed on after completing 30 months of a jail sentence for assaulting a promoter at a Connecticut nightclub (the verdict was later overturned when his attorney, Joseph Moniz, found eyewitness Corey Pace, who claimed he hadn't come forward in the original trial because the plaintiff's family offered him money). He was still under contract to Jive for another two albums, but Cohen offered sufficient money to release him. In typically pensive post–incarceration rapper mode, he told MTV: "Months, years passed by. I thought about a lot of things, and I realised that I'm a poet. I made a commitment to embrace the tragedy and fulfil the fate of life, so I'm more honest and emotional. I still have fun. I'm still lyrical. I've just grown to be well-rounded." A founder member of the Def Squad, alongside Erick Sermon and Redman, Def Jam was a natural destination once Murray was out of contract. "The impact of Def Jam can be felt wherever you go," Murray shrilled of his new employers, "whether it's in a playground up in Harlem or in a club in downtown Tokyo. Being part of such a precedent-setting music and lifestyle-making organisation is what I'm about. What made me choose Def Jam over everyone else was that Lyor and his team believed in my vision as an artist, songwriter and musician. Within Def Jam, there exists a sense of creative freedom that you simply don't find anywhere else. What more could any artist want?"

Funkmaster Flex (Aston Taylor), the son of a Jamaican DJ, has been part of the fixtures and fittings of New York rap for over a decade. His show on Hot 97 wielded huge influence among the hip hop cognoscenti, inheriting the throne vacated by Chuck Chillout (for whom he used to carry crates) and DJ Red Alert in setting the agenda for national sales. His playlist at New York's Tunnel club was almost as trend-setting, and he had a show syndicated on LA's Power 106 and a daily spot on MTV, *Direct Effects*. His remix clients included Erykah Badu, Missy 'Midemeanor' Elliott, Busta Rhymes and Foxy Brown. But he maintains that "spinning records is what I'm all about". His mix album series, *60 Minutes Of Funk*, primarily inaugurated because he was tired of hearing bootlegged copies of his radio show, helped re-establish the viability of the hip hop DJ as artist, though in truth it was his ear for hot new jams and clever sequencing that distinguished the series.

After releasing a series of mix albums for Loud, he transferred to Def Jam for 2000's *The Tunnel*, rated by some critics as "the most star-studded rap album ever", with everyone from Eminem to Snoop Dogg to Def Jam stalwarts Jay-Z, LL Cool J and DMX offering freestyle verses over tracks produced by Flex himself, or Roc-A-Fella's Rockwilder. But Funkmaster Flex was that rarest of things in the hip hop community, a modest man. He repeatedly downplayed his role as taste-maker. "We don't decide what's hot," he deferred, "we let the Tunnel decide." The highlight was a minute-and-a-half-freestyle between Tupac Shakur and Notorious B.I.G., recorded in 1993, long before their respective corners got riled with each other, resulting in the demise of both.

While Def Jam hadn't covered itself in glory in nurturing R&B talent previously, it was a market too complementary to hip hop to abandon completely. There followed a concerted effort to establish Def Soul as a viable and distinct entity, with artists including Case, Kelly Price and Sisqó. Case, a native New Yorker, had already sung back-up for Usher before signing with the label in the mid-Nineties. His three albums, *Case* (1996), *Personal Conversation* (1999) and *Open Letter* (2001) didn't set the world alight, though the latter was mildly diverting for its policy of writing each song with a specific person in mind (from his relatives to Stevie Wonder), with production from seasoned pros Jimmy Jam and Terry Lewis. Like many of Def Soul's would-be R&B stars, he's been a regular on various Def Jam soundtracks – one of Russell Simmons' and Lyor Cohen's favourite cross-promotional devices.

Kelly Price also served an apprenticeship as a backing singer for better established artists, including divas Aretha Franklin, Faith Evans and Mariah Carey. Her booming, theatrical voice also featured on three notable rap records, Notorious B.I.G.'s 'Mo Money, Mo Problems', Ma$e's 'Feels So Good' and Puff Daddy's 'No Way Out'. Comparisons to Mary J. Blige dogged her 1998 début album *Soul Of A Woman*, but *Mirror Mirror* (2000) embraced gospel and hip hop beats as well as traditional soul-sister sweetness, best expressed in her cover of Shirley Murdock's 'As We Lay'.

But Def Soul's big breakthrough came via Sisquó, whose sultry good looks, dyed blond hair and perennially flirtatious lyrics were designed to appeal to a younger demographic, one that was assiduously targeted by Def Jam (Kevin Liles believed he could be the new Michael Jackson or Prince). Born Mark Andrews in Baltimore, his libidinous 'Thong Song' and flouncy 'Incomplete' were fixtures on MTV throughout 2000, building on his reputation as the cutest member of teen R&B faves, Dru Hill (the other members of whom, Nokio, Jazz and Woody also signed with Def Soul with the idea of keeping the core group alive). His début album *Unleash The Dragon* topped the charts before he graced singles by DMX (truly a rough and smooth pairing) and Lil' Kim. By the advent of 2001's Teddy Riley-produced *Return Of Dragon* he, like so many of his rapping peers on Def Jam, was mulling over scripts, appearing in the comedy *Get Over It* and signing a five-picture contract with Miramax.

Def Soul's roster also includes Montell Jordan, who returned with a self-titled album early in 2002, Sisquó protégé Kandice Love, Musiq Soulchild, signed by Kevin Liles and touted as the new D'Angelo, Christina Milian, who has written songs for Jennifer Lopez and guested on Ja Rule's 'Between Me And You', and Playa, the southern hip hop/soul trio who are part of Timbaland and Missy Elliott's Da Bassment collective.

But of greater import than a slew of unremarkable R&B singers was Def Jam's latest crop of new MCs, hungry to take their tilt at Jay-Z's crown. Chief amongst the new pretenders was Ja Rule, five foot and six inches of hyperactive, attention-seeking but instinctively humane walking Napoleon complex. An only child born to a doting mother in Queens, Jeffrey Atkins grew up in Russell Simmons' backyard, Hollis, where he traded battle rhymes with, among others, the undiscovered DMX (whom he rivals in all of hip hop for rasp-throated gruffness). He first appeared on 'Time To Build' in 1995, the B-side to Mic Geronimo's 'Masta I.C.', produced by Hollis neighbour Irv Gotti. Thereafter Ja and his friends formed the Cash Money Click and signed an album deal with TVT Records. It was a 'bullshit deal', reckoned Ja, retrospectively, and the fact that the label retained all publishing royalties on his first two albums before releasing him support that theory. Only one single escaped, 'Get The Fortune' backed by '4 My Click', before Gotti set up a meeting with Lyor Cohen, who'd caught a Cash Money Click promo video on TV. Gotti was hired as an A&R executive, with his first mission to persuade Ja Rule to come on board (events which mirrored the way Rick Rubin used Bill Stephney to court Public Enemy).

Ja first connected with audiences via a hair-raising guest spot on Jay-Z's 1998 single 'Can I Get A . . .' His début album, *Venni Vetti Vecci*, went platinum on the back of breakthrough single 'Holla Holla', whose Rio De Janeiro-shot video, featuring a bevy of half-naked women and Gotti and Ja cruising in a low-rider, scored big time on MTV. However, some critics wrote him off as a one-hit wonder, à la Craig Mack, who scored the first platinum single for Puff Daddy's Bad Boy label with 'Flava In Ya Ear' before hitting the career obituary columns. "People were saying I got lucky with 'Holla Holla'," he protested, hurt. "I was getting a lot of disrespect." While the macho chest-beating prompted comparisons to Tupac, more introspective moments on his début such as 'Only Begotten Son' and the self-explanatory 'Daddy's Little Baby' highlighted a greater range. The guests included Jay-Z, DMX (both appearing on 'It's Murda') and Memphis Bleek. Affiliations straddling Jay-Z's Roc-A-Fella camp and DMX's Ruff Ryders saw him guest on a series of hit singles, while his exposure on the *Hard Knock Life* tour, the biggest grossing concert series in rap's history, increased his visibility substantially, and may even have won a few of the jigsta's fans over to his side.

But nothing suggested, at this stage, that he was anything beyond a competent second generation thug rapper with a strange affection for Alanis Morissette. That impression changed radically via second album *Rule 3:36*, recorded over four months while he chilled out in Beverly Hills with Gotti and the Murder Inc crew. The informal setting seemed to infect the album's grooves, wherein R&B hooks soothed the traditional gangsta rhetoric. The album débuted at number one in the American charts after the soft-focus Christina Milian duet 'Between You And Me' siphoned teenage pocket money after becoming an unexpected radio hit.

Where once you could cut open a hardcore rapper and find 'keep it real' printed through him like a stick of rock, these days, it seems, it's all about keeping several balls in the air at once. Atkins was as keen to demonstrate his versatility as the next man, acting in the hit film *The Fast And The Furious* and writing J-Lo (Jennifer Lopez)'s R&B chart-topper, 'I'm Real

(Remix)'. He flourished as a ghost-writer, proving particularly popular with female R&B artists. Macy Gray, Mariah Carey and Mary J. Blige have all benefited from his writing skills. "You can give me any track, and I'll give you a song," he deadpans. "It may not be a song for me, but I can give you something somebody can use." Murder Inc boss Irv Gotti, someone who is a little prone to exaggeration, it must be said, talked about him as "the best songwriter in the rap game". Atkins had always possessed an affinity for words. At a sixth grade production of *A Christmas Carol* his school picked two Ebeneezer Scrooges for fear a single incumbent wouldn't be able to digest all the lines. Ja had to perform both parts anyway when his fellow thesp bottled it.

Post-Dickensian show-stealing, Ja Rule started to deliver on the grandiose claims made on his behalf with 2001's *Pain Is Love* – especially on the hit singles 'Livin' It Up' and 'I'm Real'. Female hooks agreeably counterpointed Ja's sandpaper snarl to provide the album's dominant musical motif. However, the collaboration with the late Tupac Shakur, 'So Much Pain', resurrected for the occasion through digital technology, wasn't the smartest idea (and it's not as if Tupac's been quiet in terms of posthumous releases lately). 'Lost Little Girl', a track he originally composed for R&B star Brandy before electing to keep it for himself, and a cover of Stevie Wonder's 'Do I Do' featuring Case, served him better.

With Def Jam's strike rate showing no sign of decline, the album topped the US charts. Ja Rule was the latest multi-platinum rapper to have his imperious stare immortalised on the front cover of *The Source* and *Vibe*, but he also earmarked the first tentative footsteps away from the 'bling-bling' materialism of old. "We're taking steps in a conscious direction," Ja told *Rolling Stone*. "I think artists are smart enough to get together and talk out problems they've had in the past; there's a lot of bigger issues than beefs. Hip hop itself is just growing up. A lot is going on, so you want to be more conscious of what you say, anyway. My lyrical direction has become more uplifting, more spiritual, more passionate; I'm looking to live, but I'm not afraid of death." An unlikely convert was U2's Bono. "He's tough, but he can get out of the way of his ego," was Bono's expert assessment, being something of an authority on the issue, "and that's hard. You have to be really tough to do that." It was Bono's 13-year-old daughter Jordan who persuaded him to invite Ja Rule to take part in the remake of Marvin Gaye's 'What's Going On', to raise money for the Aids crisis in Africa and the World Trade Center terrorist attacks. Kevin Liles, meanwhile, reckoned he'd "found his zone". "Now he's got niggas saying,

'That's a Ja Rule record.' I'm not surprised. He's worked tremendously to make sure he defines himself as being more than just a guy who raps. He is becoming his own business, and people want to be in the Ja Rule business."

The label's other millennial breakthrough artist was also the first major success for Def Jam South, an enterprise inaugurated to capitalise belatedly on the new talent pool forming around America's southern states (much of whom had been snapped up by Jermaine Dupri's So So Def label – a business that owed more to the Def Jam model than simply its suffix). The president of Def Jam South was Scarface, the solo artist and founder member of Houston's scurrilous, Rubin-affiliated Geto Boys. Unlike the leaders of several Def Jam outposts, his mentor and inspiration was not Simmons, but Rap-A-Lot founder James Smith. However, the mantra was pure Russell Simmons. "My focus is based on building careers. I don't want to focus on just making records. I want to be responsible for helping to build someone's career just as Rap-A-Lot was responsible for building mine." He continued: "[Being CEO of Def Jam South] is kinda like watching a clock, rather than watching it from this side, I want to see it from the back. Open it up and see the parts that make the second hand work, the parts that make the minute hand work. I want to see the parts that make the hour hand work. I want to know what's behind the clock running. I want to know the reason. I feel like being appointed the president of Def Jam South is broadening my mind." His very first signing was Ludacris, aka Chris Bridges.

Ludacris, with his flamboyant afro, platinum dentures and nicknames including 'the incredible ho-man', offered welcome respite from the mundanity of most hardcore rappers, while his records owed as much to Richard Pryor and Cheech & Chong as Q-Tip and fellow Atlantians OutKast. An only child, Bridges had grown up with his mother in Chicago before moving to Atlanta to stay with his father, aged 12. His rhyme skills developed in the playgrounds of Banneker High in College Park, alongside another 'dirty south' breakout artist, Slimm Calhoun. "We used to rap in school, just beating on garbage pans to make beats," he told *HHC*. "We'd be so excited about rapping in our breaks that we'd forget about eating our lunch."

Later he enrolled on a music business course at Georgia State University. His demos found a way to Atlanta's Hot 97-FM radio station, where he worked as an intern, recording intros for each of the station's DJs. Those tapes reached producer Timbaland, who recruited him for

'Fat Rabbit', from his 1998 album *Tim's Bio* (reprised as 'Phat Rabbit' for his Def Jam début). Local music mogul Jermaine Dupri also enlisted him to be the voice of the *John Madden 2000* PlayStation game. But with both Dupri and Timbaland busy with other projects, Bridges became impatient and saved up his own money to buy studio time. He also set up his own back-street marketing operation, printing promotional T-shirts and flyers. That helped his independently released début *Incognegro* to an impressive sales tally of 30,000, and attracted the attention of several majors. But he chose to go with Def Jam because, "[With Def Jam South] I'd be like a pioneer. Def Jam as a whole never signed anyone from the South."

His début was repackaged as *Back For The First Time*, which boomed to double platinum status. The emphatic 'Southern Hospitality', produced by the prolific Neptunes team of Chad Hugo and Pharrell Williams, got his mirror-ball rolling, while international acclaim greeted his signature song 'What's Your Fantasy?' – in which he and collaborator Shawna documented all the places they'd like to 'get it on'; taking in everywhere from public libraries to the White House.

Word Of Mouf followed in 2001 and repeated the trick, again providing belly laughs aplenty. The opening track, 'Coming To America' set the Eddie Murphy-esque tone, a female voice intoning, "The royal penis is clean, your highness". The album wasn't all flippancy, however, with sombre pieces such as 'Cold Outside' counterweighting his more skittish side. "I don't worry about being typecast as one type of rapper," its creator rationalised, "because if they really listen to the album, then they'll find that there's more to [me than] acting crazy and being stupid. Sometimes it's being dead-ass serious and talking about real-life situations on stuff that I go through." The big single this time round was 'Area Codes', a southern rapper's little red book set to music, featuring Nate Dogg as his partner in lascivious crime. Elsewhere OutKast collaborators Organized Noize appeared with Timbaland on 'Rollout (My Business)'. Like seemingly every other MC in the business, Ludacris started to bring through his own stable of artists, and sought to establish his own subsidiary imprint, Disturbing The Peace.

That embryonic ideal mirrored the situation with Jay-Z's fast-rising Roc-A-Fella roster, jointly headed by Damon Dash, where Beanie Sigel, Memphis Bleek and DJ Clue were all making big commercial strides. Dash is one of the new breed of hip hop impresarios, with an ego and presence to rival any of his stable of artists. There's an arresting moment in the 2000

Backstage film where Kevin Liles catches heat for providing the tour members with jackets prominently featuring the Def Jam logo, enraging the image-conscious Dash, who believed this would deflect focus away from Roc-A-Fella. The exchange, which is loud, heated and looks as if it didn't occur merely for the benefit of the camera, impressively takes place while Dash is having his hair cut.

Queens native DJ Clue came up through the New York mix tape scene, becoming the only 'pure' DJ to secure a platinum album in the Nineties, surpassing even his Hot 97 peer Funkmaster Flex. As house DJ for the Roc-A-Fella family, he had all the right connections, which the album exploited expertly. He made his début in 1998 with *The Professional* before serving as resident DJ on the *Hard Knock Life* tour, which led to his second release, *DJ Clue Presents: Backstage* (which soundtracked a documentary film of the same title). *The Professional, Part 2* followed in 2001, again featuring a stellar cast drawing on the abilities of stablemates Jay-Z, DMX, Beanie Sigel, Redman and Foxy Brown as well as Nas and Tha Dogg Pound. The fact that many of the tracks were exclusive remixes, often bettering the originals, helped push the album to a place on the *Billboard* Top Ten.

Philadelphian MC Beanie Sigel first made his mark on 2000's *The Truth*, but more emphatically on the following year's *The Reason*. This expanded his repertoire to encompass more involved subject matter, revealing a meditative streak that frequently contemplated the price of fame. 'Mom Praying' featured Def South boss Scarface as guest MC, while 'Still Got Love For You' teamed him with Jay-Z. There was also a clever remake of EPMD's back-in-the-day classic 'So What Cha Sayin'?', featuring Memphis Bleek, another Roc-A-Fella alumnus. But elsewhere the focus remained squarely on street narratives, albeit with some vivid interludes and intricacies, while some adeptly placed soul samples and 808 drum kicks kept the music fresh-faced and vigorous.

Soon enough, Beanie was bringing *his* family to the party, the State Property posse. Sooner rather than later, the bloodline concept is going to reach saturation point. Too many rappers are indulging friends and relatives in a market where the barriers to entry are low and the expectations astronomical. Everybody wants their sedan, their clothes line, their bling bling (as Chuck D will point out, mined in horrific conditions by their impoverished black brethren in Africa). But consumer gullibility will run dry at some time, and some of those posse members, who couldn't ride a beat if their behinds were superglued to it, are going to come unstuck.

And fallout of the nature that followed the Shyne/Puff Daddy incident (though Shyne is comfortably one of the better examples of the species) could become the next ugly chapter in rap.

For further evidence of limitless ambition superceding quantifiable talent, see Murder Inc, masterminded by former Def Jam consultant Irv Gotti. Gotti had proved his A&R skills by signing both DMX and Jay-Z to Def Jam. Like Simmons a native of Hollis, he had big plans for Murder Inc, a franchise rather than merely a record label. "There are other things that we're developing," he told *The Source*. "I want to get into other businesses, because we could do anything in hip hop; we set the trends. We could take over this whole shit. If I made toilet paper and said that Jay-Z wiped his ass with that kind of wrapper, people will buy that brand of toilet paper. We could do anything, and hip hop is going to support it. My mind is set on taking over this whole shit, it's more than just the music. I'm passionate about that." Big words, but *Irv Gotti Presents The Murderers* (2000) was as poor an example of the dilettante posse format as it's possible to conceive of, and fell a long way short of delivering on the hubris.

Another Def Jam intern to follow in Simmons' footsteps by establishing his own business empire is former Jungle Brothers tour manager Chris Lighty, who runs Violator management and temporarily counted LL Cool J among his clients. Having grown up in the Bronx, he was part of [Kool DJ] Red Alert's inner sanctum, carrying his record crates to shows. He won a University of Maryland basketball scholarship in the Eighties, but turned it down to pursue music. He took whatever job was on offer. "I was a slash – slash DJ, slash road manager, slash . . ." He'd signed Capone-N-Noreaga to Def Jam as well as Busta Rhymes to J Records, while Violator also handled management for Foxy Brown, Missy Elliott, Cam'ron, Fat Joe, the Beatnuts and Mobb Deep. He too was building the company up to comprise management, marketing and film ventures as well as a record label, the first fruits of which came with the *Violator: The Album* showcase, released through RCA's Loud subsidiary in 1999 after Lighty invoked a buy-out clause to leave Def Jam, and followed two years later by a second volume.

But the daddy of all Simmons' protégés is not Andre Harrell, Chris Lighty, Irv Gotti or Damon Dash, but Lyor 'Lansky' Cohen. "I know Lyor doesn't like risk," Jay-Z once observed, over a poker hand. "He doesn't cross the street if it doesn't say walk." Yet Cohen's sturdy grip has ensured the baton passed to him by Simmons has never slipped. Shrewd, composed and self-confident, he is also steely enough to have prospered in a world where he was often the only white face in the crowd. "Here was this guy in the midst of all these black rappers and a very black rap movement," recalled Bill Stephney. "They didn't care that he was white." And Cohen didn't fret too much either.

It was Cohen who was responsible for devising the street marketing practices that gave Def Jam its original word-of-mouth cachet, instituting the now standard technique of generating thousands of posters and handbills to promote releases, plastering telephone poles and buildings. He would further ensure that news of any release had spread prior to its release date by co-opting DJs and other taste-makers. Efforts that were eventually honoured by an Entertainment Marketer of the Year award.

That concentration of resources is something he's carried forward to his current position as president of Def Jam/Island. The projected release schedule for Universal in 2002 is 30 acts, less than half of its competitor, Sony. That gives Cohen double the money, about £2 million per project, to promote each release. It's a policy which makes the success of each act far more crucial than is conventional for a major label, but it also means he'll be backing his hunches. Something which has been the hallmark of Def Jam's success so far.

He also retains the absolute trust of Simmons in a smooth working partnership that has endured for over 15 years and overseen three generations' worth of classic American hip hop, media scrums and countless acts of reckless criminal behaviour on behalf of his artists. He has now superceded his mentor as the most powerful executive in hip hop, advancing purposefully into the corporate upstream, with his responsibilities now incorporating Island Records, home to the biggest rock band in the world, U2. His new position means artists as diverse as Hanson, PJ Harvey, Ryan Adams, Def Leppard, Pulp and Bon Jovi fall under his jurisdiction, which must be a big contrast after so many years at an upstart rap label.

He's now swapped that desk for one at the head office of the Def Jam-Island group, which he calls "the oasis of truth". "Whenever they want pure, unadulterated truth," he told Q, "they seek me out." Evidence that he's beginning to believe some of his own publicity, though his business-speak is still shot through with an expletive-heavy bluntness born of his years promoting rap groups. And he's taken to smoking cigars, which is a bad sign in anyone's book. But he insists his new responsibilities will not impact on Def Jam's trajectory. "I talk loudly and directly. If the corporation tries to take me and Def Jam and mould us into their image of what a music company should be, then Def Jam will wilt." He's widely respected throughout the industry, albeit for different reasons than Russell Simmons. "Lyor Cohen is just as big," reckons Chris Lighty, who cites him as an influence on the way he conducts business at Violator. "I'm just trying to get the job done and not be in the limelight. We're trying to build the company. I'd rather be respected than idolised."

Yet Cohen's future is not entirely clear. Seagram's putsch on the music industry, a $10 billion shopping spree by chief executive Edgar Bronfman Jr, whose father once crossed swords with Minister Farrakhan, raised eyebrows in the business community as well as the world of 'old money' from whence Bronfman came (though he actually writes pop songs under the pseudonym Junior Miles, and has more sympathy for musicians than some might have thought). He'd used the proceeds from Seagram's sale of its stake in DuPont to fund the Universal purchase, though when DuPont's stock market value subsequently doubled and Seagram's fell, he won few friends on Wall Street. By bringing A&M, Interscope, Geffen, MCA, Mercury, Motown and Polydor into the Universal fold, Bronfman Jr was taking a major gamble. Those fears were realised when French group Vivendi, formerly a waste management and utilities concern that had diversified into media, took over Seagram in December 2000 for $35 billion, and the Bronfman family disposed of a fifth of their shares as soon as the lock-in period expired. Edgar Bronfman Jr resigned as head of the group in May 2001, keeping a position on the board until December. Where that leaves Cohen and Def Jam-Island is, frankly, anyone's guess, but perhaps taking a few French lessons might be wise.

And while there were rumblings on the top table, the new, gerrymandered musical family didn't necessarily integrate seamlessly, either. Jimmy Iovine, of Interscope, immediately trod on Cohen's toes by trying to lure away Def Jam's big-name acts, including new Def Soul breakthrough artist, Sisquó. Cohen retaliated by offering Limp Bizkit's Fred Durst a position in the Def Jam-Island hierarchy and his own label if he swapped sides, but Cohen backed down after Iovine offered Durst a similar deal within the Interscope structure, though there were rumours of a peace-making intervention by the conglomerate's 'suits'.

Inevitably, Cohen's focus is going to be drawn away from rap acts. He simply won't have the time, and some would question whether he still has the inclination. He recently signed the retro punk rock band Sum-41 and mounted a concerted multi-media campaign to promote them. "I think teenagers in the year 2000 are the same teenagers that were running around a thousand years ago," he noted of his marketing rationale. "Hormones start splattering all over the place. They start hating their parents. They want to take chances, and they don't want everybody to be in their game." But a little of the 'devil may care as long as the accountant is happy' attitude instilled in him at Def Jam prevailed. "I told them, the more fun you have, the more you will, by osmosis, be important to kids who buy your records. I said I'd pick up the tab for the carnage. I pick up all carnage expenses. I'm a man of my word."

His other clients include Jon Bon Jovi, who gave this testimony for Cohen: "If he gets behind a project, he'll go to war." But is he still fighting the good fight? Not if he's foisting another Bon Jovi album on the world, he's not. Another new project was the all-white hip hop girl group Shorty 101, an answer to Bad Boy's Dream or the UK's All Saints, for whom Ja Rule penned 'My Sweet Baby'. While a much more cautious operator than Simmons, Cohen has also brokered deals with far-reaching consequences. He and Kevin Liles signed a contract with mp3.com and Brilliant Digital Entertainment for a joint venture entitled Digital Hip Hop to produce interactive rap videos. And he's played his part in expanding Universal's empire, buying half of Cees Wessels' Roadrunner for $33 million, thereby bringing extreme metal acts such as Fear Factory and Slipknot into the fold. There were several other interested parties, but Wessels, an opera buff by nature, was sharp enough to know that any loss of identity for the label would alienate fans. Having known Cohen for several years, he believed the work he'd done with Def Jam demonstrated the requisite insight into the importance of brand awareness and niche marketing under which those groups originally prospered. Cohen and his Def Jam-Island chairman Jim Caparro also purchased the Lost Highway catalogue, including country stars Lucinda Williams and William Topley. Now, of course, he also has Rick Rubin's American Recordings as a near bedfellow under the Universal umbrella, which should prove interesting.

Whether Cohen can radicalise Bon Jovi or sell all-white female hip hop groups to suburban Americans remains to be seen, but he had the reassurance of knowing that Def Jam itself has never been in better shape. The last few months of 2001 lined up something like this: In its first week of release on 19 September (the week after the World Trade Center bombings) Jay-Z's *The Blueprint* sold 427,000 copies. It was knocked off the top of the charts by Ja Rule's *Pain Is Love*, selling 361,000 units in its week of release in October. By the end of October it was the turn of

DMX and *The Great Depression*, which sold 439,957 copies in its début week. A performance saluted in Grammy Award nominations, three each for Ja Rule and Jay-Z, two for Ludacris. All of which confirmed Def Jam as by far the most visible and successful rap label. Indeed, its market share, estimated to be a finger below 30 per cent in a hugely lucrative sector, represents a dominance unequalled in any era of popular music.

Epilogue

"I felt that I was lucky to be around smarter people. I am kind of a collaborator, that is my formula for success. I was lucky enough to align myself with the right people."
— Russell Simmons

Russell Simmons' achievements are indisputably colossal. Without him, hip hop may never have transported itself from its Bronx hatchery to the world frequency it currently inhabits – whatever you want to say about the dilution of the original ethic that occurred in the process. We would not be bothered, frankly, discussing rap music here and in countless other media outlets, were it not for his input.

Simmons has always been the mouth and face of Def Jam, rather than the ears. None of the star names with whom he is associated would ever have entered a recording studio on Def Jam's behalf, save for the intervention of those with a better grasp of hip hop's possibilities. He had to be convinced that his younger brother and his friend, who together would become Run-DMC, had a future. At Def Jam he initially thought LL Cool J, that other harbinger of the new school aesthetic, was dated. It was Rubin who first recognised the potential of The Beastie Boys. Simmons didn't recognise the appeal of the 'black punk rock' of Public Enemy at all, and thought they'd never sell a record. He even discouraged them from releasing 'Rebel Without A Pause', arguably the greatest rap single of all time. And the hugely successful acts of the Nineties – Jay-Z, DMX, Ja Rule – who helped Def Jam reassert its standing as rap confounded those who'd put a sell-by date on the medium, were signed by others within the organisation. It's potentially a catalogue of missed opportunity that rivals Dick Rowe's decision to pass on the Beatles for Decca in 1962. And one averted by an innate serendipity that is unsurpassed in the history of popular music.

Yet without Simmons as the motor behind Def Jam, no one outside of New York would ever have heard of the label and its artists, or possibly even hip hop. As any independent label owner can tell you, there's a seismic difference between making great records and getting the world to notice them. At a juncture when rappers fixated on the size of their members, Simmons was worried solely about membership, his global mindset refusing to accept the limitations of operating in a 'black' market. He gave the label its *esprit de corps*, hectoring and chivvying his often recalcitrant charges along, and hyping the label's importance whenever the wolf was at the door – usually in the shape of unwelcome major label intrusion.

The principal criticism that can be levelled at him is that the music he likes most is the ringing of tills. Too often he speaks of his artists simply in terms of units shipped and chart positions. And he glories more in his status as one of the pre-eminent black businessmen than he does hip hop pioneer. He's routinely described as a music mogul, but the reality is, he wants to be an everything mogul – music, fashion, comedy, poetry, the internet and, most recently, social responsibility. He started with music, but that's been a springboard to sticking a finger in every pie on the trolley.

Contrast that with Rick Rubin, a man whose focus has never shifted far from music. He was a punk at the outset, because that was the most exciting thing happening around him. He got involved in rap when that supplanted punk's urgency and honesty. And he got out when he thought its course had run. Not because he thought the market was shrinking (indeed, it was expanding), as Simmons might have done, but because it bored him.

Rubin was less the public face of Def Jam than Simmons in his time with the label, doing most of his talking in the studio. His success with rap allowed him to diversify into anything that interested him. (Def) American Recordings merely serviced his love of music, and the fact that its owner was an artist-orientated producer meant that it would never enjoy comparable success to Simmons' ventures. Rubin was not averse to selling large quantities of records, but it was never his primary focus. But his association with a slew of truly remarkable records, especially his Johnny Cash trilogy, and his willingness to engage with whatever strain of contemporary music interests him, confirms his stature as one of America's great maverick producers.

Most partnerships have a hierarchical basis, but this was not the case with Simmons and Rubin. As Jennifer Livett notes in her essay on 'odd couples', "one of the pair may at times seize cunning advantage, but this is brief and always reversible. It has nothing to do with any essential difference in rank, wealth or fame. Neither partner is a lone hero and neither a 'sidekick or faithful retainer'." The tensions within Rubin's and Simmons' relationship were primarily ones of taste, in the final analysis. And they still get along fine and respect each other's abilities. Both are restless men, ensuring that any business partnership was destined to be temporary, but spectacular. Their unlikely association lasted only four years but produced a musical legacy of unchallenged calibre. More importantly, as Def Jam established itself, it also established rap as the dominant form of American youth music.

In that four years Def Jam released at least five milestone albums, and at least two dozen wondrous singles. That's without counting the creative impact they jointly wielded on Run-DMC. By the time Rubin walked away in 1988, the project, from his viewpoint, had been completed. Yet Simmons went on to turn Def Jam into the world-class business concern he'd always hoped it would be. The fact that someone else owns it – he never saw the multinationals as natural enemies like Chuck D and others did, simply as investors – doesn't rob him of any sleep.

Def Jam eventually outgrew both its parents. It is now in the keeping of Lyor Cohen, a custodian who is a businessman first and foremost, cast most definitely in the image of Simmons, even though he shares a background closer to Rubin's. Now, with LL Cool J finally departed, nothing remains of the acts which built the label's foundations, but if anything it is stronger than it ever has been. Its current stable of star rappers makes it the envy of the music industry. There is no indication that its fabulous history is nearing closure.

Def Jam: The Hot 75
Recommended Listening

LL Cool J
Radio (1985)
Bigger And Deffer (1987)
Walking With A Panther (1989)
Mama Said Knock You Out (1990)
14 Shots To The Dome (1993)
Mr Smith (1995)
Phenomenon (1997)
G.O.A.T featuring James T. Smith: The Greatest Of All Time (2000)

Beastie Boys
Licensed To Ill (1986)

Public Enemy
Yo! Bum Rush The Show (1987)
It Takes A Nation Of Millions To Hold Us Back (1988)
Fear Of A Black Planet (1990)
Apocalypse '91 . . . The Enemy Strikes Black (1991)
Greatest Misses (1992)
Muse Sick-N-Hour Message (1994)
He Got Game (1998)

Oran 'Juice' Jones
Juice (1986)
GTO: Gangsters Takin' Over (1987)

Slick Rick
The Great Adventures Of Slick Rick (1988)
The Ruler's Back (1991)
Behind Bars (1994)
The Art Of Storytelling (1999)

Def Jam

3rd Bass
The Cactus Album (1989)
Derelicts Of Dialect (1991)

EPMD
Business As Usual (1991)
Business Never Personal (1992)

Nice 'N' Smooth
Ain't A Damn Thing Changed (1991)

Redman
Whut? Thee Album (1992)
Dare Iz A Darkside (1994)
Muddy Waters (1996)
Doc's Da Name 2000 (1998)
Malpractice (2001)

Erick Sermon
No Pressure (1993)
Double Or Nothing (1995)

Domino
Domino (1993)

Onyx
Bacdafucup (1993)
All We Got Iz Us (1995)

Boss
Born Gangstaz (1993)

Method Man
Tical (1994)
Tical 2000: Judgement Day (1998)
Blackout! (1999)

South Central Cartel
'N' Gatz We Truss (1994)

Def Jam: The Hot 75 Recommended Listening

Warren G
Regulate . . . G Funk Era (1994)
Take A Look Over Your Shoulder (1997)

Montell Jordan
This Is How We Do It (1995)
More . . . (1996)
Let's Ride (1998)
Get It On . . . Tonite (1999)

Jay-Z
Reasonable Doubt (1996)
In My Lifetime Vol. 1 (1997)
Vol. 2: Hard Knock Life (1998)
Vol. 3: Life And Times Of S. Carter (1999)
The Dynasty: Roc La Familia (2000)
The Blueprint (2001)

Foxy Brown
Ill Na Na (1996)
Chyna Dolla (1998)
Broken Silence (2001)

DMX
It's Dark And Hell Is Hot (1998)
Flesh Of My Flesh, Blood Of My Blood (1998)
And Then There Was X (1999)
The Great Depression (2001)

DJ Clue
The Professional (1998)
DJ Clue Presents: Backstage (1999)
The Professional, Part 2 (2000)

Beanie Segal
The Truth (1999)
The Reason (2001)

Funkmaster Flex
The Tunnel (1999)

Def Jam

Sisquó
Unleash The Dragon (1999)
Return Of Dragon (2001)

Ja Rule
Venni Vetti Vecci (1999)
Rule 3:36 (2000)
Pain Is Love (2001)

Ludacris
Back For The First Time (2000)
Word Of Mouf (2001)

N.O.R.E.
Grimey . . . God's Favorite (2002)

Important Def Jam Soundtracks
Less Than Zero (1987)
The Show (1995)
How To Be A Player (1997)
Rush Hour (1998)
Belly (1998)
Nutty Professor II: The Klumps (2000)
Rush Hour II (2001)
The Fast And The Furious (2001)
How High (2001)